T0288273

Civil War

CAMPAIGNS
in the
HEARTLAND

STEVEN E. WOODWORTH
SERIES EDITOR

The

SHILOH

Campaign

Edited by Steven E. Woodworth

Southern Illinois University Press
Carbondale

12   11   10   09   4   3   2   1

Library of Congress Cataloging-in-Publication Data
The Shiloh campaign / edited by Steven E. Woodworth.
      p. cm. — (Civil War campaigns in the heartland)
Includes bibliographical references and index.
ISBN-13: 978-0-8093-2892-5 (cloth : alk. paper)
ISBN-10: 0-8093-2892-5 (cloth : alk. paper)
1. Shiloh, Battle of, Tenn., 1862. 2. Tennessee—History—
Civil War, 1861–1865—Campaigns. 3. United States—His-
tory—Civil War, 1861–1865—Campaigns. I. Woodworth,
Steven E.
E473.54.S575 2009
973.7'31—dc22   2008034311

Printed on recycled paper. ♻
The paper used in this publication meets the minimum re-
quirements of American National Standard for Information Sciences—Permanence of Paper for Printed Library
Materials, ANSI Z39.48-1992. ∞

CONTENTS

ACKNOWLEDGMENTS

Special thanks are due to Jason M. Frawley, Charles D. Grear, and David Slay for coming up with the original idea for this book and the series of which it is part. They know exactly what I mean when I say that none of this would have happened without them.

To no less degree, thanks are due, and gladly rendered, to Sylvia Frank Rodrigue for her patience and gentle persistence in shepherding the project through to completion on behalf of Southern Illinois University Press.

INTRODUCTION

Shiloh represented the nation's first bloodletting on the scale that was to become typical of major Civil War battles. Perhaps its best-known statistic is that more Americans died in that two-day battle than had died in all the battles in all the nation's previous wars put together. Shiloh also represented the Confederacy's first great counteroffensive in the western theater, the first attempt to regain all that was lost in the opening debacles of forts Henry and Donelson, and it was also very likely the Confederacy's last, best hope to turn the tide in the West and save the Southern heartland for the Rebellion. There would be other attempts thereafter, but each would be more desperate and have less chance of success than the one before, until finally such efforts at creating a turning point in a war that, it seemed, simply would not turn concluded in John Bell Hood's disastrous foray to Franklin and Nashville. If the Confederacy was to turn the tide of the war in its favor, it had few better chances than Shiloh.

In a sense, the Shiloh campaign began with the fall of Fort Donelson, February 16, 1862, or at least in the immediate aftermath of that great Union victory and almost irremediable Confederate disaster. The fall of forts Henry and Donelson opened the Tennessee River to Union boat traffic, including gunboats, all the way to northern Alabama, and the Cumberland River to the head of navigation above Nashville. This cut Confederate east-west communication and effectively gave Union forces control of all of Kentucky and half of Tennessee. The next Union goal was the rail-junction town of Corinth, Mississippi. Situated in northeastern Mississippi, Corinth lay at the crossing of the Mobile & Ohio Railroad—the most important north-south line in the Confederate heartland—with the Memphis & Charleston Railroad—probably the most important rail line in the Confederacy. The Memphis & Charleston ran east and west between the cities of its name, but its greatest significance was that it joined at Chattanooga with the East Tennessee & Virginia Railroad, thus forming a continuous line of rails between the Confederacy's main eastern and western armies. Its loss would cripple the Confederacy's ability to shift men and supplies, both from one end of the front to the other and within the confines of the northern Mississippi theater of the conflict.

Like many significant military goals, the importance of Corinth was readily apparent to informed observers of the strategic situation. Several Confederate generals, including western-theater commander Albert Sidney Johnston, recognized the need to concentrate Confederate forces there. On the Union side, Gen. Henry W. Halleck, recently elevated to command of all the Union armies in the West, also recognized the desirability of having Corinth and began laying his plans to take it. The way in which Halleck designed to capture Corinth and the way that Johnston chose to defend it set the stage for the battle of Shiloh.

Halleck was methodical, thorough, and very cautious. He determined to unite the three Union armies between the Appalachians and the Mississippi into a single grand force that would crush all resistance in its way. John Pope's Army of the Mississippi, which had previously cooperated very successfully with Union naval forces on the river of that name, would come east to join Halleck's campaign. Gen. Don Carlos Buell's Army of the Ohio, which had recently occupied Nashville, would likewise join in the advance. Ulysses S. Grant's Army of the Tennessee, which had won the victories at the forts that had made Pope's and Buell's smaller successes possible, would be the largest component. The three armies would rendezvous at a point on the Tennessee River as close as possible to Corinth, which was about twenty miles from the river's nearest point. The Army of the Tennessee, which was already operating near the lower reaches of that river, would be the first to ascend it and to establish a position on its banks at which the other armies were to join it.

Halleck had a low opinion of Grant and was jealous of the success his junior had achieved. He did his best to claim credit for Grant's victories but was annoyed that those triumphs had won Grant promotion over other officers whom Halleck much preferred. Grant's aggressive style of warfare unnerved Halleck—raising for him the specter of the equally undesirable outcomes either of Grant blundering into a defeat or of his forging ahead to a victory that would further eclipse his commander. Halleck therefore was especially eager to rein Grant in after forts Henry and Donelson. He briefly relieved Grant of command on contrived charges but had to reinstate him when Grant's congressman prompted Washington to demand explanations of Halleck, which Halleck knew full well he could not produce.

Stuck with Grant, at least for the time being, Halleck ordered his renowned subordinate to resume command of the Army of the Tennessee's expedition up its namesake river, to encamp that force somewhere along that river's banks near Corinth, and, above all, not to do anything at all that might bring on a battle. There Grant and his army were to remain inert, doing nothing that might tend to diminish Halleck's glory or contribute to winning the war, while Pope's and Buell's army made their way to join them. Grant's subordinates had already selected a position for the army at Pittsburg Landing and Crump's Landing, on the west side of the Tennessee, and the nearby village of Savannah, on the east bank, where Union troops had begun arriving in mid-March 1862.

Buell's force would be the first to join the Army of the Tennessee, and it should have arrived much sooner than it did. Halleck wanted Buell to put his army in steamboats and take it to Pittsburg Landing by river, in the same

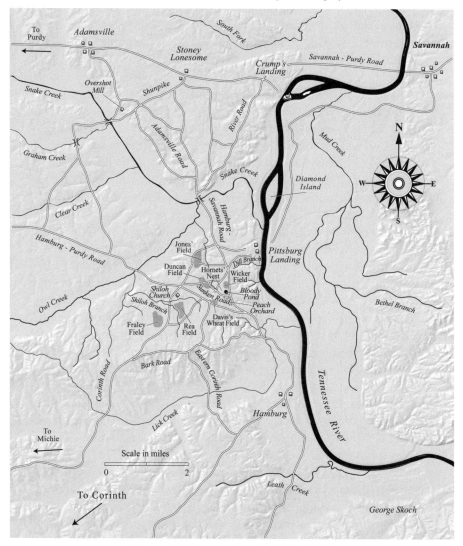

Map 1. Shiloh—overview of the battlefield.

way the Army of the Tennessee had traveled. Buell, however, had other ideas, and he persuaded Halleck to let him march his army overland from Nashville to Pittsburg Landing, a distance of about 140 miles. It was a bad decision. Roads were poor, and Buell was never a fast-moving commander at the best of times. His slowness, coupled with Halleck's insistence that the war, or at least Grant's army, stand still until all was prepared to his liking, had the effect of surrendering the initiative to the Confederates and leaving the Army of the Tennessee sitting exposed to a Rebel counterstroke. Compounding the vulnerability of Grant's army, Halleck's stringent orders against doing anything that might tend to bring on a battle practically forbade the Army of the Tennessee from patrolling aggressively toward Corinth so as to detect the approach of an enemy force.

This played directly into Johnston's hands. The Confederate general had come under severe criticism since the fall of forts Henry and Donelson on his watch. He retained the confidence of his close friend Confederate president Jefferson Davis as well as that of his troops, and he was determined to regain what the Confederacy had lost in the West. He ordered the concentration of his previously scattered forces at Corinth, and Davis lent his aid by ordering reinforcements to him from several less seriously threatened sectors including some ten thousand men under Braxton Bragg from Pensacola. By late March, Johnston had at Corinth an army of about forty-two thousand men. What he needed to do with them was, as Davis pointed out in a letter about that time, too obvious to require explanation. He must strike and destroy Grant before Buell could join him, then do the same to Buell, and finally Pope. It was tall order, but Halleck's enforcement of Union inaction and Buell's tedious march gave Johnston the opportunity to try.

Johnston needed as much time as possible to organize and drill his newly assembled collection of mostly green, untested units into a cohesive army, so he determined to wait until the last possible moment, when Buell had almost reached Grant, before launching his attack on the Army of the Tennessee at Pittsburg Landing. On April 2, he learned from scouts that Buell's army was within a few days' march of joining Grant, and he issued orders for his army to march the following morning. His plan was for his army to proceed to the vicinity of Pittsburg Landing on April 3 and attack Grant early on the morning of April 4. Poor roads, bad weather, undisciplined troops, and poorly conceived orders, drawn up by Johnston's second-in-command, P. G. T. Beauregard, made the march much slower than planned. On the evening of April 3, with his army still far from being in position to launch an attack, Johnston had to postpone the assault to the morning of the fifth. Then the following evening, with preparations still not complete, he had to order yet another delay, shifting the planned attack to Sunday morning, April 6.

Johnston's conduct of the Shiloh Campaign, from the fall of forts Henry and Donelson until his own death on the battlefield of Shiloh, is the subject of the current volume's opening chapter, written by John R. Lundberg.

Federal units on the front lines of the encampment at Pittsburg Landing detected the presence of Johnston's army but could not convince their superiors, especially General William Tecumseh Sherman, of the threat. A Union patrol made contact with the Confederates in the predawn hours, sparking a firefight that merged into the broader battle when the entire Rebel army advanced to the attack around 7 A.M. Each Union division had time to get under arms, form its line, and advance some distance in front of its camps before engaging the enemy. A couple of divisions even waited for some time in position before the tide of battle reached them. None of the Union troops were caught in their tents or bayoneted in their blankets as some overheated newspaper accounts claimed, but the strategic surprise for the Union generals was complete. The Army of the Tennessee was not entrenched (entrenchment was not customary at that stage of the war), and throughout much of the day, it was unable to form a continuous, coherent battle line from one side of the field to the other. Gaps in the Union line were often the means by which Confederate attackers were able to drive the Federals out of otherwise strong and stoutly defended positions.

One of the most significant of these gaps was near the left end of the Union line, near the river, between Brigadier General Stephen A. Hurlbut's Fourth Division and a detached brigade of Sherman's Fifth Division under the command of Colonel David Stuart. The gap there was ultimately the main factor that allowed the Confederates to drive the Federals in a large section of the battlefield out of the positions they had held for a good part of the day and back to Grant's final line of resistance. However, the fight that Stuart put up on the extreme Union left served to delay that event for several hours and was a key factor in the Army of the Tennessee's survival that day. Alexander Mendoza analyzes the crucial fight of Stuart's brigade in chapter 2 of the current volume.

While Confederate pressure during most of the day pressed most heavily on both ends of the Union line, only a relatively small number of Confederate brigades assailed the center. This is ironic in view of the fact that the center was the scene of the famous "Hornets' Nest," where, as legend has it, the fiercest fighting took place. In chapter 3 of the current volume, Timothy B. Smith examines the validity and origins of that legend.

Throughout the first day of the battle, the Fifth Division of the Army of the Tennessee, commanded by Major General Lew Wallace, on orders from Grant, was attempting to make its way to the battlefield from a position only six miles away by road. Yet, it did not arrive until night had fallen, and the firing had ceased. In chapter 4, I analyze the reasons for Wallace's delayed arrival and the lingering effects on Wallace's Civil War career.

The Battle of Shiloh was fought on the ground it was because of the proximity of the river. The river had brought the Army of the Tennessee to Pittsburg, and Union power continued to be especially strong on this inland waterway in the form of the brown-water arm of the U.S. Navy. Especially during the latter stages of the fighting on April 6, Union gunboats on the Tennessee added the fire of their heavy cannon to the defensive barrage being put out by the artillery on Grant's final line of resistance. In chapter 5 of this book, Gary D. Joiner sizes up the important role of the gunboats in the campaign and battle of Shiloh.

Controversy has long surrounded Beauregard's order to his forces to break off the attack on the evening of April 6. While such controversy can be couched in terms of "Lost Cause" wistfulness—in this case, the persistent assertion that the Confederacy would certainly have won the war if not for the unaccountable foolishness of this or that individual—it need not be examined in such a spirit. The question for military historians is whether the rather small chance of achieving a stupendously large result—the capture of Grant and his army—would have been worth the losses that would likely have resulted from a continuation of the assault. In chapter 6 (originally published in the *Journal of Southern History*), the late Grady McWhiney argues that a realistic chance of success existed and that Beauregard was premature in calling a halt. One need not agree that Grant's lines were likely to be broken that evening to believe that given the astronomical stakes involved, Beauregard ought to have continued his efforts until nightfall necessarily put a close to operations.

In some ways, at least from the Confederate point of view, Shiloh was a turning point where the course of the war stubbornly refused to turn. Johnston had struck his hardest blow at Grant, aiming to destroy his army and begin the process of regaining all the Confederacy had lost in the West by the fall of forts Henry and Donelson. The result was the bloodiest battle in American history to date. Grant's army and reputation were damaged, but both would survive. Johnston did not. Once Halleck arrived at Pittsburg Landing and gathered in the forces of Buell and Pope, his combined army of a hundred thousand men advanced slowly and steadily toward Corinth, more or less as Halleck had been planning to do all along, and compelled its evacuation at the end of May. What did the Battle of Shiloh mean to the average Confederate soldier in the ranks? What did the men write to their wives, parents, or sweethearts back in Texas, Louisiana, Arkansas, Mississippi, Alabama, or the rest of Tennessee, giving the Southern home front its impression of the great battle? Charles D. Grear explores this question in chapter 7.

In the final chapter of the current volume, Brooks D. Simpson examines the Grant-Sherman relationship—how it was affected by the Battle of Shiloh and what impact it had on the future careers of both men. In doing so, he casts doubt on some of the long-held beliefs about the relationship as well as some of its more famous anecdotes.

Much more could be written on the Battle of Shiloh. Two or three volumes this size could easily be put together, with each chapter adding to knowledge about one of the most important clashes fought on the North American continent. This volume represents a start, however, toward a fuller understanding of one of the key events in deciding the outcome of the Civil War with all its momentous issues, above all, the future of human slavery. The authors hope that other scholars will be inspired to take up the further study of the western theater of the war, where such decisions were ultimately made.

1

"I MUST SAVE THIS ARMY"

ALBERT SIDNEY JOHNSTON AND
THE SHILOH CAMPAIGN

John R. Lundberg

On the evening of February 15, 1862, General Albert Sidney Johnston received intelligence from General John B. Floyd that Floyd had won a great victory at Fort Donelson. Encouraged by this information, Johnston went to bed at midnight at his headquarters near Edgefield, Tennessee, on the Cumberland River across from Nashville. Just before daybreak, an aide awakened him with news that Donelson and its garrison would be surrendered at dawn. Stunned and bewildered, Johnston exclaimed, "I must save this army," and throughout the rest of the early morning hours marched the forces under his command into Nashville.[1]

This alarming predawn incident on February 16, 1862, marked the beginning of the Shiloh Campaign for Johnston. Just weeks earlier, he had been hailed by Jefferson Davis and the rest of the South as the man who would save the Confederacy. But after the fall of forts Henry and Donelson, almost everyone in the Confederacy except Davis turned on this erstwhile savior. Many modern historians have picked up on this theme, almost vilifying Johnston as a highly overrated commander responsible for early Confederate defeat in the West. Yet, Johnston has also had his defenders, who persist that he indeed was the commander that Davis had hoped for and that his efforts to save Tennessee were undermined by inexperienced and insubordinate officers. The Shiloh Campaign is so important to the outcome of the Civil War and the debate over Johnston so heated that periodically it is necessary to reevaluate the issue in light of current scholarship and what is now known about the campaign.[2]

Johnston has been unjustly criticized for much that occurred in the Shiloh Campaign. Despite his failings in the Henry-Donelson Campaign, Johnston's conduct between the fall of Fort Donelson and his death at Shiloh evinced all of the potential credited to him by Davis and an admiring public when he took command in the West. Johnston's execution of the retreat from Nashville and junction with Beauregard at Corinth was nothing short of brilliant. Contrary to the claims of some historians, Johnston never lost confidence in himself or his plans at any point during the campaign. His primary flaw remained his somewhat naïve trust of his subordinates, most of whom failed him time and again. Johnston's dependence on these subordinates doomed the Confederate effort at Shiloh when they disobeyed or ignored his orders. Because Johnston had learned he could not trust his subordinates, he began near the end of the campaign to take command in person as often as possible, and this ultimately led to his death at the head of a charge on the first day of battle.

Other than perhaps Robert E. Lee, no soldier of the old army stood higher in the country's expectations than Albert Sidney Johnston. Union General Winfield Scott even favored Johnston to command all U.S. forces at the outbreak of the war. Johnston led a distinguished military career between his graduation from West Point in 1826 and the outbreak of the Civil War. At West Point, Johnston compiled an enviable academic record, graduating eighth in the class before winning an appointment as a brevet second lieutenant in the infantry. After serving in the Black Hawk War of 1832, Johnston resigned his commission and returned home to care for his ailing wife. She died shortly thereafter, and Johnston moved to Texas, where he took part in the Texas Revolution and became the senior general in the Army of the Republic of Texas. Johnston went on to serve as Secretary of State of the new Republic and then led a regiment of Texas volunteers in the Mexican War. In 1849, he reentered the U.S. Army as major and paymaster to the military posts in Texas. Six years later, he received a promotion to colonel and was given command of the Second U.S. Cavalry Regiment, a unit whose officers included, among others, Robert E. Lee, Earl Van Dorn, and George H. Thomas. Johnston then assumed command of the Department of Texas and in 1857 headed the U.S. forces dispatched to deal with the Mormons. The Mormon expedition garnered him a promotion to brevet brigadier general, and after its conclusion, he took command of the Department of the Pacific with headquarters in San Francisco.[3]

Though born in Kentucky, Johnston adopted Texas as his home state because of his service during the Texas Revolution. When he received word of Texas's secession, Johnston resigned his commission to join the Confederacy. In the fall of 1861, Jefferson Davis faced a dilemma; he had no officer to command Department No. 2, the vast expanse of Confederate territory west of the Appalachian Mountains. Johnston, who had just arrived from the west coast, seemed the perfect choice, and on September 10, Davis issued orders appointing him to the command. Davis and Johnston were old friends from their days at West Point and then as comrades-in-arms in northern Mexico when they fought in the Mexican War, and the president entertained the utmost confidence in the adopted Texan. For four months after Johnston's appointment to the western command, little occurred to shake that assurance, as Johnston's defensive line held against minor Union probes. Then in mid-February 1862 came the twin debacles of Henry and Donelson.[4]

Ulysses S. Grant's victory at Fort Donelson handed Johnston with an awkward strategic situation. After the fall of Donelson, the Union army stood in between the two primary wings of Johnston's forces. At Columbus, Kentucky, General Leonidas Polk remained with approximately fourteen thousand men under the direct command of General P. G. T. Beauregard, with whom Johnston had split command of the Confederate forces in Department No. 2.[5] After Donelson's fall, Beauregard moved his headquarters to Jackson, Tennessee, and after lengthy verbal sparring with Polk, succeeded in ordering him to bring his men south into Tennessee in order to concentrate forces in the Mississippi Valley. Beauregard also sent messages to Generals Braxton Bragg in Mobile, Mansfield Lovell in New Orleans, and Van Dorn in Arkansas to join him. Lovell responded by sending some of his men, as did Bragg, but Van Dorn refused the direct orders given him. Instead, he launched an offensive against Union Major General Samuel Curtis in northwest Arkansas.

Meanwhile, Johnston had personal command of the eastern half of Department No. 2's forces, approximately seventeen thousand men who had been stationed at Bowling Green, Kentucky, only weeks before. Johnston's Confederates had faced approximately seventy thousand Federals in two armies under Generals Don Carlos Buell and Grant. From Donelson, Grant prepared to move up the northward-flowing Tennessee River into southern Tennessee while Buell moved south from central Kentucky toward Middle Tennessee. At the direction of the Union's new western theater commander, Major General Henry W. Halleck, Grant and Buell planned to unite their forces in southern Tennessee before moving on into northern Mississippi. To stop them, Johnston had to do something quickly.[6]

Immediately following the news of Donelson's fall, Johnston's primary concerns revolved around Nashville. The Tennessee capital stood second only in prominence to New Orleans in the western Confederacy and served as Johnston's logistical and strategic headquarters. However, with Donelson gone, Johnston immediately decided that Nashville should be abandoned for a point farther south. At this point, Johnston had apparently not yet decided whether he should abandon the Mississippi Valley and fall back on Chatta-nooga or whether he should make a stand somewhere in northern Alabama or Mississippi. In any event, he hedged his bets by retreating with his forces out of Nashville southeast toward Murfreesboro, giving the impression at least that he would fall back on Chattanooga. On Sunday and Monday, February 16 and 17, the Confederate army slipped across the Cumberland, through Nashville and out on the Murfreesboro Pike. The next day, Johnston himself ignominiously departed the capital by buggy to join his men.[7]

Up to this point, Johnston had had few options in the campaign. Nashville was obviously untenable with Grant and Buell sweeping down from the north and northwest. The first real decision he made, however, did not bode well for the campaign. After the fall of Donelson, Johnston had graciously re-ceived that garrison's erstwhile commander, General Floyd, perhaps without realizing Floyd's almost criminal behavior in the surrender of the garrison. When Johnston abandoned Nashville on February 18, he put Floyd in charge of evacuating the supplies and munitions from the city. No sooner had the last soldier in Johnston's column departed than stragglers and civilians be-gan looting the commissary stores. By Tuesday, February 20, Floyd's efforts to stop the riots and looting had proven almost as thorough a failure as his command of ill-fated Fort Donelson. Then, Nathan Bedford Forrest arrived with his Tennessee cavalry regiment. Forrest formed his men in ranks and charged the rioters three times, finally restoring order. Floyd then completed his task by evacuating the much-needed supplies south toward the retreating army. Johnston's first decision had been a poor one; had Forrest not arrived in the nick of time, it is likely that none of the precious stores in Nashville would have been saved.[8]

Some historians have maintained that with the presence of Beauregard in western Tennessee, command of the Confederate forces in the West be-gan to slip from Johnston's fingers. In his *Army of the Heartland*, historian Thomas Lawrence Connelly states, "When Johnston left Nashville, his con-trol of the troops was visibly slipping from his grasp." As proof, he cites that Johnston moved his army west toward Beauregard's force rather than east toward Chattanooga. Connelly states that Beauregard "drew" Johnston out of Middle Tennessee and into the Mississippi Valley by encouraging him to come to Corinth with his column.[9]

Connelly's conclusion rests on faulty logic. It would only stand to rea-son that Johnston would want to unite his forces rather than keeping them divided, and there is no reason to see this as an abdication of his command. Connelly's claim that Johnston moved into Beauregard's "territory" also makes little sense, because Johnston never relinquished command of the department; he merely divided the field command. Furthermore, the assertion that command was slipping from his fingers ignores that both Johnston and Beauregard seem to have concluded, independently and more or less simultaneously, that Corinth would be the best place to reorganize.[10]

Critics have also charged that Johnston relinquished his command by staying with the eastern half of his forces rather than directing the operations from a more central location. It appears that Johnston stayed with the eastern wing in order to raise the soldiers' morale himself and keep them in line. By staying with his army, Johnston began a pattern of behavior that lasted through the rest of the campaign. Because his subordinates had failed him before, at Columbus with Polk, at Donelson with Floyd and Gideon J. Pillow, and again with Floyd at Nashville, Johnston seems to have felt that the only way to see that his orders were carried out and to hearten his men was to take command personally.[11]

Johnston's subordinates, including Bragg and Beauregard, urged him to form a junction of the two wings of the army in northern Alabama or Mississippi. Despite the hardships entailed by this move, Johnston remained optimistic. General W. C. Whitthorne, the Adjutant General of Tennessee, visited Johnston's headquarters at Murfreesboro and later recalled that Johnston "at once inquired as to the feelings and views of the people of Tennessee . . . but concluded, by saying 'General Whitthorne, go tell your people that, under the favor of providence, I will return in less than ninety days and redeem their capital.' I remember well his confident tone, his smile, and the earnestness of his manner."[12]

On February 23, Johnston took over the immediate command of his seventeen thousand men at Murfreesboro and five days later began moving them south toward Shelbyville, Tennessee. Along the way, Johnston organized his forces into three compact divisions under Generals William J. Hardee, George B. Crittenden, and Gideon J. Pillow, with a reserve brigade under Major General John C. Breckinridge. Johnston also carefully masked his movements with the cavalry at his disposal, primarily the commands of Forrest and John Hunt Morgan. The Confederate troopers succeeded in preventing Union discovery of Johnston's true destination.[13]

Johnston's men, especially the Kentuckians and Tennesseans, resented what they viewed as a retreat, but Johnston's discipline and morale helped keep their spirits high. One soldier wrote, "When the line of march was taken up, and the heads of the columns were still turned southward, the dissatisfaction of the troops broke out into fresh and frequent murmurs. Discipline, somewhat restored at Murfreesboro, had been too much relaxed by the scenes witnessed at Nashville, to impose much restraint upon them.

. . . Officers and men concurred in laying the whole burden of blame upon General Johnston." Another soldier said, "But everything went on with a regularity and a degree of order that seemed to have been the result of circumstances working in entire harmony with the plans of a great general, instead of having been adverse at every step; and he reached Corinth with so little loss of men or [am]munition as to mark him one of the first administrative minds of his age in the country."[14] Gradually, as they moved south, Johnston restored the confidence of his men and performed nothing short of a miracle in restoring his forces to fighting trim. Major Jeremy F. Gilmer, the chief engineer who had failed Johnston at Donelson, noted that the general "expresses confidence that better fortunes await us."[15] Colonel St. John R. Liddell wrote while at Murfreesboro, "At all events, I was satisfied that Johnston's clear head was grasping the state of things rapidly. . . . He listened to, and yet was not confused by, the various opinions of his subordinates."[16] From Shelbyville, Johnston proceeded south to Fayetteville, Tennessee, and then crossed the Tennessee River at Decatur, Alabama.

During the march, President Davis worked hard defending Johnston from his critics. On March 12 from Richmond, he began an informal letter to his favorite general in the West: "We have suffered great anxiety because of recent events in Kentucky and Tennessee. . . . In the mean time, I made for you such a defense as friendship prompted, and many years of acquaintance justified; but I needed facts to rebut the wholesale assertions made against you. . . . I respect the generosity which has kept you silent, but would impress upon you that the question is not personal but public."[17]

On March 18, Johnston replied from Decatur, explaining that he had not had the time to reply to Davis with a full report of the Henry-Donelson fiasco. After giving a sketch of what had occurred, Johnston informed Davis,

> I ordered the command to Murfreesboro. . . . The weather was inclement, the floods excessive and the bridges washed away; but most of the provisions and stores were saved, and conveyed to new depots. This having been accomplished, though with great loss, in conformity with my original design I marched southward and crossed the Tennessee at this point, so as to cooperate or unite with Beauregard for the defense of the valley of the Mississippi. The passage is almost completed, and the head of my column is already with General Bragg at Corinth. The movement was deemed too hazardous by the most experienced members of my staff, but the object warranted the risk. The difficulty of effecting a junction is not wholly overcome, but it approaches completion. . . . I observed silence, as it seemed to me the best way to serve the cause and the country. . . . The test of merit in

my profession with the people is success. It is a hard rule, but I think it right. If I join this corps to the forces of Beauregard . . . then those who are now declaiming against me will not have an argument.[18]

Johnston's letter is notable for several reasons. First, he withheld censure of generals Floyd and Pillow for the Donelson fiasco. He also failed to criticize any of his other subordinates for their complicity in the disasters. Second, the silence he maintained in the face of criticism is remarkable, especially considering the penchant of other generals in the western theater to gripe incessantly and take recriminations against them personally. Third, that few thought it possible for Johnston to effect a junction with Beauregard says much about Johnston's audacity and skill.

On March 25, Johnston completed the concentration of his forces with Beauregard at Corinth. His gamble had paid off. In the face of overwhelming odds, Johnston had succeeded in uniting his forces in the face of the enemy to meet Grant and Buell head on. Despite this accomplishment, many have criticized Johnston for not directing all of his forces from a more central location. Yet, Johnston had good reasons for acting as he did. His subordinates conjectured that a junction at Corinth would be nearly impossible for the column marching south out of central Kentucky, and Johnston in all likelihood felt that he could best serve his cause by remaining with that column to hearten the men and see to it personally that the junction at Corinth was completed effectually.

By March 25, Johnston had reached Corinth and joined Beauregard, making their effective total forty-two thousand men. Johnston then made what, on the surface, seemed like a foolish decision. Instead of immediately taking command himself, he offered command of the army to Beauregard, and Johnston volunteered to move his departmental headquarters to Memphis or Holly Springs. This decision was not a hasty one, and many of Johnston's friends even begged him not to offer Beauregard the command. Confederate Governor George W. Johnson of Kentucky wrote, "You must not do this. I beg that you will not do it, both for your own fame and the good of the country. If I hear that you are resolved in this course, I will despair of our cause. It will sink under the curse of Heaven, upon a people, who joined like wolves . . . to hunt down the noblest and purest man it has been my good fortune to know."[19]

Despite these pleadings, Johnston did offer Beauregard the command, but the Creole graciously turned it down. Instead, Johnston named him second-in-command. Historians have debated ever since Johnston's motivations in making this unusual move. His critics have argued that Johnston had lost confidence in himself, but as the letter of Governor Johnson implies, Johnston probably felt that the people and soldiers had lost confidence in him and that the cause and the army would best be served by a change in command. At the time, wild rumors also swirled about that Davis was about to relieve Johnston of command, showing that the president had lost faith in him. Johnston had already shown a high respect for Beauregard by splitting the command with him in early February and felt that the Confederacy might best be served if he stepped back. Johnston clearly never lost confidence in himself and perhaps even anticipated Beauregard's response. Additionally, Beauregard had taken much control since his arrival, and perhaps the offer constituted a passive-aggressive move on Johnston's part to reassert command over the army. Historian Stanley Horn notes, "At any rate he [Johnston] seems not to have insisted on his offer once Beauregard refused it, so it may have been nothing more than a perfunctory gesture which Beauregard magnified into an admission of weakness."[20] With Beauregard's refusal, Johnston set about organizing his forces to face Grant's Federals.

Johnston delegated the task of organizing and training the army to Beauregard and Bragg. To Beauregard, he gave the task of organizing the various commands into three army corps and a reserve force, while he appointed Bragg his chief of staff with the task of getting the men into fighting trim. After the war, Beauregard claimed that he came up with the plan of organization of what became known as the "Army of Mississippi." However, Beauregard himself admitted that he conferred with Johnston beforehand; his organization of three corps and a reserve force closely resembled Johnston's earlier organization at Murfreesboro. It is possible that Beauregard came up with corps designations for the four parts of the army to spite Jefferson Davis, who had earlier denied his request to organize the Confederate forces in Northern Virginia into corps in the fall of 1861. Johnston placed Polk in command of the First Corps, which consisted of 9,163 men in four brigades. Bragg took command of the Second Corps, in addition to his duties as chief of staff. The Second Corps constituted the largest of the three, with 13,589 soldiers in six brigades. General Hardee took command of the Third Corps, a smaller force with 6,789 men in three brigades. Finally, Johnston designated Crittenden to command the reserve force with 6,439 men in three brigades. On March 31, under orders from Bragg, Hardee went to Crittenden's headquarters at Iuka (near Corinth) and arrested him, along with Brigadier General William H. Carroll, for drunkenness and dereliction of duty. Major General John C. Breckinridge replaced Crittenden as commander of the reserve.[21]

Bragg found himself with the far more difficult tasks of maintaining discipline, arming and properly equipping the soldiers, and in general working them into fighting shape. In appointing Bragg chief of staff, Johnston for the first time in his Confederate career showed an aptitude for choosing the right man for the right task. Despite his character flaws that would become apparent later as commander of the Army of Tennessee, no one ever doubted Bragg as an organizer and administrator.

He faced an almost impossible situation, especially providing ammunition for the widely varied armaments the Confederate volunteers brought with them. In a typical plea, Hardee sent a message to Bragg on April 1: "I am greatly in want of 73,000 Enfield cartridges and 6,000 Minie. I have 1,060 Enfield guns and only 31,000 cartridges. . . . I learned this evening that 47,000 Enfield cartridges would be here tomorrow, and this is all the Ordnance Department had, and this was subject to your order. Can I [have] ammunition when it arrives?"[22]

"Rifles," ranted Bragg to Johnston, "rifled and smooth bore muskets, some of them originally percussion, others hastily altered flint locks by Yankee contractors, many still with the old flint and steel, and shot guns of all sizes and patterns, held place in the same regiment." The new chief of staff considered the entire Confederate army at Corinth a disorganized mob, "a heterogeneous mass in which there was more enthusiasm than discipline, more capacity than knowledge, and more valor than instruction. . . . The task of organizing such a command in four weeks and supplying it . . . was simply appalling." Despite the appalling, heterogeneous mass of men, Bragg managed, in a month, to bring the soldiers in the Army of Mississippi to the point of being a reasonably well-organized, disciplined, and supplied force capable of giving battle. In retrospect, Albert Sidney Johnston's choice of Bragg as chief of staff proved to be the most insightful and effective appointment he made during the Shiloh Campaign.[23]

As soon as Johnston reached Corinth, he decided, even before the organization of the army began, to attack Grant at Pittsburg Landing along the west bank of the Tennessee River before Buell could effect a junction with him there. Before Buell's arrival, Grant and Johnston possessed roughly the same number of men, and Johnston determined that the only way to stop the Federal incursion would be to defeat them in detail. After the war, Beauregard again took credit for convincing Johnston to attack Grant before Buell arrived, but this is clearly the strategy Johnston had adopted by concentrating his forces at Corinth in the first place. Furthermore, in a March 17 letter to Bragg, Beauregard advocated a "defensive-offensive" course of action by which Grant could be drawn away from his base and attacked. In light of this correspondence, it seems that Beauregard may not even have agreed with Johnston's decision to attack at all.[24]

In the meantime, both Lee and Davis wrote to Johnston supporting his plan of action. Writing from Richmond, Virginia, on March 26, Lee expressed sympathy with Johnston in the criticism he was then facing. He also voiced his approval of Johnston's action in combining his forces with Beauregard at Corinth. "I need not urge you," he added, "when your army is united, to deal a blow at the enemy in your front, if possible, before his rear gets up from Nashville. You have him divided, and keep him so, if you can. Wishing you, my dear general, every success and happiness, with my earnest prayers for the safety of your whole army."[25] Davis concurred with Lee's opinion and urged Johnston to strike Grant quickly before Buell could join him. Johnston needed no urging, but this correspondence reveals the high regard that Davis and Lee still held for Johnston. "My confidence in you," Davis wrote to his western commander, "has never wavered."[26]

Even though Johnston had decided to attack, he still wanted Van Dorn to join him with his twenty thousand men from the Trans-Mississippi Department. Despite orders from Beauregard and then from Johnston for Van Dorn to march for western Tennessee, the Trans-Mississippi general launched his own offensive in another direction in late February. At the Battle of Pea Ridge, in northwestern Arkansas on March 7–8, Van Dorn's Confederate army met defeat at the hands of a smaller force under Union Major General Curtis. After this defeat, Van Dorn retreated to Van Buren, Arkansas, near Fort Smith. Beauregard had originally intended Van Dorn to relieve the Confederate garrison at New Madrid, Missouri, but since the town had already fallen, Van Dorn wrote to the Creole and requested instructions. Beauregard received this communication while at Jackson, Tennessee, on March 23 and again urged Van Dorn to move east. Van Dorn did not receive Beauregard's new orders until March 27 and at that time began marching his troops the two hundred miles to Des Arc, Arkansas, on the White River, where they could board boats for Memphis and thence overland to Corinth. However, the roads proved so terrible that Van Dorn estimated it would take him three weeks to reach Johnston and Beauregard.[27] Again, one of Johnston's subordinates had failed him by disregarding orders. Short of Van Dorn's arrival, Johnston decided to attack when he received word that Buell was approaching Grant's encampment at Pittsburg Landing.

Shortly before 10 P.M. on April 1, Johnston received a forwarded communication through Beauregard from General Benjamin F. Cheatham, one of his division commanders, posted twenty miles north of Corinth. Cheatham warned that a part of Grant's forces was threatening his position, and Beauregard scribbled on the communication, "Now is the moment to advance, and strike the enemy at Pittsburg Landing." Around the same time, Johnston received intelligence from Nathan Bedford Forrest that Buell's army was not far from Pittsburg Landing. Johnston wired Davis and informed him of the developments: "Confederate forces, 40,000 ordered forward to offer battle near Pittsburg. . . . Hope engagement before Buell can form junction." At the same time, Johnston issued an order to his commanders to be ready to move within twenty-four hours. At 1 A.M. on April 3, Johnston gave the order to begin the advance.[28]

He delegated the responsibility of planning the march to Beauregard, which turned out to be his second error of the Shiloh Campaign. Beauregard immediately issued verbal orders to the four corps commanders with a promise that written orders would reach them on the march. Two roads—the Ridge Road and the Monterrey Road—led from Corinth to where Grant's army was encamped around Pittsburg Landing. These two routes converged five miles from Pittsburg Landing, and lateral roads connected the two along the entire route. Beauregard intended the three corps to bivouac on the night of April 3 in the vicinity of a farmhouse known locally as Mickey's, with the attack to take place at dawn on April 4. As Johnston and Beauregard understood their enemy's position, Grant's army remained encamped with Lick Creek to the south, Owl Creek to the north, and the Tennessee River to the east, with the two roads leading into the camp from the west. Beauregard and Johnston intended the main attack to fall on the Union left, to cut them off from Pittsburg Landing on the Tennessee, and crush them against Owl Creek.[29]

Despite these seemingly simple plans, Beauregard's written instructions to the corps commanders were extremely complicated, completely unsuitable to green, untried troops. The results were predictable. Hardee's Corps, which Beauregard intended to spearhead the assault, blocked in the road by the wagons and artillery of Polk's corps, did not even get out of the streets of Corinth until mid-afternoon on April 3. Hardee's men rested on the road that night and did not reach Mickey's until the morning of April 4, twelve hours late. Braxton Bragg had even more problems. He had only reached the hamlet of Monterrey, halfway between Corinth and Pittsburg Landing, by noon on April 4. At an informal 5 P.M. conference at Monterrey, Johnston and Beauregard agreed to push the assault time back to the morning of April 5.[30]

Johnston realized that morale would play a key role in the coming battle. On April 3, he issued a circular to the "Soldiers of the Army of Mississippi." He began by telling them, "I have put you in motion to offer battle to the invaders of your country. With the resolution and disciplined valor becoming men fighting, as you are, for all worth living or dying for, you can but march to a decisive victory over agrarian mercenaries, sent to subjugate and despoil you of your liberties, property, and honor. Remember the precious stake involved. Remember the dependence of your mothers, your wives, your sisters, and our children on the result. . . . With such incentives to brave deeds, and with the trust that God is with us, your generals will lead you confidently to the combat, assured of success."[31] Johnston also rode from regiment to regiment along the line of march, encouraging the men. Speaking to a Louisiana regiment, Johnston said, "I'm glad to find you in such good spirits. I think we will beat the Yankees out today." To another unit, he advised, "Aim low; today you will have warm work to do." Everywhere Johnston went, the men broke into cheers, belying the claim that they had lost confidence in him and making it unlikely that he would have lost confidence in himself.[32]

Rain poured down in torrents on the night of April 4. Added to the inexperience of the troops, the rain caused massive confusion and delay. As Hardee's men moved into position less than a mile from the encamped Federals, the men began to discharge their weapons to see if their powder was still dry. When deer popped from the woods, the men would raise a shout that could be heard for miles. The attack, which depended on surprise, now seemed destined to fail. Finally by mid-morning on April 5, Hardee had his men in position. Meanwhile, Bragg couldn't get his last division into place for hours. In frustration, Johnston exclaimed, "This is perfectly puerile! This is not war! Let us have our horses." The commander and some of his staff members then rode off to find the missing division. Eventually, they found it, blocked in the road by some of Polk's wagons and artillery. Clearing the jam, Johnston sent the division forward. It was already 4 P.M. The attack clearly could not now take place on April 5. Reluctantly, Johnston pushed the time for the assault back again, to the morning of April 6.[33]

Much of the blame for the seventy-two-hour delay in launching the assault at Shiloh can be laid on the inexperience of the men and officers and the deplorable weather, but a greater degree of responsibility rests on the shoulders of Beauregard. Johnston seriously erred in placing him in charge of drawing up the plans for advance. Beauregard's plans were clearly unsuited for untried troops on this scale, and this serious oversight contributed more to the delay than did the rain and raw troops.

Beauregard also erred in issuing specific attack orders. His orders were unique in that they called for an advance with a single corps occupying the entire front line, while the other three corps followed at intervals of about one thousand yards. This cumbersome attack scheme proved difficult for several reasons. First, with a corps spread out over a front that stretched several miles, it would be nearly impossible for a corps commander to maintain control and contact with his entire line. Second, such an arrangement provided no extra strength at the point Johnston and Beauregard ostensibly wished to strike hardest—the Union left-center. Third, this plan necessarily entailed the early entanglement of men from the different corps as they advanced at different speeds across the battlefront. In all, it was a terrible plan, but Beauregard issued orders to the corps commanders that Hardee would lead off, with Bragg behind him, Polk behind him, and Breckinridge with the reserve bringing up the rear.[34]

Controversy has followed this attack scheme ever since. In his telegram informing Davis of the advance on April 3, Johnston indicated that Polk would advance on the left, Hardee in the center and Bragg on the right, with Breckinridge in reserve.[35] Such a plan of action made much more sense than that drawn up by Beauregard; Bragg's corps numerically possessed the most men and would be in position to smash the Federal left, as planned. Meanwhile, Polk's command had the fewest soldiers, next to the reserve, and would keep the Union right occupied while Hardee did the same in the center. Breckinridge could then be brought up in whatever sector he was most needed. Why Johnston's plan was never carried out is not entirely clear. Supporters of Johnston after the war claimed that Beauregard simply ignored Johnston's plan and issued his own orders, but in all likelihood, in the rush of the moment, Johnston and Beauregard probably did not have time to compare notes, and Johnston did not fully realize Beauregard's tactical thinking, or lack thereof, until it was too late. In any event, it is clear that Johnston made a serious error in judgment by placing the details for the advance and assault in the hands of Beauregard. Once again, a key subordinate had failed him.[36]

About 4 P.M. on April 5, Beauregard arrived at Bragg's headquarters near the intersection of the Corinth and Bark roads and began discussing the state of affairs. Breckinridge's command still lagged in the rear, and many of the men had exhausted their rations. Beauregard and Bragg also assumed that Grant had been alerted to their presence by the noisy displays of Hardee's men earlier in the day. The two generals agreed that the offensive should be canceled and the army returned to Corinth. Polk arrived next at this council of war and began exchanging heated words with Beauregard about the necessity of going through with the attack. This exchange lasted for some time before Johnston arrived and inquired as to the nature of the discussion. He was taken aback and utterly flabbergasted at the notion that the army should retreat. Beauregard, who at this point had clearly lost his nerve, exclaimed to Johnston, "Now they will be entrenched to the eyes." Johnston, though, stood firm, finally retaking the reigns of control. Retreat, he stated, "will never do." Polk, for once, made a sound decision in concurring on this point, and Johnston broke off the conversation: "Gentlemen, we shall attack at daylight tomorrow." As he walked away, he stated to a staff officer, "I would fight them if they were a million."[37] In these decisive remarks, Johnston continued to show confidence in himself, his plans, and his men, as had been his pattern throughout the campaign.

Historian Larry Daniel records this conversation in his book *Shiloh* but downplays its importance, stating that Johnston remained "pathetically insecure." On the contrary, it is clear that Johnston retained his self-confidence throughout the campaign. His actions continued to evince a robust confidence in himself, even if at times he did not feel that this confidence was shared by his men, civilians, or the government in Richmond.[38]

At 8 P.M., the Confederate generals again gathered around a fire. By this time, Bragg had changed his opinion, leaving Beauregard the only commander who favored retreat. After some perfunctory conversation, the meeting broke off at 10 P.M. In his defense, Beauregard's objections did have some merit. It certainly appeared as if the Federals should have gotten wind of the Confederate attack because of the rash behavior of the troops. Nevertheless, again it seems that Beauregard overestimated the training of the soldiers. A retreat to Corinth would have sent morale plummeting and relegated the Confederates to a wait-and-see policy while Grant and Buell united for a crushing blow. Despite the risks, Johnston clearly made the right decision in proceeding with the attack, notwithstanding the Creole's objections. As they fell asleep that night, Johnston, his subordinates, and many of his men felt that the next day would decide the war.

The Battle of Shiloh began at 5:00 A.M. on April 6 when a Federal reconnaissance party from the Twenty-fifth Missouri Infantry ran into the Third Mississippi Infantry Battalion of Hardee's Corps in front of the Union right-center. Johnston ordered a general advance for 6:30 A.M., and the forty thousand Confederates moved forward, taking Grant's men by surprise in their camps. For various reasons, the Federals had not been alerted to the Confederate presence, and the element of surprise remained intact as screaming Confederates charged through the tents of the Union army. Even though the Confederates had achieved strategic surprise in that Grant's men had neither entrenchments nor a coherent defensive alignment, they did not achieve tactical surprise because by the time they reached the Union camps, all of the Federal units were already under arms. As he rode toward the front after the skirmishing began, Johnston stopped Colonel John Marmaduke of the Third Arkansas Infantry and said, "My son, we must this day conquer or perish." As the battle began, Johnston instructed Beauregard to remain in the rear and funnel troops toward the front. Johnston decided to lead from the front astride his horse, Fire Eater.[39]

Why Johnston chose to lead from the front has been a matter of conjecture ever since. Because Beauregard had drawn up the plan of attack, perhaps Johnston felt that Beauregard should take care of the administrative details while he, Johnston, tried to correct the Creole's faulty battle plan by directing the Confederate effort on the right, fulfilling his original battle plan. His subordinates had failed him so many times that Johnston probably supposed that he had to lead from the front, on the spot, in order to get anything done right.

Johnston's actions during the battle are somewhat difficult to track but can be reasonably pieced together using various sources. Johnston made his headquarters on the night of April 6 along the Bark Road and rode forward after the first sounds of firing at 5:15 A.M. At this time, Johnston spoke to Brigadier General Randall Gibson, just to the west of Bark Road. Sighting his son's friend, he said, "Randal, I never see you but I think of William. I hope you may get through safely this day, but we must win a victory."[40] At this point, Johnston became concerned about Greer's Ford to the east on Lick Creek and decided to send reinforcements to that point in case Buell's army should arrive and flank his army. Riding west from Gibson, he addressed the First Tennessee Infantry, sending five companies of the regiment east toward Lick Creek.[41]

By 7 A.M., Hardee's assault had begun to falter, and Johnston ordered Bragg to bring his corps into action. Soon, Bragg's men had become entangled with Hardee's men as they struggled forward through the woods. As S A. M. Wood's Confederate brigade charged into the camps of Colonel Everett Peabody's brigade around 7:30 A.M., they absorbed a volley from the Federals, and the Fifty-fifth Tennessee and Third Mississippi battalions broke and ran, stampeding the Seventh Arkansas of Thomas Hindman's brigade. Johnston personally assisted Hindman and Wood in rallying their regiments and sending them back to the front.[42] From Peabody's position, Johnston rode east, toward the Confederate right. Seeing the widening gap on the right as Bragg's men advanced northwest away from the Tennessee, Johnston, at 8:30 A.M., ordered up General James Ronald Chalmers's brigade to press the attack. After setting Chalmers in motion, Johnston moved back toward the center to direct the advance there.[43]

Johnston entered Rea Field just in time to see Brigadier General Patrick Ronayne Cleburne's brigade come reeling back at about 9 A.M. after a bloody repulse. Speaking to Brigadier General Charles Clark, whose brigade was coming up behind Cleburne, Johnston instructed him merely to keep his men in place. From Clark, Johnston proceeded back east toward the Federal camp of Colonel Madison Miller's brigade just after Adley Gladden's and Chalmers's Confederate brigades had routed the occupants.[44] Riding into the captured bivouac at roughly 9:15, Johnston discovered some of the undisciplined troops looting the camp. Recognizing the need to press the advance, Johnston berated a young officer who had stopped to collect spoils. Then, noting both the youth and the contrition of the officer, Johnston softened, picked up a tin cup, and said, "Let this be my share of the spoils today." He then encountered a group of Federal prisoners who begged for their life. Johnston replied by assuring them that the Confederates would not kill prisoners. Then he rode on to confer with Hardee. From Miller's Camp, Johnston watched Chalmers's brigade disappear over the ridge and exclaimed to those around him, "That checkmates them."[45] Johnston assumed that Chalmers's men were in place to cut off Grant's men from Pittsburg Landing. In reality, Chalmers's brigade was much too far west to accomplish this goal.

For the first three hours of combat at Shiloh, Johnston had ridden along his line from left to right and back again, conferring with various commanders and observing enemy positions. At approximately 10:30 A.M., he received a note from one of the engineers on his staff, Captain Samuel H. Lockett, roughly mapping out the enemy positions.[46] By this time, a hard knot of Federal resistance had started to develop in the Union right-center in what became known as the Hornets' Nest, its successful defense facilitated by the fact that the assaulting Confederate lines in this sector had become extremely thin due to transfers of various brigades to other sectors on the left and right. Riding into a nearby ravine, Johnston dismounted, studied Lockett's map for a while, listened to the battle, and determined that he had to see to it personally that his men broke through the Hornets' Nest. To this end, he ordered up the two brigades under Breckinridge still being held in reserve. Johnston then rode to the right in advance of Breckinridge's men to inspire his troops in the critical sector of the battlefield.[47]

When he neared the front, Johnston encountered a group of wounded men, mostly Union, left unattended. He instructed his own personal surgeon, Dr. D. W. Yandell, to remain with the prisoners and care for them. Yandell objected, but Johnston overruled him, stating that he would send for him if needed. Johnston then proceeded with the rest of his staff, placing units in line and inspiring the morale of the troops, especially those on the right. When Breckinridge's two brigades came up around 1 P.M., Johnston personally placed them in front of the Peach Orchard, where the Union troops in that sector had anchored their left flank—just to the Confederate right of the Hornets' Nest. As the men of the Second Confederate Regiment moved into position, Johnston told them that with a few more charges, the day would be theirs.[48] At 1:30, Johnston began placing Brigadier General John S. Bowen's brigade into position.[49]

By 2 P.M., the Confederate assault had begun to falter, and Breckinridge approached Johnston in the rear to inform him that he could no longer prevail on the Forty-fifth Tennessee to advance. Johnston sent Tennessee Governor Isham Harris, who was on staff, to address the regiment. Soon, Breckinridge approached him again and informed him that he could not prevail on Bowen's brigade to advance. Johnston decided to do it himself. He rode to the ravine where the brigade, in line of battle, was sheltering from Union fire. Riding up and down the line, he impressed on the men the urgency of the moment. As he rode along the line, he touched their bayonets with the tin cup he had picked up in Miller's camp. "Men of Missouri and Arkansas," he said, "the enemy is stubborn. I want you to show General Beauregard and General Bragg what you can do with your bayonets." Then, impetuously, Johnston cried, "I will lead you!" and the regiments rushed forward with the army commander at their head. The men carried the position in front of them, and Johnston fell back mid-charge. What is clear is that Johnston received some close calls during the charge when a bullet tore off the sole of one of his boots, and Fire Eater sustained two slight wounds. He shouted to Harris, "They didn't trip me up that time!" in reference to his boot sole, which he flapped to show Harris the damage. Johnston then sent the governor off to the right to redirect a brigade in the correct direction.[50]

When Harris returned, he found Johnston almost alone, with most of his staff carrying messages to different parts of the field. The governor saw Johnston reel in the saddle. Asked if he was wounded, Johnston replied, "Yes, and I fear seriously." Leading Fire Eater to a nearby ravine, Harris and a Captain Wickham of Johnston's staff helped their commander dismount. Unaware of the wound in Johnston's leg, Harris tore the general's clothing, searching for a wound. Finding none, he tried to administer some brandy, but it simply ran out of Johnston mouth. The general was losing consciousness. Soon, other members of Johnston's staff arrived just in time to see their venerated commander expire from loss of blood. A Minnie ball had penetrated behind his right knee and severed the popliteal artery. Johnston bled to death within fifteen minutes. Ironically, he had a tourniquet in his pocket that Dr. Yandell could have utilized to save his life had Johnston not selflessly sent him to care for enemy wounded.[51]

Would the Confederates have won Shiloh had Johnston not been killed? Probably not. Beauregard's faulty plan of attack probably ensured that they would lose. The real loss to the Confederate cause by the death of Albert Sidney Johnston came in the long run, when a series of ineffective commanders blundered through command of the Army of Tennessee while Federal forces systematically destroyed Confederate resistance in the West. Johnston certainly had his failures in the Shiloh Campaign, primarily his willingness to trust his subordinates too much, but he had shown by Shiloh that he was beginning to overcome this defect in his leadership. Compared to his performance in the Henry-Donelson Campaign, the Shiloh Campaign showed vast improvement in Johnston's abilities as a field commander, particularly his strategic vision. Had he continued to improve at this rate, he might conceivably have become as great a field commander as Lee or Jackson and could have greatly enhanced the Confederate war effort in the West. His death at Shiloh lengthened the odds against Confederate success in the West and thus ultimately in the war as a whole. After the war, Jefferson Davis wrote of Johnston's death at Shiloh, "In his fall the great pillar of the Southern Confederacy was crushed, and beneath its fragments the best hope of the Southwest lay buried."[52]

Notes

1. Charles Roland, *Albert Sidney Johnston: Soldier of Three Republics* (Lexington: University Press of Kentucky, 2001), 298. Johnston had already anticipated that he would have to withdraw from his Bowling Green line with the assault on Fort Donelson, placing his army opposite Nashville. William Preston Johnston, *The Life of General Albert Sidney Johnston: His Service in the Armies of the United States, the Republic of Texas, and the Confederate States*, with a new introduction by T. Michael Parrish (1879; repr., New York: Da Capo, 1997), 501. Colonel William Preston Johnston was the son of the general.

2. The most complete biography of Johnston is Charles P. Roland, *Albert Sidney Johnston: Soldier of Three Republics* (Austin: University of Texas Press, 1964; with a new introduction by Gary Gallagher, Lexington: University Press of Kentucky, 2001). Roland also published a smaller volume, *Jefferson Davis's Greatest General: Albert Sidney Johnston* (Abilene: McWhiney Foundation, 2000). For a pro-Johnston stance, see Johnston, *Life of General Albert Sidney* Johnston. For other interpretations of Johnston in the campaign, see Gabor Borritt, ed., *Jefferson Davis's Generals* (Oxford: Oxford University Press, 1999); Thomas L. Connelly, *Army of the Heartland: The Army of Tennessee 1861–1862* (Baton Rouge: Louisiana State University Press, 1967); Larry Daniel, *Shiloh: The Battle That Changed the Civil War* (New York: Simon and Schuster, 1997); Stephen D. Engle, "'Thank God He Has Rescued His Character': Albert Sidney Johnston, Southern Hamlet of the Confederacy," in *Leaders of the Lost Cause*, ed. Gary Gallagher and Joseph T. Glathaar (Mechanicsburg: Stackpole, 2004), 133–64; Stanley Horn, *The Army of Tennessee* (1941; repr., Norman: University of Oklahoma Press, 1953); James McDonough, *Shiloh: in Hell before Night* (Knoxville: University of Tennessee Press, 1977); Wiley Sword, *Shiloh: Bloody April* (New York: William Morrow, 1974), and Steven E. Woodworth, *Jefferson Davis and His Generals: The Failure of Confederate Command in the West* (Lawrence: University Press of Kansas, 1990), and "When Merit Was Not Enough: Albert Sidney Johnston and Confederate Defeat in the West, 1862," in *Civil War Generals in Defeat*, ed. Woodworth (Lawrence: University Press of Kansas, 1999) 9–28.

3. Roland, *Jefferson Davis's Greatest General*, 14–15. Confederate legislation of September 1861 established a list of five individuals who initially held the rank of full general in the Confederate service. The first on the list was Adjutant General Samuel Cooper, considered too old for field command, followed by Albert Sidney Johnston, Robert E. Lee, Joseph E. Johnston, and P. G. T. Beauregard. Johnston's line rank as brigadier general made him the ranking officer from the old army who had resigned his commission to join the Confederacy.

4. Ibid., 20–21.

5. Johnston split the department with Beauregard in a council of war on February 7, 1862. Beauregard was assigned all of the troops and territory between the Tennessee and Mississippi Rivers, and Johnston had command of everything from the Tennessee River to the mountains in east Tennessee. Johnston, *Life of General Albert Sidney Johnston*, 500.

6. Roland, *Albert Sidney Johnston*, 301. U.S. War Department, *The War of the Rebellion: A Compilation of the Official Records of the Union and Confederate Armies*, ed. Robert N. Scott, 128 vols. (Washington, DC: GPO, 1884), 10.2:91. (This source is hereafter referred to as "*OR.*" All references are to series 1 unless otherwise noted.)

7. Daniel, *Shiloh*, 41.

8. Ibid., 43. Despite Forrest's efforts, Johnston lost 575,000 pounds of pork, 500 barrels of whiskey, 10,000 pairs of shoes and boots, 500 tents, and over 50 cannon. In Johnston's defense, Floyd apparently misled those around him as to whose idea the surrender at Donelson was. In his memoir, Colonel St. John Richardson Liddell of Johnston's staff came away with the impression that Simon Bolivar Buckner had urged surrender over the objections of Floyd and Pillow. Liddell, *Liddell's Record*, ed. Nathaniel C. Hughes Jr. (Baton Rouge: Louisiana State University Press, 1997), 52–53.

9. Connelly, *Army of the Heartland*, 138.

10. Roland, *Albert Sidney Johnston*, 306. Connelly's bias is shown in the very title of part 5 of *Army of the Heartland*, "The Beauregard Interlude." Liddell wrote at Murfreesboro, "Here the conclusion is almost universal that he [Johnston] is totally unfit for the position he holds in the Confederate army, and if he does nothing to retrieve his character very soon, he will be regarded as hopelessly embicile [*sic*]." Connelly, *Army of the Heartland*, 137. After the war, Liddell wrote, "I knew enough of Johnston's private views and the efforts he had quietly made to avert disasters, not to abandon myself to such want of confidence. I must confess, though, that my faith for the moment was somewhat shaken." Liddell, *Liddell's Record*, 54.

11. Connelly, *Army of the Heartland*, 138; Woodworth, "When Merit Was Not Enough," 10.

12. Johnston, *Life of Albert Sidney Johnston*, 506.

13. Ibid., 510.

14. Ibid.

15. Gilmer quoted in Roland, *Albert Sidney Johnston*, 303–304. Gilmer failed to carry out Johnston's orders to strengthen the Henry and Donelson defenses and also failed to construct defenses at Nashville as ordered.

16. Liddell, *Liddell's Record*, 59.

17. *OR*, vol. 7, 257–58.

18. Ibid., 258–61.

19. Roland, *Jefferson Davis's Greatest General*, 52.

20. Horn, *Army of Tennessee*, 120. For Colonel William Johnston's view on his father's actions, see Johnston, *Life of Albert Sidney Johnston*, 549–551. It is curious that Beauregard should consider Johnston's offer a sign of weakness, because just weeks earlier Beauregard, alarmed by the split of his forces from Johnston by the fall of Donelson, offered his command to his subordinate Braxton Bragg. Bragg, of course, declined.

21. Horn, *Army of Tennessee*, 119, 446. *OR*, 10.2:379.

22. *OR*, 10.2:379.

23. Roland, *Albert Sidney Johnston*, 314–15.

24. Ibid., 312–13.

25. Johnston, *Life of Albert Sidney Johnston*, 552–53.

26. Davis to Johnston, March 26, 1862, *OR*, 10.2:365.

27. Daniel, *Shiloh*, 98–99.

28. Roland, *Jefferson Davis's Greatest General*, 59–60.

29. *OR*, 10.1:392–97. In reality, the Tennessee River runs roughly north to south here, with Lick Creek to the east, Owl Creek to the West, and the roads leading into the encampment from the south. In general at Shiloh, the Confederates attacked facing north.

30. Roland, *Albert Sidney Johnston*, 318–19.

31. *OR*, 10.1, 396–97.

32. Roland, *Albert Sidney Johnston*, 320.

33. Ibid., 319; Woodworth, "When Merit Was Not Enough," 24.

34. Roland, *Albert Sidney Johnston*, 321.

35. *OR*, 10.2:387.

36. Woodworth, "When Merit Was Not Enough," 25. Historian James McDonough notes regarding Beauregard's plan, "The Confederates may well have lost the opportunity to break the Union army at Shiloh when they adopted this program of battle." McDonough, *Shiloh*, 73.

37. Daniel, *Shiloh*, 128.

38. Ibid.

39. McDonough, *Shiloh*, 86–87, 98–99. Why the Confederates took Grant's army by surprise is beyond the purview of this article. For a more complete explanation, see McDonough, *Shiloh*.

40. Johnston, *Life of Albert Sidney Johnston*, 582.

41. Daniel, *Shiloh*, 145.

42. *OR*, 10.1:577, 591.

43. *OR*, 10.1:532, 536, 545, 548.

44. *OR*, 10.1:414–15.

45. Roland, *Albert Sidney Johnston*, 332. *OR*, 10.1:404.

46. Most of the other sources mentioning Lockett's note state that Johnston received it at 9:30, but there are several facts that militate against this time frame. First, Federal resistance in the Hornets' Nest had not yet started to develop by 9:30. Second, Johnston was busy watching Chalmers's Brigade advance at this time. Third, in his official report, Johnston's aide-de-camp Colonel William Preston stated that Johnston received Lockett's report at "half past 9 or 10. . . . " This indicates that time was very confused and that Johnston probably received the communication at 10:30 A.M. *OR*, 10.1: 404.

47. *OR*, 10.1:335.

48. Ibid., 335; ibid., 621.

49. *OR*, 10.1:554, 621.

50. McDonough, *Shiloh*, 153. Johnston led the charge of Bowen's Brigade at approximately 2:15 P.M.

51. Roland, *Albert Sidney Johnston*, 337–38.

52. Jefferson Davis, *Rise and Fall of the Confederate Government*, vol. 2 (New York: Appleton, 1881), 67.

2

A TERRIBLE BAPTISM BY FIRE
DAVID STUART'S DEFENSE OF THE UNION LEFT

Alexander Mendoza

Shortly after 6 P.M. on April 6, General P. G. T. Beauregard halted the attack of his Confederate Army of Mississippi on the lines of Grant's Army of the Tennessee. "The victory is sufficiently complete," explained Beauregard to one of his subordinates. The Creole general was confident that if Grant's army did not withdraw during the night, as Beauregard rather expected, his own Confederate army would drive it into the river. He was wrong, and the Rebel assault on the evening of the sixth represented in some ways a high-water mark of Confederate hopes.[1]

Several key junctures in the battle figured largely in this final result, this Union victory, and none of these was more important than the fight that took place near Lick Creek and the Hamburg-Savannah Road area two miles to the southwest of that high-water mark.[2] There Colonel David Stuart's lone brigade of a little more than twenty-one hundred raw troops from Ohio and Illinois stood off a larger Confederate force for five vital hours when retreat would have brought about the collapse of the Union position and the likely surrender of at least a significant part of the Army of the Tennessee.

Several weeks before the battle, General William Tecumseh Sherman had selected the ground around Pittsburg Landing for the Union army's camps and deployed his own division to cover its approaches. Three of his four brigades he deployed near his division headquarters at Shiloh Church, on the Corinth Road a little more than two and a half miles from the landing. The fourth brigade, Stuart's, consisting of the Fifty-fifth Illinois and the Fifty-fourth and Seventy-first Ohio, he deployed two miles to the east of Shiloh Church to guard the Hamburg-Savannah Road, which was the other primary southern approach to Pittsburg Landing.[3] During the weeks between that deployment and the battle, three other divisions moved into the area between Sherman's and the landing, and Brigadier General Benjamin Prentiss's Sixth

Division began to organize along the outer edge of the Union encampment between the main body of Sherman's division at Shiloh Church and Stuart's separated brigade. Stuart remained in his original position, assigned to guard the extreme Union left.[4] Prentiss's left flank was about eight hundred yards from Stuart's right, and a similar gap separated Prentiss's right from the left of the main body of Sherman's division.[5]

Stuart, a former Illinois lawyer and railroad solicitor whose prewar reputation took a serious blow when he was involved in a sordid divorce case, epitomized the inexperienced officers who dominated both armies early in the war. Successful in their professional lives, many of these untrained soldiers failed in the heat of battle, a problem that was not lost on the rank and file as they carefully observed the performance of their commanders.[6] Stuart may not have possessed the professional military education many believed necessary, but he did at least have the one intangible benefit that the common soldier appreciated—courage. "Colonel David Stuart . . . had no military training but he was brave to a fault," wrote one Ohio soldier, "and if he committed errors in posting and handling his brigade, it was in the endeavor to obey the orders that were given him."[7] Yet, bravery was not always an adequate substitute for preparedness, and Stuart often had his subordinates drill the men in his place, thus assuring himself limited experience in leading his men during battle.[8]

Lick Creek, which ran just north of a series of steep hills that dominated the area, flowed eighty to a hundred feet wide at , Lick Creek Ford, just south of Hamburg-Savannah Road. While not particularly imposing, the stream could still be a significant barrier to an attacking force, especially after the recent wet weather.[9] The Fifty-fifth Illinois, bivouacking in a peach orchard in the field of Noah Cantrell, held the easternmost position of Stuart's brigade. A few hundred yards to Fifty-fifth's right stood the tents of the Fifty-fourth Ohio, along the western edge of Larkin Bell Field. About three hundred yards farther to their right, just south of the junction of the Hamburg-Purdy and Savannah-Purdy roads, the Seventy-first Ohio encamped as the westernmost element of Stuart's brigade.[10] Approximately a quarter mile away from Stuart's front and parallel to the Hamburg-Purdy Road was a tributary of Lick Creek called Locust Grove Run. The area that Stuart guarded, like the rest of the field of battle, was filled with dense thickets that were interspersed with fields and orchards.

Even though the natural terrain on the Union left might have seemed imposing and an ideal defensive position, the Federals realized it also had its drawbacks. For one thing, the sharp ravines and steep bluffs that marked the area could also prove perilous to the Union defenders, as the rough terrain could prevent them from moving quickly to aid a threatened position. Adding to the woes on the Union left, Stuart's brigade, like the rest of Grant's army, had neglected to entrench and fortify its positions, because at this early stage of the war, when most of the army's raw recruits had never seen combat, it was perceived as demoralizing to dig with pick and spade. "No effort was made to fortify at any point, and the very highest of the surrounding bluffs . . . were left for the enemy to occupy," observed a veteran of the battle.[11] Without entrenching, Stuart did his best to prepare for a possible Confederate assault by posting pickets to his front and reconnoitering to the south and east of Lick Creek. The brigade commander ordered one company to remain at Lick Creek Ford, while another company guarded the area near the intersection of the Bark and the Hamburg-Savannah roads, where the latter crossed Locust Grove Run.[12] Additional pickets were stationed along Locust Grove Run where it meandered northwesterly to its mouth at Lick Creek, which flowed southward before veering to the southeast itself. In the days preceding the battle, Sherman showed concern for this sector and ordered the Fifty-fourth Ohio, along with a detachment of cavalry, to advance along Lick Creek toward the home of Jack Greer and drive any Rebel pickets in the vicinity.[13] While the operation failed to uncover any substantial information as to the Confederates' intentions, it at least gave the green Federal troops some activity beyond drill and exercise.

When the initial wave of the Confederate battle line struck Prentiss's troops at about 7:00 A.M., Stuart's men were casually preparing for another day of drill and exercise. As they woke from their weary slumber, and the cooks began to prepare for breakfast, some members of the Fifty-fourth Ohio were reporting on sick call while the officers of the Seventy-first Ohio were checking in with Colonel Rodney Mason to organize their morning drill.[14] Captain George Stone's artillery battery had been ordered away from the brigade the day before, and all that remained were the three infantry regiments assigned to the sector. No one reported any enemy activity near their camps. Much like the rest of Grant's army, Stuart's men would be caught completely unaware. If the Federal soldiers initially ignored the sound of firing to the southwest of their camps, it was because Stuart had given his men permission to clear their weapons by firing toward a bluff on the opposite side of Locust Grove. Consequently, as the Confederates hit Prentiss's line in full force, the initial sounds of battle were largely ignored by the members of Stuart's brigade.[15]

Unbeknownst to Stuart's men, they had been watched by a Confederate patrol probing the Lick Creek sector to ascertain what Union forces might be lurking on the extreme eastern end of the battlefield. Captain Samuel H.

Lockett of General Braxton Bragg's staff observed Stuart's brigade closely the morning of April 6. Bragg had ordered Lockett along with a small detachment of cavalry to scout the Union left "to get all the information possible about the enemy's position and condition."[16] It was about 4:00 A.M. when Lockett first made his way along the Bark Road to the area of Locust Grove Run before taking a position on a bluff overlooking the Union camp north of the creek. In his initial trip beyond the Union pickets, the Confederate captain witnessed the smoldering fires of an otherwise inactive Federal camp. Dispatching a note of warning to his commander, Lockett continued to advance eastward another quarter mile when he saw the Yankee cooks beginning to prepare for breakfast and reveille being sounded as the men readied for inspection. On a third foray, Lockett emerged from the hills south of Locust Grove still farther to the east and heard the sound of firing from the distance. He detected that the initial sounds of the morning's battle were "not understood" until "couriers began to arrive." At that point, Lockett observed, the long roll was beaten, and the Union soldiers began to prepare for battle. When Lockett saw the activity of Stuart's men, he made the egregious error of assuming he had reconnoitered an entire division (six thousand to eight thousand men) rather than a single brigade (about two thousand men). Fearing that this large Union force would flank the Confederate right, the engineer, after a brief survey of his front, retreated at about 9:00 A.M. from his precarious perch to report his distressing news personally to Johnston.[17]

While the Confederate reconnaissance of the Union left began too late to provide adequate intelligence to the Rebel commander, Lockett's misinterpretation of Stuart's force was actually aided by the Federal activity that morning. When the firing opened up on the Union center, General Prentiss personally made his way to Stuart to apprise him that the army was under attack.[18] Private John Wheeler of the Fifty-fourth Ohio probably echoed the sentiments of most of the rank and file, however, when he assumed that the long roll was meant for morning drill. Colonel Thomas Kilby Smith of the same regiment quickly ascertained the true meaning of the early morning firing. "They are fighting," he announced, as the men quickly moved into line and readied for battle.[19] Stuart's inexperience in maneuvering his troops caused some delay as his men remained standing for about half an hour before moving to their left and then advancing toward Lick Creek Ford. The Federals' pause before advancing along the Hamburg-Savannah Road unintentionally gave Lockett the impression that the Union left was preparing to attack the Confederate right flank to the southwest.[20] The Rebel engineer likely assumed that the initial delay and the additional movement of Stuart's troops as they readied for battle meant that a division was making the march to get to the Confederate left and rear. If successful, such a movement could prove disastrous for Johnston's army.

The battle thus far had gone splendidly for the Rebels. The initial impact of General William J. Hardee's assault had overwhelmed Prentiss's Federals. Once Hardee's troops had engaged Sherman, Johnston ordered Bragg's troops and the initial brigades of General Leonidas Polk's corps into battle. By the time Johnston received Lockett's initial message, Prentiss's Sixth Division was retreating northward toward Pittsburg Landing.[21] The Union lines were stiffening around the Shiloh Church sector as Lockett arrived sometime around 11:00 A.M. at Johnston's makeshift headquarters at the captured camp of Prentiss's Second Brigade with the dire news of a Union division advancing on the Confederate right. Johnston informed Lockett that he had received the engineer's prior messages alerting him to the danger on the right, and he had already ordered troops to that sector. The commanding general had dispatched couriers to send the brigades of James Chalmers and John K. Jackson, about forty-five hundred men in all, to meet the Union force by Lick Creek Ford.[22] If these men could get there in time, they could potentially help the Confederates push the Federals back.

By focusing his attention to the Union left, Johnston was in effect returning to the original battle plan he had envisioned in the days prior to the battle. Yet, the problem for the Rebels remained the lack of adequate and accurate intelligence about the Federal dispositions in the area near Lick Creek. Johnston probably did not intend the forty-five hundred men he thus dispatched to cut off Grant's army from the river. He seems to have believed, thanks to inaccurate maps, that he had substantially accomplished that already by taking Prentiss's camps. Chalmers and Jackson would have the task of securing the Confederate flank against this errant Union "division." It would be no light job. Not only would they supposedly have to deal with a force of equal or greater size (according to Lockett's flawed intelligence report) but they would also have to disengage themselves from their positions on the battlefront and march a roundabout journey in arguably some of the battlefield's roughest terrain. Moreover, the lack of Confederate intelligence regarding the area around Pittsburg Landing would be a major element in the battle.[23]

Standing on the Confederate right flank, Generals Chalmers and Jackson received Johnston's orders to withdraw from the battle line and move to the southeast at around 9:30. Chalmers, a former district attorney from Mississippi, commanded the Second Brigade in Bragg's Second Division, while Jackson, a Georgia lawyer prior to the war, led the Third Brigade in the same division. Jackson's Brigade comprised the Seventeenth, Eighteenth, and Nineteenth Alabama regiments and the Second Texas. The brigade had been engaged with Prentiss's line along the Hamburg-Purdy Road for about an hour when Johnston's order arrived. On Jackson's right stood Chalmers's brigade, composed of the Fifth, Seventh, Ninth, and Tenth Mississippi regiments and Fifty-second Tennessee. The Rebel force had been veering to the left as it advanced against the Federal lines in what amounted to a left-wheel movement. Unbeknownst to Johnston, who was depending on Lick Creek to anchor the Confederate right, that stream, where it met the Hamburg-Savannah Road, veered sharply to the east, toward the Tennessee River. The gap between the Johnston's right flank and the stream would thus keep increasing the farther the Confederates advanced against the Union lines. And if Lockett's report was accurate, having a Federal division come up against the Rebel rear would be devastating. So, before the two brigades could continue to exploit their gains against the Union lines, Johnston's instructions to move to the right seemed prudent. Joining the brigades were two artillery units: Charles P. Gage's Alabama Battery, which accompanied Chalmers, and Isadore Girardey's Georgia battery, which followed Jackson. Within minutes of receiving Johnston's orders, they had disengaged and begun the march south toward Locust Grove Branch.[24]

The Confederate troops who began the circuitous journey to the right were in one important respect similar to the Union force they aimed to meet: they were equally inexperienced.[25] Chalmers's brigade had not seen battle thus far. Jackson's troops had served on the Gulf Coast prior to being transferred to Johnston's army. The Second Texas had been mustered in less than a month prior to the campaign and arrived in Corinth on April 1.[26] Inexperience did not subdue the Confederates' confidence in the days leading up to the battle. One soldier in the Eighteenth Alabama claimed that in drill and exercise, his regiment "is surprisingly proficient" despite their rawness. This skill gained from military preparation gave many of the Rebels extreme confidence, regardless of the setbacks at forts Henry and Donelson. As one soldier from the Seventh Mississippi said, "If we do not whip the Federals this time I shall always think we ought."[27] Certainly the gains of the morning's battle had only reinforced the Rebels' morale, as they had overwhelmed the Union camps during the early hours of battle. Some soldiers, like those of the Second Texas, even used the notoriety of the frontier experience to instill a sense of fear among the Federals, who, according to one captured Yankee, feared "they would be shown no quarter" if captured by troops from the Lone Star state.[28] As Chalmers's and Jackson's brigades launched their roundabout march to the south bank of Locust Grove, they were likely buoyed by the resounding success of the early morning.

While the Rebels made their way southward from the battle line along the Hamburg-Purdy Road, Stuart's brigade continued to await the Confederate assault as it had since being alerted to the action on its right front early that morning. The Ohio and Illinois regiments grew anxious when they received orders to move to and fro while waiting for the enemy. "These aimless spasmodic changes of position coupled with the realizing sense that should we be attacked it would naturally be by a strong force," wrote one veteran of the Fifty-fifth Illinois, "worked the men up to a high nervous pitch."[29] After this time of indecision, Stuart tried to deploy his brigade to meet all possible threats to his sector, moving his men slightly to the southeast in the direction of Lick Creek Ford. The Fifty-fourth Ohio, which previously held the center position in Stuart's encampment, moved farthest toward Lick Creek Ford, jumping over the previous camp of the Fifty-fifth Illinois before straddling the Hamburg-Savannah Road at the north end of McCuller Field. About two hundred yards to their right stood the Fifty-fifth Illinois, holding the brigade's new center, just southeast of the Larkin Bell Field. Stationed on the brigade's right flank, the Seventy-first Ohio's line spanned the Larkin Bell Field, just south of the Hamburg-Savannah Road. Stuart also ordered two companies from each regiment sent toward Locust Grove Run to watch for a Rebel advance.[30]

Still more complicated maneuvers followed, especially for the hapless Fifty-fifth Illinois, further exacerbating the disorder among the green troops. Stuart had given Lieutenant Colonel Oscar Malmbourg most of the responsibilities for that regiment's field maneuvers, and on the morning of battle, according to one member of the Fifty-fifth, the lieutenant colonel seemed to "have the idea that the main use of infantry was to repel the attacks of cavalry." The native Swede put his regiment through an elaborate set of movements that consisted of forming a hollow square he called "column by file." While the Federal soldiers would ultimately have to wait about three hours for the Rebels to make contact, the maneuvers and redeployments Malmbourg ordered during the interim certainly did not strengthen the confidence of his raw troops. To make matters worse, the gap of about a quarter mile between Stuart's right flank and the rest of the Federal force farther west, seemed to be growing larger once the Rebels dispensed with Prentiss's division and moved on to confront the Union center. Stuart's brigade was on its own.[31]

Yet, despite the initial mismanagement of his brigade, Stuart stuck to his original orders of guarding Lick Creek Ford while conforming to the battle at hand and preparing to meet any potential Confederate advance on Locust Grove Run. With one regiment watching the ford of Lick Creek while two others faced the smaller stream to the south, the brigade was thus ready to meet the Confederate onslaught. At the same time, without additional orders and instructions, Stuart's force maintained a line of retreat to the north and Pittsburg Landing.

While Stuart's men prepared for the inevitable Confederate attack, Chalmers and Jackson had begun their march south from the Hamburg-Purdy Road through the roughest terrain of the battlefield, crossing the western end of Locust Grove Run before veering to the east and making a roundabout journey to the Lick Creek sector. The Rebel troops commenced an undulating march, descending approximately fifty feet, as they moved south to Locust Grove, before ascending another fifty feet as they completed their march and prepared to meet Stuart's brigade. As Colonel John C. Moore of the Second Texas recollected, the difficulty of marching on the battlefield was exacerbated by the inexperience of the "raw troops" that often led them to break their lines in the thick undergrowth of the battlefield.[32] Some of the Rebels also broke ranks to plunder the Union camps in search of spoils, ranging from food and stationery to the medical supplies.[33]

Adding to the challenges of terrain and indiscipline, the Confederate troops also had to deal with the ever-mounting fatigue of hours of marching and fighting. Although Chalmers's and Jackson's brigades had been engaged in battle only a short while, the men had made quick gains against the Union lines, capturing prisoners, provisions, and even a Union battery as they advanced more than half a mile against Prentiss's lines.[34] The march was particularly arduous for the two Confederate batteries accompanying the brigades, as they had to maneuver through "thickly wooded country over ravines and hills almost impossible to ordinary weapons."[35]

As Chalmers's and Jackson's brigades moved to find the Union left, they were accompanied by Colonel James H. Clanton's First Alabama Cavalry, which had been assigned to Chalmers's rear that morning. Clanton, a veteran of the Mexican-American War and a former congressman from Alabama, had been ordered to reconnoiter the area of Lick Creek and protect the Rebel right from attack. Chalmers's Brigade and Clanton's cavalry had actually engaged the Federals three days prior to the battle in a small skirmish that netted no significant results other than having a dozen Confederate horsemen taken prisoner. Now, as the battle progressed and intelligence was limited within the Confederate high command, the Alabama cavalry unit advanced along Lick Creek toward the Tennessee River with orders to prevent an envelopment of the Rebel right.[36]

Chalmers and Jackson had to wait about half an hour for a guide, and then their brigades took about an hour to traverse the difficult ground and redeploy in order to advance against the Federal left. It was between 10:30 and

11:00 A.M. as the vanguard units of the Confederate force first began to receive fire from the Union skirmishers on the north bank of Locust Grove Run. As the Confederates began their left wheel to face north, Jackson's Brigade held the left flank, directly south of Larkin Bell Field, while Chalmers advanced on the Confederate right toward McCuller Field. Meanwhile, Girardey's and Gage's batteries took position on Jackson's left and right, respectively, on the high ground south of Locust Grove Creek.[37]

During the long wait for the Confederates to arrive, Stuart's skirmishers had advanced across Locust Grove Creek and all the way to the top of the bluff that overlooked the stream from the south. Now, with their backs to the steep slope just behind them, the Federal skirmishers watched as the Confederate brigades deployed and moved up to within a hundred yards of their position. Members of the Fifty-fifth Illinois's skirmish detachment saw the Rebels opposite them, standing in ranks, the officers "riding up and down the line, talking to their men, who cheered vociferously." One of the Federals, attempting to pick off a Confederate officer on horseback, inadvertently initiated a general volley from the Union skirmishers, which shook the Rebel lines. The skirmishers had fired on Chalmers's men as they were forming, inflicting some damage on the Confederate troops. "We commenced firing upon them," wrote Captain S. B. Yeoman, a skirmisher from the Fifty-fourth Ohio, "and I had the pleasure of seeing seven of them 'bite the dust.'"[38] Particularly hard hit by that initial volley, the Fifty-second Tennessee broke and ran away in what Chalmers described as "most shameful confusion," while the remaining Mississippi regiments of the brigade stood their ground. After repeated efforts to rally the Tennessee regiment, Chalmers ordered it out of the line for the remainder of the battle, with the exception of two of its companies that fought in the ranks of the Fifth Mississippi for the rest of the day.[39]

The Federal skirmishers had done well, but once the Rebel batteries deployed, they stood no chance. Girardey's Georgia Battery quickly maneuvered to within one hundred yards of the Union skirmishers and began firing canister at the Yankees. Masked by the thick undergrowth and the sharp ravines of the battlefield, the Federals were not ready to give up yet. They returned fire, wounding several of the cannoneers. Captain Girardey requested infantry support, and Jackson's men moved up and forced the stubborn skirmishers to retreat. With the Union pickets silenced, Girardey was able to place his guns at the north edge of the bluff, overlooking the ravine of Locust Grove Run, where his fire quickly eliminated Federal resistance. The Rebel guns could now focus on the Union force near the Hamburg-Savannah Road.[40]

Chalmers and Jackson waited for almost half an hour as Clanton's cavalry probed the Lick Creek sector to their right in search of additional Federal units, and the Rebel batteries finished planting their field guns on the bluffs over-looking Locust Grove Run. "Satisfied that there was no enemy on our right," Brigadier General Jones Mitchell Withers, the Second Division commander, later reported, "the order was given to advance."[41] The two brigades—more than four thousand men—pushed forward, brushing aside a few remaining Union skirmishers, who continued to fire while retreating. The Confederate infantry advanced to the bottom of the ravine, largely unimpeded in their progress, before they "were ordered to charge." Yelling and cheering as they crossed Locust Grove Run, the Rebels were pleased and perhaps surprised by what they saw. The Bluecoats were running away without firing a shot. In his postbattle report, Jackson was charitable when he wrote that the "enemy fell back, and the camp was ours."[42]

For Stuart's men, the tension had been building since the morning's early futile maneuvering. Now, it reached the breaking point. As firing first began to erupt from the bluffs south of Locust Grove Run, an obviously nervous Lieutenant Colonel Malmbourg had continued to maneuver the Fifty-fifth Illinois with increasing urgency. Unsure as to the direction from which the Rebels would approach, the Swedish martinet, hitherto ferociously confi-dent in his military knowledge, now seemed entirely out of his depth as he issued a stream of orders shifting the regiment's formation first one way and then another. The confusion and uncertainty culminated in panic as the companies of the Fifty-fifth began to "crowd and overlap each other," provoking at last a "wild stampede" as the regiment "broke and ran in the most inextricable confusion."[43]

The Illinois troops were not alone in their search for safe haven as the Seventy-first Ohio, holding the right, or west, end of Stuart's line, also broke once the Rebel guns unlimbered and commenced firing from their position south of Locust Grove Run. Initially organized in Troy, Ohio, in October 1861, the Seventy-first was led by Colonel Mason, whose father, Samuel Mason, was a five-term congressman and a highly respected public figure from the Buckeye State. Many of the men in the regiment despised their command-ing officer: "They cannot ask him a civil question without getting a cursing for an answer."[44]

Although Mason might have received the command of the regiment due to his father's political connections to Governor David Tod, the heart and soul of the Seventy-first undoubtedly remained Lieutenant Colonel Barton S. Kyle, who actually recruited and organized the regiment in his hometown. Like many units at Shiloh, the Ohio regiment had not previously experienced battle. Rather, the Seventy-first had traveled from Cincinnati down the Ten-nessee River to set up its first camp in the field near Shiloh. During the move to join Grant's army in February and March, many soldiers of the regiment fell ill due to the dietary changes and the river water, reducing their force to less than five hundred effectives.[45]

No sooner did the Confederate artillery begun to thunder from across Locust Grove Run than the Seventy-first Ohio regiment and its commander, Colonel Rodney Mason, fled in terror. Mason had been complaining to Stuart about his regiment's inability to withstand artillery fire when the brigade commander rode off without further discussion. Once the Rebel batteries opened on them, the Seventy-first fired a few shots before falling back in disorder. Mason later tried to explain his regiment's apparent failure to remain steadfast against enemy fire and lamented that many of his men went into battle untrained and unarmed. Justifications notwithstanding, Mason could not help but regret that his troops "did not bear themselves with greater steadiness."[46]

Stuart, for his part not as charitable as his regimental commander, pointed out in his official report that he did not see Mason or his regiment for the remainder of the fight. In the days following the battle, the Illinois press disparaged the Ohio regiment that "ran at the first fire or without a shot," going as far as to claim that members of the Seventy-first had commandeered a steamboat waiting for the Union wounded.[47] Although shattered after the initial artillery bombardment, the unit did not entirely disappear, despite the later claims of Illinois veterans who bitterly denounced the entire regiment in their postwar reminiscences while conveniently forgetting that some of their own comrades also ran.[48] A few of the junior officers of the Seventy-first took charge and rallied dozens of soldiers and continued to fight—some attaching themselves to the other two regiments—while the rest of the Buckeyes attempted to re-form about 150 to 200 yards behind their original position.[49] Although they might not have played a major role in the fight, their mere appearance near the Hamburg-Purdy and Hamburg-Savannah intersection probably kept the Rebel units at least alert to an enemy presence on that front.[50]

In the meantime, the only unit in Stuart's brigade that remained resolute during the initial fighting was the Fifty-fourth Ohio. The Fifty-fourth, one of a few Zouave regiments in the Army of the Tennessee, had been originally organized by Colonel Smith in the fall and winter of 1861 before joining Sherman's division prior to the Battle of Shiloh. Holding the far left of Stuart's line with about four hundred men, the Buckeyes of the Fifty-fourth had been waiting several hours for the Rebel assault. When Chalmers's brigade advanced toward the Federals, the Fifty-fourth, with its right on the Hamburg-Savannah Road, stood ready to meet the Confederate wave behind a fence at the northern end of McCuller Field, a six-hundred-yard-long parallelogram tilting to the northwest. A 350- to 400 yard-wide peach orchard stood toward the southern edge of the field. North of McCuller Field, a sharp trace, which originated near the Hamburg-Savannah Road, ran east before turning north toward the Tennessee River.[51]

After crossing Locust Grove Run, Chalmers's brigade moved cautiously against the Union position. The Confederates recognized that their force was in full view of the Federal lines from the time it crossed the stream and advanced northward, gradually ascending McCuller Field. With the Ninth Mississippi Regiment on its far left, approximately thirty yards from the Hamburg-Savannah Road, the brigade marched forward, Gage's battery offering support from its position on the bluff above the run. Chalmers noted in his after-action report that he was surprised "not a shot was fired until we came to within 40 yards of the fence." The Fifty-fourth Ohio was merely biding its time before launching a vicious volley that slammed into Chalmers's brigade with deadly effect. While the Confederates reeled from the hail of enemy fire, the Federals sent a column down the Hamburg-Savannah Road to flank the Rebel force. At this point, Gage's battery began to hammer the Fifty-fourth, scattering the flanking column and allowing Chalmers enough time to redeploy his men and charge the Union lines.[52] Captain Yeoman noted that the Fifty-fourth was soon overwhelmed by "both artillery and infantry" and was forced to withdraw.[53] To some of the Rebels, the retreating Federals were plum picking. "As they retreated I gave it to one old blue belly about where his suspenders crossed sending him to eternity," a private in the Seventh Mississippi related.[54]

By now it was noon, and Chalmers's and Jackson's men had had things very much their own way. Yet, they could not closely pursue Stuart's fleeing Federals. The Rebels had been marching since dawn, and their circuitous journey from the center of the battle line to arrive at a position from which to assault the Union left had winded them. he fight for McCuller Field had taken its toll, leaving them exhausted and short of ammunition. Moreover, with their wagons far to the rear, across Locust Grove Run, Chalmers's men would have to delay their advance once again while they waited for details to bring up cartridges.[55]

Thus far, the day had not gone particularly well for Stuart's brigade. The Fifty-fifth Illinois and Seventy-first Ohio were in full retreat while the Fifty-fourth Ohio barely hung on against a numerically superior foe. In the face of impending crisis, Stuart reasserted his authority as he witnessed his panic-stricken brigade disintegrate before his eyes. "Halt! Men, halt!" Stuart bellowed from atop his horse, sword in hand. The men of the Fifty-fifth Illinois along with some members of the Seventy-first Ohio stopped and began to re-form their lines about a quarter mile behind their original position. The brigade commander's early-morning jitters had not dissipated and grew as reports about Confederate cavalry once again threw the Federals into disarray. Stuart figured that he now had about eight hundred men to face more than five times that number. In the confusion, Malmbourg gave the order to form another hollow square in anticipation of the Rebel horsemen. When no attack materialized, the Federals withdrew once more, this time to a position on the brow of a hill with a sharp ravine to their rear. "[W]e did not have long to wait for the deadly work to begin," recalled Lieutenant Elijah Lawrence.[56]

The Confederates advanced—Jackson's brigade this time. The Fifty-fifth, some of whose members had taken cover in old log houses, "opened fire and checked the advance of the Confederate forces after they crossed the open fields unmolested and entered the woods," said a Union officer. Joining the Illinoisans in the log houses were remnants of the Seventy-first Ohio under Captain Thomas K. Brown, who had taken over one of the cabins previously used as a hospital by the Fifty-fifth.[57] The Confederates grumbled about the Yankees "who fired through the cracks at us" from those log cabins.[58]

Girardey's and Gage's batteries, about eight hundred yards to the south, continued to pour solid shot and shell into the Federal lines, but the Confederate long arm lost some of its earlier effectiveness as the rolling terrain to which the Union troops had retreated provided the Yankees some cover from the Rebel artillery. In the meantime, Chalmers stopped momentarily.[59] Chalmers's delay had an impact on Jackson's brigade as it was "unexpectedly ordered to halt and await further orders . . . due to our advancing in front of the line on our right occupied by Chalmer's [sic] brigade," recalled Colonel Moore of the Second Texas.[60] While the Confederate brigade commanders paused to regroup and re-form their lines, the rank and file rummaged through the abandoned Federal camps in search of plunder, a pattern that was repeated throughout the field of battle that day.

Members of the Second Texas Regiment, however, feared a loss of momentum the longer they delayed. The Texans came from a hardscrabble unit who had endured an arduous three-week journey from Houston (some of them took pride in being known as the "*dirtiest* troops in the command"), arriving ill-equipped at Corinth just days before the campaign, and they were not to be denied a victory at Shiloh. Without waiting for orders from Jackson, Colonel Moore led his men in a charge, overcoming a withering fire from the Federals in the log houses as the Rebels advanced northward.[61] According to one Texan, "Our men fell back a short distance and formed again and charged with a terrible yell. The Yankees dropped guns, cartridge boxes, and even threw off their coats, to get beyond our reach."[62] The Confederate attack forced the Union troops to withdraw from their position in the log cabins and yielded several prisoners.[63] In defending the Federal position, Lieutenant Colonel Kyle was mortally wounded while attempting to rally the men of the Seventy-first Ohio.[64]

Advancing across the ground from which the Texans had just driven the Federals, the Confederates found remnants of Stuart's brigade along the near edge of a deep ravine, about one hundred feet wide and about fifty feet deep, a natural defensive barrier that the Federals would use to their advantage. Not only were the Yankees largely impervious to the Rebel batteries firing ineffectively over their heads but they were also able to regain their confidence as they squared off against the advancing Confederate force.[65] Lieutenant Lawrence of the Fifty-fifth noted, "The men would drop down the hill to load, and crawl up to the top to fire, in almost every case taking deliberate aim, with good effect."[66] The Rebels, for their part, advanced to the edge of a tree line bordering an open field about 150 yards south of the ravine, took cover, and commenced firing. Chalmers reported that "a very stubborn fight ensued" as the two forces battled for control of the fields along the Hamburg-Savannah Road. Frustrated by the stalled advance, the Confederate brigade commander ordered Gage's battery brought up, despite the rough terrain, while his troops continued exchanging volleys of musketry with the stubborn Yankees.[67]

The battle on the Union left had resulted in devastating bloodshed. Even though the most famous remembrances of the Battle of Shiloh would concentrate on the fighting in the Union center, emphasizing the struggle in the "Hornets' Nest," the fight on the Union left was just as vicious, if not more so.[68] A Mississippian described how the Southerners "fought like Indians behind trees, logs, lying down behind the ridges, or hills" as they pushed against the Federals.[69] The fierce fighting and mounting casualties obviously took their toll, as J. H. Cravey of the Second Texas later claimed to have "seen the blood flowen down the sides of the hilles like water."[70] The Union soldiers, however, were not easily deterred. "Eighteen hundred of us stood our ground," wrote a captain in the Fifty-fourth Ohio.[71] The bloody conflict left its mark on all participants. Corporal Robert Oliver, of Company C, Fifty-fifth Illinois, later recalled how his lieutenant, Theodore Hodges, bent to one knee to give him instructions during the fight when a canister shot hit the lieutenant in the head. Hodges had placed the tip of his sword into the ground to balance himself while bending over to talk to Oliver, and when the shot struck him, he clung with a death grip to the hilt of his sword. The weight of Hodges's body bent the sword nearly in two until the lieutenant's grasp finally let go, catapulting the sword six feet into the air while the horrified corporal looked on.[72] William Kennedy, a private in Company G, Fifty-fifth Illinois, remarked that the withering enemy fire caused his comrades to seek cover even where there were no natural defensive barriers. "I have often heard of men in battle laying down but never thought they hug[ged] the ground as close as they did on the 6th and 7th," Kennedy wrote.[73]

The carnage near the Hamburg-Savannah Road devastated on the Stuart's force, but the brigade's refusal to yield their ground readily to Chalmers and Jackson had bought precious time for the Federals on the right and center who continued to fend off the repeated Rebel assaults. Earlier that morning, Brigadier General John A. McArthur of W. H. L. Wallace's Division had moved down the Hamburg-Savannah Road toward Stuart's right and promised to reinforce Stuart if the brigade could only hold on. The reinforcements never came—by that time McArthur had all he could do to hold his own position against the Confederate onslaught—but as the two Federal brigades remained within six hundred yards of one another, the presence of McArthur's three regiments discouraged the advancing Confederates from exploiting the gap on Stuart's right.[74]

Left alone for the better part of the day's battle, Stuart decided sometime around 3:00 P.M. to withdraw across the sharp ravine and re-form on a hill north of the Hamburg-Savannah Road, slightly northeast of Larkin Bell Field. The fight north of Locust Grove Run had lasted a little more than three hours before the Federals, who had run short of ammunition and resorted to rummaging the cartridge boxes of their dead comrades, received the order to withdraw to a stronger position to the north. "Our ammunition gave out, and they were trying to flank us, which compelled us to leave the field," wrote an officer in the Fifty-fourth Ohio.[75] The bloodshed continued as the Federals retreated. One young Illinois private was struck seven times by Rebel musket fire, turning him "as red as if he had been dipped in a barrel of blood."[76] The general consensus among the Federals was that the "Rebels fought like devils."[77]

Their line of retreat would have them crossing another ravine, one hundred feet deep by one hundred yards wide. Elements of Jackson's brigade had already plunged into this second ravine, between Stuart's right and McArthur's force, when the Federals began to fall back. As the Yankee troops rushed to cross the gulch, they were exposed to a blistering crossfire from the west and south, as vanguard units from Jackson's Brigade rushed to the lip of the ravine and fired down on the retreating Federals. "It was like shooting into a flock of sheep," later recounted Major F. Eugene Whitfield, of the Ninth Mississippi, about the devastating barrage loosed on the Federals. "I never saw such cruel work in the war." The Confederate musketry volleys were aided by Rebel artillery, which added grape and canister to the "veritable cyclone" of fire through which the Federals retreated.[78]

Stuart's survivors struggled across the ravine as best they could, "leaving bleeding victims at every step."[79] The brigade commander was able to regroup a few hundred yards north of the gulch. He was joined by Captain James Hart, who led remnants of the Seventy-first Ohio, Colonel Malmbourg of the Fifty-fifth Illinois, and Colonel Smith of the Fifty-fourth Ohio. Stuart, who had been wounded earlier in the day, turned over the command of his brigade to Smith, the next-ranking officer, and Stuart went to the Union camp at Pittsburg Landing to have his injury treated. Smith quickly recognized his precarious situation with ammunition running short and the Confederates continuing their advance. Fortunately for the Federals, an officer from Grant's staff arrived and directed Stuart's brigade toward the rear to receive ammunition and to support the Union batteries near Pittsburg Landing. "At last an orderly from General Grant came up to promise the required supply and to order us to a position at which we could cover a battery," wrote Colonel Smith, a few days after the battle.[80] Before leaving the field, Stuart sent word to Brigadier General Stephen A. Hurlbut's headquarters, warning him that Stuart's left would soon be flanked. Then the brigade withdrew to the area of Pittsburg Landing, where its remnants regrouped a final time to face the enemy once more.[81]

While Union officers strove to reestablish a defensive line, the Confederate advance stalled once more. The Rebel troops were pillaging whatever goods they could find in the abandoned Federal camps. Although the Southern soldiers basked in a brief lull in the fighting, the fury of the battle had not dissipated. A company of the Second Texas was rummaging through the Yankee plunder when a squad of Union soldiers bearing a white handkerchief approached. The Texans naturally assumed that the Federals wished to surrender, especially after the bloody fighting that had just taken place. The Union soldiers approached to within fifty feet of the Texans before launching a volley, to the Confederates' surprise, that killed two and wounded several others. Recovering from the initial blow, the Texans pursued the dozen or so Yankees, shooting every one of them and leaving no survivors.[82]

It was close to 3:00 P.M., and Chalmers's and Jackson's men were exhausted as they waited for their ordnance wagons. It had taken them approximately four hours to advance a little less than a mile, from the south bank of Locust Grove Run to their position just north of the Hamburg-Savannah Road, slightly east of Sarah Bell's Old Cotton Field. The Rebels were now only about a quarter mile east of the position they had reached almost six hours earlier, when they had received orders to move against Stuart's brigade. That small change of location had cost Chalmers's Brigade about four hundred casualties; Jackson's force probably lost a similar number. Adding to the Confederate predicament, Union gunboats in the Tennessee River had begun to lob shells onto the Rebel positions. Although many Rebels considered the shooting from the Yankee vessels largely ineffective due to the steep trajectory of fire, the constant bombardment was still another challenge in an already difficult day.[83]

Once they got in motion again, Chalmers and Jackson moved to exploit their hard-won position. With Stuart's brigade effectively eliminated from their front, they veered to the northwest along the Hamburg-Savannah Road, against McArthur's exposed right flank. McArthur's men put up a stout fight, suffering some of the battle's highest casualty rates, but finally had to yield to overwhelming pressure in front and flank. McArthur's retreat exposed Hurlbut's left flank in the sector around the Peach Orchard on the north edge of Sarah Bell's Cotton Field. By the late afternoon, Hurlbut's divisions gave way, and Sherman's and Major General John A. McClernand's had to fall back on the Union right. In the center, Prentiss, with a small remnant of what had been his division, along with the still-solid division of W. H. L. Wallace, continued to hold their ground, their lines bending back to roughly resemble a horseshoe, with the open end facing north.

Major General John C. Breckinridge, acting on instructions from Johnston, ordered Chalmers and Jackson to reinforce his reserve corps, which had been engaged against the Federals since about 12:30 P.M. General Johnston had taken charge of the battle, personally directing Brigadier General John S. Bowen's brigade north along the Hamburg-Savannah Road. Yet, with Chalmers and Jackson engaged against Stuart's brigade, it would be more than two hours before Bowen's men received reinforcements, and it would take another hour before they resumed their advance against the Union lines.[84]

While the Confederates launched repeated assaults on Hurlbut's line, Johnston was wounded, the bullet severing an artery, which caused the Confederate commander to die from blood loss. The Rebels continued to fight, Beauregard taking charge of the Confederate army around three o'clock. By 4:30, the full weight of the Confederate assault, "with the force of a hurricane," was brought to bear on the Union line at the Hornets' Nest. W. H. L. Wallace, having learned that Hurlbut and McClernand were falling back, determined to withdraw his division as well but was killed before he could do so. Elements of his division reached the new Union line near the landing. The left and right wings of the Confederate army converged in Prentiss's rear, forcing the surrender of 2,250 men of his and Wallace's division. Colonel Moore of the

Second Texas, who had led the assaults against Stuart's brigade for a large part of the battle, helped capture a contingent of Prentiss's division.[85]

While Chalmers's and Jackson's brigades, along with most of the rest of the Confederate army, celebrated the largest single capture of Federal troops to date, the remnants of Stuart's force—along with Hurlbut's men—had begun to receive ammunition and support near the river.[86] Grant had positioned the remnants of his shattered army at Pittsburg Landing, facing south and southwest, across the mouth of the Dill Branch and along the Corinth Road. Gunboats *Tyler* and *Lexington* anchored the left of the line while Sherman and McClernand held the right. While Beauregard reorganized his troops and sent prisoners to the rear after the collapse of the Hornets' Nest position, Grant further buttressed his line. The line held that evening, and the next day, reinforced by Lew Wallace's Third Division of the Army of the Tennessee, as well as three divisions of Don Carlos Buell's Army of the Ohio, Grant drove the Rebels back across the same ground the armies had contested April 6. On the afternoon of April 7, Beauregard disengaged his army and marched it forlornly back to Corinth.[87]

In a battle whose outcome hung by many threads of contingency, the presence of the men of Stuart's brigade and their spirited resistance against the brigades of Chalmers and Jackson likely prevented Johnston's army from turning the Union left, cutting the Army of the Tennessee off from the river, and driving it into Owl and Snake creeks. Even though Beauregard modified Johnston's original plan for a flanking maneuver on the battle's first day in favor of a linear assault, the midmorning assault against Stuart's brigade at least had the potential to resurrect the commanding general's original plan.

The question of what Johnston knew or intended became much more difficult to answer when he died on the field of battle during the first day. The commanding general moved to the front of battle to direct troop dispositions while Beauregard remained at the rear, his responsibilities unclear and ultimately relegated to postwar conflicts between his supporters and Johnston's sympathizers.[88] Throughout the battle, Johnston and his commanders knew very little about the field of battle or the positions of the Union army that morning.

Johnston erred in directing Chalmers and Jackson against the Hornets' Nest sector after disposing of Stuart's brigade in the midafternoon, rather than allowing them to follow their original line of advance toward the landing. Even though it is improbable that the two Confederate brigades could have dislodged the Union troops preparing a defensive line near the landing, they could at least have added to the panic and disorder that had characterized the Federals' fight thus far. Yet, at the same time, the Confederates were unclear as to the terrain and the direction of the battle itself.

The Union high command also failed their soldiers during the Shiloh Campaign. Simply put, the Union generals were surprised and caught completely off guard on the sixth. Although Sherman's failure to entrench his forces might be chalked up to the general aversion most Civil War generals had to fighting behind defensive positions during the early stages of the war, the sprawling deployment of the Federal troops along such a wide front showed more concern for healthy and comfortable camp sites than for a possible defense, which none of the top Union generals expected. In particular, Stuart's brigade, holding the Federal left was not connected to the rest of the army, much less its own division, which stood on the Union right flank. The rough, broken terrain of the battlefield, coupled with the densely wooded and thicketed area, prevented timely reinforcements and coordination among the Federals. Without information or contact with Sherman, Stuart chose to remain near his original post by the Lick Creek Ford rather than to withdraw his brigade farther north to a less-exposed position. The brigade commander chose to cover all his bases: protect the ford, watch for enemy movement across Locust Grove Run, and maintain a line of retreat to Pittsburg Landing, rather than pull back to a stronger defensive position that could have helped his men, none of whom had seen combat prior to Shiloh. Consequently, the challenging task proved too much for Stuart's inexperienced troops, many of whom broke at the first sign of battle. The brigade commander, however, was able to rally his men and offer the Confederates some stiff resistance as they advanced north along the Hamburg-Savannah Road.[89]

The true credit for the resolute defense of the Union left and depriving the Confederates an unobstructed path to Pittsburg Landing goes to the junior officers and enlisted men who fought boldly against superior numbers. Some veterans of Stuart's brigade lamented that the commanding generals "had left us alone to our fate" by leaving them exposed on the Union left.[90] And while many noted the courage of their commander, they also recognized that it was the soldiers' battle to win or lose. As a captain in the Fifth Ohio Independent Battery observed about the battle in general: "It was a private soldiers' battle, fiercely fought by unskilled, uninstructed and inexperienced volunteers, supported by the indomitable energy, desperate courage and marvelous staying qualities of the rank and file."[91]

The postwar battles of the memoirs were fierce. While veterans of Stuart's brigade would bemoan the fact that most of the postwar attention was fixed on the fight for the Hornets' Nest, the accusations and recriminations between Illinoisans and Ohioans would in some ways diminish the recognition of the brigade in helping win the battle.[92] Several stories in the *Chicago Tribune* launched the opening salvos of the campaign by supporters of the Fifty-fifth Illinois to portray the Seventy-first Ohio as shirkers and cowards with the Illinoisans conveniently forgetting some of their own transgressions. The Ohioans recognized their own blunders and some observers informed Governor Tod that the regimental officers had lost the confidence of the troops.[93] That the Seventy-first Ohio ran at the first sight of combat was not in question, but what was overlooked in the postbattle accounts was that several contingents from the regiment joined the rest of the brigade in opposing the Rebel brigades.

Yet, one concept that was not entirely lost in the ranks was keeping a proper perspective on Stuart's brigade in the campaign as a whole. In postwar accounts, veterans of Stuart's brigade noted how truly lucky they had been in stopping Chalmers's and Jackson's brigades from plowing through the Union position and on to Pittsburg Landing. They noted that the Rebel failure to launch an all-out assault against the isolated Federal brigade was due to a combination of the Confederates' fatigue, the difficulties presented by the terrain, and the general uncertainty as to how big a force the Rebels faced. Lieutenant Lawrence suggested that the Stuart's struggle for the left was "aided by a combination of favorable accidents" that kept the Confederates at bay.[94] Adding to this sense of awe of how a mangled Federal brigade was able to fend off a force more than twice its size was how raw and inexperienced all of the troops at Shiloh were. As one Union veteran maintained, Stuart's brigade "suffered a terrible baptism by fire" in saving the Union left that day.[95]

Notes

1. Samuel H. Lockett, "Surprise and Withdrawal at Shiloh," in *Battles and Leaders of the Civil War*, ed. Robert Underwood Johnson and Clarence C. Buell (New York: Yoseloff, 1884), 1.605.

2. Pierre G. T. Beauregard to Samuel Cooper, 7 April 1862, U.S. War Department, *The War of the Rebellion: A Compilation of the Official Records of the Union and Confederate Armies*, ed. Robert N. Scott, 128 vols. (Washington, DC: GPO, 1884), 10.1:384. (This source is hereafter referred to as "*OR.*" All references are to series 1 unless otherwise noted.) For the post-battle recriminations over the evening of 6 April, see Daniel, *Shiloh*, 250–53, 255–56; McDonough, *In Hell before Night*, 168–83. For an excellent study of Shiloh and Civil War memory, see Timothy B. Smith, *The Great Battlefield of Shiloh: History, Memory, and the Establishment of a Civil War National Park* (Knoxville: University of Tennessee Press, 2004).

3. William T. Sherman to William McMichael, 15 March 1862, William T. Sherman to William McMichael, 17 March 1862, *OR*, 10.1:22, 25. Larry J. Daniel argues that Sherman was actually more concerned with Federal left flank than the Shiloh Church sector in the army's center. *Shiloh*, 137.

4. "Special Orders No. 36," *OR*, 10.2:67.

5. Sword, *Shiloh: Bloody April*, 23, 27, 28; Daniel, *Shiloh*, 137; McDonough, *In Hell Before Night*, 50.

6. "General Stuart," in T. M. Eddy, ed., *The Patriotism of Illinois: A Record of the Civil and Military History of the State in the War for the Union, with a History of the Campaigns in Which Illinois Soldiers Have Been Conspicuous* (Chicago: Clarke, 1865), 272–74; Ezra J. Warner, *Generals in Blue: Lives of the Union Commanders* (Baton Rouge: Louisiana State University Press, 1964), 784–85; Joseph Allan Frank and George A. Reaves, *"Seeing the Elephant": Raw Recruits at the Battle of Shiloh* (Westport, CT: Greenwood, 1989), 53.

7. Ephraim C. Dawes, "The Battle of Shiloh," in *Campaigns in Kentucky and Tennessee, Including the Battle of Chickamauga, 1862–1864* (Boston: Military Historical Society of Massachusetts, 1908), 126.

8. Elijah Lawrence, "Stuart's Brigade at Shiloh," in *Military Order of the Loyal Legion of the United States, Massachusetts Commendery*, vol. 2 (Boston: For the Commendery, 1900), 493; Woodworth, *Nothing but Victory*, 18; Frank and Reaves, *"Seeing the Elephant,"* 53.

9. Sword, *Shiloh: Bloody April*, 23, 27, 28; Daniel, *Shiloh*, 137; McDonough, *In Hell before Night*, 50.

10. Crooker, *Story of the Fifty Fifth*, 68.

11. Lawrence, "Stuart's Brigade at Shiloh," 490.

12. Dawes, "Battle of Shiloh," 154.

13. William T. Sherman to Colonel Stuart, 2 April 1862, *OR*, 10.2:87.

14. Dawes, "Battle of Shiloh," 157–58.

15. Daniel, *Shiloh*, 198; Lawrence, "Stuart's Brigade at Shiloh," 490.

16. Lockett, "Surprise and Withdrawal at Shiloh," in *Battles and Leaders*, 1:604. Bragg gave the engineer simple instructions: do not make contact with the enemy, and report the information of the Union left as soon as possible.

17. Ibid.

18. Benjamin Prentiss to J. C. Kelton, 17 November 1862, *OR*, 10.1:277–78.

19. Quoted in Daniel, *Shiloh*, 198.

20. Lawrence, "Stuart's Brigade at Shiloh," 490.

21. Allen, "Shiloh," 19–24.

22. Lockett, "Surprise and Withdrawal," 604; Allen, "Shiloh," 46; Daniel, *Shiloh*, 195; Thomas Connelly, *Army of the Heartland: The Army of Tennessee, 1861–1862* (Baton Rouge: Louisiana State University Press, 1970), 164. Connelly writes that while Johnston was concerned with the Union center, Beauregard had received a reconnaissance report from Colonels Numa Augustin and George Brent advising him of the situation on the Confederate right flank. Beauregard, in effect, had preceded Johnston's order and sent two Brigades to the threatened sector shortly before the commanding general received Lockett's personal report.

23. See Connelly, *Army of the Heartland*, 162.

24. "Report of Brig. Gen. John Chalmers," 12 April 1862, and "Report of Brig. Gen. John K. Jackson," 26 April 1862, *OR*, 10.1:548–54; Allen, "Shiloh," 46; Ezra J. Warner, *Generals in Gray: Lives of the Confederate Commanders* (Baton Rouge: Louisiana State University Press, 1959), 46, 150–51.

25. Stuart's Brigade had not seen action prior to the Battle of Shiloh, and, in fact, the Fifty-fourth Ohio had only been armed four weeks prior to the campaign. See Dawes, "Shiloh," 161.

26. Alex Frazier of Co. E Memorandum, 2nd Texas Infantry, Second Texas Infantry File, Texas Confederate Archives, Hill College, Hillsboro, Texas; Charles I. Evans, "The Service of Texas Troops," in Dudley Wooten, ed., *A Comprehensive History of Texas, 1685–1897*, 2 vols. (Dallas: Scarff, 1898), 2:578; Joseph Chance, *The Second Texas Infantry: From Shiloh to Vicksburg* (Austin: Eakin, 1984), 24. Evans was a private in Company G of the Second Texas.

27. Quoted in Frank and Reaves, *"Seeing the Elephant,"* 62.

28. S. Fisher, "The Amenities of War," Second Texas Infantry File, Texas Confederate Archives, Hill College, Hillsboro, Texas.

29. Lawrence, "Stuart's Brigade at Shiloh," 491. Lawrence served in Company B of the Fifty-fifth.

30. Dawes, "Shiloh," 158; "Report of Col. David Stuart," 10 April 1862, *OR*, 10.1:258.

31. Lawrence, "Stuart's Brigade at Shiloh," 493; Woodworth, *Nothing but Victory*, 177.

32. John C. Moore, "Shiloh Issues Again," *Confederate Veteran* 10 (July 1902): 316.

33. One officer in the Second Texas, for instance, later described how he grabbed a skillet of fried meat as he pursued the retreating Federal troops. Chance, *Second Texas Infantry*, 27–28.

34. "Report of Brig. Gen. John K. Jackson," 26 April 1862, *OR*, 10.1:553–54; Wooten, "Texas Troops," 579–80.

35. Daniel, *Cannoneers in Gray*, 33.

36. "Report of Brig. Gen. Jones M. Withers," 20 June 1862, W. J. Hardee to Braxton Bragg, 4 April 1862, *OR*, 10.1:93, 532; Thomas Worthington, *Shiloh; Or, The Tennessee Campaign of 1862: Written Especially For the Army of the Tennessee in 1862 . . . by a Comrade on That Battle-field and a West-Point Graduate of 1827* (Washington, DC: McGill and Witherow, 1872), 101; Warner, *Generals in Gray*, 50–51. See also "Report of Col. William H. H. Taylor" [Fifth Ohio Cavalry], 3 April 1862, and "Report of Brig. Gen. James R. Chalmers," April 12 1862 *O.R.*, 10.1:86–87.

37. "Report of Brig. Gen. James R. Chalmers," 12 April 1862, "Report of Brig. Gen. John K. Jackson," 26 April 1862, *OR*, 10.1:548, 554.

38. S. B. Yeoman to Dear Friend Pearce, 12 April 1862, in *Washington Register*. Yeoman wrote, "My company was now sent out as skirmishers. We had not gone over half a mile when I saw a regiment of infantry: but the Colonel told me, before I started, that one of our regiments was in that direction. Then I saw two more regiments, with a 'Secesh' flag."

39. Lawrence, "Stuart's Brigade at Shiloh," 491–92; "Report of Brig. Gen. James R. Chalmers," 12 April 1862, *OR*, 10.1:549. Captains J. A. Russell and A. N. Wilson commanded the two companies of the Fifty-second, who were reassigned to the Fifth Mississippi.

40. "Reports of Col. John C. Moore, Second Texas Infantry," 19 April 1862, "Report of Capt. Isadore P. Girardey," 12 April 1862, *OR*, 10.1:561, 565.

41. "Report of Brig. Gen. Jones M. Withers," 20 June 1862, *OR*, 10.1:532.

42. "Report of Brig. Gen. John K. Jackson," 26 April 1862, *OR*, 10.1:554; Lawrence, "Stuart's Brigade at Shiloh," 492.

43. Crooker, *Story of the Fifty-fifth*, 106; Lawrence, "Stuart's Brigade at Shiloh," 493.

44. Quoted in Daniel, *Shiloh*, 199.

45. Martin Stewart, "A Short History of the 71st Ohio Infantry," unpublished essay (2005).

46. Daniel, *Shiloh*, 199; W. H. McClure, "The 71st Ohio at Shiloh," *National Tribune*, 6 June 1907; "Report of Col. Rodney Mason," *OR*, 10.1:261–62.

47. *Chicago Tribune*, 14 April 1862. The *Tribune* wrote, "We would we could be spared the pain of recording the shame of some of the Ohio regiments who ran at the first fire or without a shot. One of these regiments rushed down helter skelter to the river and took possession of a steamer in waiting for the wounded." The negative reports of the Seventy-first even reached the Southern press, which reported that the regiment had been attacked while having breakfast. *(Houston) Tri-Weekly Telegraph*, 16 May 1862. See also T. J. Lindsey, ed., *Ohio at Shiloh: Report of the Commission*, (Cincinnati: Krehbiel, 1903), 37–38, which reported that the regiment "has been severely censured for its conduct in the battle of Shiloh."

48. For examples of the bitter denunciations of the Seventy-first Ohio, see Lawrence, "Stuart's Brigade at Shiloh," and Crooker, *Story of the Fifty-fifth*. For an Ohio perspective, see the *(Houston) Tri-Weekly Telegraph*, 23 May 1862, which reprinted an editorial from the *Cincinnati Gazette*, "About the Running of the Ohioans in Shiloh," which maintained, "The motley crowd that thronged the bluff and sneaked behind the river banks for protection on Sunday afternoon, were not all nor mainly Ohioans. I saw plenty of Illinoisans there, with the usual coward's story about how their regiments were cut to pieces."

49. S[ilas] B. Walker to the Honorable G. V[olney] Dorsey, 12 April 1862, Thomas Kilby Smith to Governor David Tod, 14 April 1862, David Stuart to Governor David Tod, 14 April 1862, Sampson Mason to Governor David Tod, 21 April 1862, William Sawyer, E. M. Phelps, and Ben Metcalf to Governor David Tod, in Correspondence to the Governor and Adjutant General, 1861–1866, series 147, volume 37, Ohio Historical Society, Columbus, Ohio. The letters to Governor Tod praise the conduct of Captain Gideon LeBlond and Major James H. Hart during the battle. Colonel Mason, however, disagreed with the assessment of Captain LeBlond, writing to Governor Tod and insisting that the captain had misrepresented himself amongst the Ohioans in order to obtain a promotion. See Rodney Mason to Governor Tod, 24 May 1862, in ibid. Colonel David Stuart points out that Mason and the Seventy-first fell back to "some position . . . about 150 yards to the rear." "Report of Col. David Stuart," 10 April 1862, *OR*, 10.1:258.

50. Following the battle, General Grant recalled how Mason "came to me with tears in his ayes and begged to be allowed another trial" after his performance on April 6. Grant acquiesced only a few months later to see Mason surrender six companies of his regiment in Clarksville, Tennessee, . See Ulysses S. Grant, *Personal Memoirs of Ulysses S. Grant* (New York: Da Capo, 1982), 207; Noah Trudeau, "Fields without Honor: Two Affairs in Tennessee," *Civil War Times Illustrated* 32 (August 1992): 42–49, 57.

51. "54th Infantry," in *Ohio at Shiloh*, 18; "Report of Brig. Gen. James R. Chalmers," 12 April 1862, *OR*, 10.1:549. See Woodworth, *Nothing but Victory*, 16–17, for a brief discussion of the Zouaves.

52. "Report of Brig. Gen. James R. Chalmers," 12 April 1862, *OR*, 10.1:49.

53. S. B. Yeoman to Dear Friend Pearce, 12 April 1862, in *Washington Register*.

54. Benjamin F. Wilkinson to Dear Brother [Micajah Wilkinson], 16 April 1862, in Micajah Wilkinson Papers, 1839–1958, E-39 #707, Louisiana State University, Special

Collections, Hill Memorial Library, Baton Rouge, Louisiana. Wilkinson wrote, "Sunday 6th double quicked two miles give the Yanks a warm salute. They giving us the field and honor. Double quick two miles to the right—dive into them again after half an hour we charged bayonets. As they retreated I gave it to one old blue belly about where his suspenders crossed sending him to eternity." Ibid.

55. "Report of Brig. Gen. James R. Chalmers," 12 April 1862, *OR*, 10.1:549.

56. Lawrence, "Stuart's Brigade at Shiloh," 493–94. See also "Report of Col. David Stuart," 10 April 1862, *OR*, 10.1:258; Crooker, *Story of the Fifty-fifth*, 107. Lucien Crooker later wrote, "It seems providential that no advance on the part of the enemy occurred until these tactical monstrosities [forming the hollow squares] were reduced, otherwise the laurels of the Fifty-fifth and Fifty-fourth Ohio would have withered in the infamy of a wild race to the rear."

57. "Report of Col. Rodney Mason," 10 April 1862, *OR*, 10.1:562.

58. Sioux [?] to [?], 29 April 1862, *(Houston) Tri-Weekly Telegraph*.

59. "Report of Brig. Gen. John K. Jackson," 26 April 1862, *OR*, 10.1.554; Lawrence, "Stuart's Brigade at Shiloh," 494. According to Crooker's postwar account, the tactical maneuvers of the Fifty-fifth played a role in causing the Confederates to delay their advance, arguing that "the hollow square exhibition induced extra caution, it being so ridiculous that it was looked upon as a ruse to induce an attack." *Story of the Fifty-fifth*, 109.

60. Moore, "Shiloh Issues Again," 316.

61. Chance, *Second Texas Infantry*, 24, 27. See the letter dated 28 June 1862 in the *(Houston) Tri-Weekly Telegraph*, 16 July 1862, for the quote taking pride in the state of the Texas troops.

62. Sioux [?] to [?], 29 April 1862, *(Houston) Tri-Weekly Telegraph*.

63. "Reports of Col. John C. Moore," 19 April 1862, *OR*, 10.1:561.

64. "Report of Col. Rodney Mason," 10 April, *OR*, 10.1:561; Crooker, *Story of the Fifty-fifth*, 86.

65. Crooker, *Story of the Fifty-fifth*, 97.

66. Lawrence, "Stuart's Brigade at Shiloh," 494.

67. "Report of Brig. Gen. James R. Chalmers," 12 April 1862, *OR*, 10.1:549; Lawrence, "Stuart's Brigade at Shiloh," 495; Woodworth, *Nothing but Victory*, 178.

68. For an explanation on the postwar emphasis on the "Hornets' Nest," see T. B. Smith, *Great Battlefield at Shiloh*, 69–70.

69. B. F. Wilkinson to Dear Brother [Micajah Wilkinson], 16 April 1862, Micajah Wilkins Papers.

70. "The Civil War Record of George W. L. Fly, Major Confederate States Army, 1861–1865," Second Texas Infantry File, Texas Confederate Archives, Hill College, Hillsboro, Texas.

71. S. B. Yeoman to Dear Friend Pearce, 12 April 1862, in *Washington Register*.

72. Crooker, *Story of the Fifty-fifth*, 121. The story of Corporal Oliver is also recounted in Woodworth, *Nothing but Victory*, 178, and Sword, *Shiloh*, 232–33.

73. Kennedy quoted in Franks and Reaves, "*Seeing the Elephant*," 101.

74. "Report of Col. David Stuart," 10 April 1862, *OR*, 10.1:258–59. According to a correspondent with the *Chicago Tribune*, McArthur "mistook the way, marched too far to the right, and so, instead of reaching Stuart, came in on the other side of the rebels, now closely pushing Prentiss." "The Battle of Pittsburg," Chicago *Tribune*, 16 April 1862.

75. S. B. Yeoman to Dear Friend Pearce, 12 April 1862, *Washington Register*, n.d.

76. Crooker, *Story of the Fifty-fifth*, 124.

77. J. H. Hart to W. B. McClung, 14 April 1862, in Correspondence to the Governor and Adjutant General, 1861–1866, series 147, vol. 37, Ohio Historical Center, Columbus, Ohio.

78. Crooker, *Story of the Fifty-fifth*, 110. Confederate Captain Girardey noted in his battle report that despite the devastating fire from his battery, the Federals continued to resist "with desperate valor." "Report of Capt. Isadore P. Girardey," 12 April 1862, *OR*, 10.1:565.

79. Crooker, *Story of the Fifty-fifth*, 110.

80. T. Kilby Smith to My Dear Sister, 14 April 1862, in Walter George Smith, ed., *Life and Letters of Thomas Kilby Smith, Brevet Major General United States Volunteers, 1820–1887* (New York: Putnam's Sons, 1898), 196.

81. "Report of Col. David Stuart," 10 April 1862, and "Report of Brig. Gen. Stephen A. Hurlbut," 12 April 1862, *OR*, 10.1:259, 204; Crooker, *Story of the Fifty-fifth*, 110–11.

82. Sam Houston Jr., "Shiloh Shadows," *Southwestern Historical Quarterly* 34, no. 4 (July 1930): 330–31. Sam Houston Jr. fought in the Second Texas Regiment.

83. "Report of Brig. Gen. James R. Chalmers," 12 April 1862, *OR*, 10.1:550. Ashbel Smith of the Second Texas describes his regiment "was terribly torn to pieces at Shiloh." Ashbel Smith to My Dear Friend, 31 July 1862, Second Texas Infantry File, Texas Confederate Archives, Hill College, Hillsboro, Texas. For views on the effect of the Union gunboats on the Confederate lines, see "Reports of General G. T. Beauregard," 7 April 1862, "Report of General Braxton Bragg," 30 April 1862, "Report of General Leonidas Polk," September [?] 1862, and "Report of Col. John D. Martin," 14 April 1862, *OR*, 10.1:387, 466, 410. Beauregard describes the Union gunboat fire as "annoying" while Polk maintains that they were "comparatively harmless to our troops." Even Colonel Martin, who commanded the John S. Bowen's Brigade on the Confederate right during the afternoon of April 6 reported that the Union gunboat fire "sounded terribly and looked ugly and hurt but few." The effectiveness of the Union artillery changed the closer the Rebels got to the river. Captain Girardey, for instance, reported that the Union artillery caused significant damage. "Report of Capt. Isadore Girardey," 12 April 1862, *OR*, 10.1:565–66.

84. "Report of Brig. Gen. James R. Chalmers," 12 April 1862, "Report of Brig. Gen. John K. Jackson," 10 April 1862, *OR*, 10.1:550–51, 554–55; Allen, "Shiloh!" 54. Daniel places the time that Chalmers and Jackson attacked along with Bowen's Brigade (under Colonel John D. Martin) around 4:00. *Shiloh*, 235.

85. Allen, "Shiloh!" 53–54 (quote on page 54); "Reports of General G. T. Beauregard," 11 April 1862, and "Report of Brig. Gen. B. M. Prentiss," 17 November 1862, *OR*, 10.1:386–87, 279; Moore, "Shiloh Issues Again," 317; Chance, *Second Texas Infantry*, 30–31; Evans, "Service of Texas Troops," 579.

86. S. B. Yeoman to Dear Friend Pearce, 12 April 1862, *Washington Register*, n.d.; Allen, "Shiloh!" 54.

87. Daniel, *Shiloh*, 252–53 (quote on page 253).

88. See McDonough, *In Hell before Night*, 98–99; Daniel, *Shiloh*, 95–96, 119–25.

89. Crooker, *Story of the Fifty-fifth*, 106. In their postwar accounts, veterans of Stuart's brigade noted their commander's bravery and ability to inspire his men in the face of a potentially disaster, praising the "magnificent" conduct of the colonel.

90. Lawrence, "Stuart's Brigade at Shiloh," 495.

91. Andrew Hickenlooper, "The Battle of Shiloh," in *The Battle of Shiloh, Personal Reminiscences of the Battle, Part I* (Cincinnati, OH: Robert Clarke, 1903), 25.

92. For an excellent account of the postwar struggle to memorialize the Shiloh battlefield, see T. B. Smith, *This Great Battlefield at Shiloh*. Crooker notes, "There runs a fiction through many narratives of this epoch that the best fighting and the greatest losses at Shiloh were toward the Union right." *Story of the Fifty-fifty*, 133.

93. B. Stanton to Governor Tod, 1 May 1862, in Correspondence to the Governor and Adjutant General, 1861–1866, Ohio Historical Society.

94. Lawrence, "Stuart's Brigade at Shiloh," 496.

95. Crooker, *Story of the Fifty-fifth*, 102.

3

ANATOMY OF AN ICON
SHILOH'S HORNETS' NEST IN CIVIL WAR MEMORY

Timothy B. Smith

The sweat-lathered soldier, caked with black powder and grime, peered through lengthening shadows to see if they were coming again. Along with neighboring units, his regiment, the Twelfth Iowa Infantry, had for six hours repelled at least seven or eight attacks on their position. Those rebels in butternut and gray had attacked over and over again, fresh unit after unit coming against their position only to be turned away by the thunder-like volleys from their Enfields and those of the regiments on either flank. But the enemy just kept coming, finally with heavy artillery support that caused the Iowa boys to lie down and hug the earth as close as possible. Just when it seemed the situation could get no worse, news came that the enemy was now in their rear. Orders came to fall back, but the enemy seemed to have every avenue of escape blocked. The crossfire in one area was especially dangerous, causing the soldiers to term it "Hell's Hollow." Soon, white flags began to appear. But this young soldier was spared from surrender because of a worse fate: a Confederate bullet slammed into his thigh, and he went down. He spent a miserable night watching as his comrades surrendered and were carted off as prisoners of war, and he bled from his wound and suffered on the battlefield through the long, rainy night.[1]

Forty years later, almost to the day, that same soldier stood on that same historic ground and must have felt extreme pride as he pondered what had happened all those years before. The man was David W. Reed, and although he didn't know it at the time, he and his comrades had defended the famous Hornets' Nest at Shiloh on April 6, 1862. Making him even more proud, Reed had by 1902 become the one man who wielded more power on how the Hornets' Nest would be remembered than anyone else. Of the nearly 110,000 men who had struggled at Shiloh, Reed had become the authority on the battle. He was the historian on the commission charged with establishing Shiloh

National Military Park, and his pen literally wrote volumes about what was important at Shiloh. In 1902, forty years after his miserable experience on the battlefield in 1862, Reed issued his history of the clash: *The Battle of Shiloh and the Organizations Engaged.* The Hornets' Nest, his fight, played the starring role.[2]

Today, in large part because of Reed's historical efforts, historians view the Hornets' Nest as the focal point in the Battle of Shiloh. It is Shiloh's Pickett's Charge; it is Shiloh's Bloody Lane. It is the area that most visitors want to see. Telling evidence in the Shiloh National Military Park visitor center shows just how much of an American icon the Hornets' Nest has become. On the large wall map (with battle lines located by David W. Reed, no doubt), so many visitors have pointed to the famous spots at Shiloh that at certain places the print is wearing thin. Thousands upon thousands of fingers have pointed to Pittsburg Landing, Shiloh Church, and Bloody Pond, causing small, round globes of wear on the map. In the Hornets' Nest, however, the entire Union line is worn from one end to the other. It is as if visitors make their point that this place was crucial by emphasizing their touch all up and down the line.

But was the Hornets' Nest really that important? If so, the attention is justified. If not, then the question of why it has become such an icon must be asked. Was the Hornets' Nest really the focal point of the battle, or are we the benefactors of a collective and selective memory of Shiloh veterans?

In actuality, the Hornets' Nest's iconic status is a result of a few veterans' interpretation of the facts, and that interpretation has been growing ever since. An examination of those early veterans and their efforts in singling out the Hornets' Nest, as well as later National Park Service historians in continuing that thesis, can offer many answers regarding the battle. When taken as a case study of Civil War memory, the Hornets' Nest at Shiloh can not only provide a better understanding of the battle but it can also point toward the need for further research into the historiography of other battles, examining how they were treated by veterans and historians years later. In many cases, and certainly at Shiloh, the treatment of the events after the fact has had more to do with how we view the battles today than how they were actually fought.

The Hornets' Nest—April 6, 1862

So what really happened at the Hornets' Nest on that bright spring day, and how did it fit into the battle as a whole? The Federal line in the Hornets' Nest was the result of the meeting between withdrawing front-line divisions and advancing reserve divisions of the Federal army. The two first divisions the Confederates attacked were those of Brigadier Generals William T. Sherman and Benjamin M. Prentiss, and they began to fall back from their initial lines of defense around midmorning. As they did, they met advancing divisions from the rear. Brigadier General Stephen A. Hurlbut moved his men forward on the Union left into the Peach Orchard sector, while Major General John A. McClernand moved his brigades up on the Federal right to support the Shiloh Church line. In the center, Brigadier General W. H. L. Wallace led his troops forward into what would become the Hornets' Nest, the center of the line. As

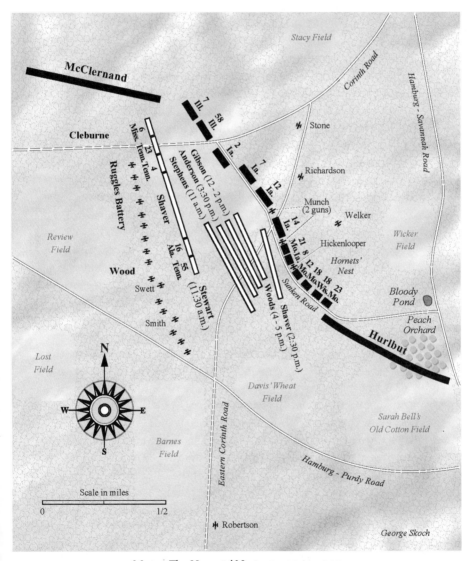

Map 2. The Hornets' Nest, 10 A.M. to 5 P.M.

the shattered divisions of Sherman and Prentiss encountered the advancing reserves, the divisions reformed and joined the developing line, thus creating a Federal line of battle that stretched almost three miles from Owl Creek on the west to the Tennessee River on the east. The Confederates would literally pound their way through most of this line but not at the Hornets' Nest.[3]

The reason the Hornets' Nest never broke under repeated Confederate assaults was not because of the strength of the Federal line but rather a result of what was occurring on other parts of the battlefield, leaving the center of the line the least-fought-over portion of the battlefield. Earlier in the day, long before any Confederates reached the Hornets' Nest area, Confederate commander General Albert Sidney Johnston had put into motion his plan of driving the enemy into the swamps of Snake and Owl creeks northwest of Pittsburg Landing. Inherent in the plan, of course, was hooking the left flank of the Federal army and then driving it. Johnston personally witnessed the fighting near Peter Spain's Field as his brigades dealt Prentiss's division a cruel morning greeting. He heard the sounds of heavy firing all along the line but realized that it stopped just inside the woods east of the field. Logically thinking that where he heard no fighting meant no enemy presence, Johnston thought he had found the Federal left flank and could thus begin his turning and driving movement. In actuality, the fighting had fallen off east of Spain's Field but not because it was the enemy left flank. There was a gap between Prentiss's division and the next unit in line to the east; Colonel David Stuart's brigade of Sherman's division. Johnston had found that gap and perceived it to be the left flank of the Federal army. The damage was done when Johnston sent his hard-charging brigades surging to the northwest to drive into the swamps the Federals he had flanked. Feeling confident in his victory, Johnston remarked to a staff officer, "That checkmates them."[4]

The result of Johnston's predetermined plan was that almost all the Confederate Army of the Mississippi moved off to the northwest to drive the Federals in one mass attack into the swamps. The eventual contact between this Confederate surge and the advancing units of McClernand's division was the bloody and brutal fighting between 10:30 and 11:00 A.M. around what is today known as the Crossroads. Most of the assaulting Confederates, in this move, went well west of the Hornets' Nest, thus placing as many as nine Confederate brigades on that western third of the battlefield.[5]

But Johnston soon learned, to his dismay, that he had acted too quickly. An engineer sent to scout the Federal left early that morning returned after Johnston had ordered the final push and reported that an entire Federal division was still lurking farther to the east. In actuality, it was only the badly frightened and understrength brigade commanded by Stuart, not a full division, but Johnston did not know that at the time. Acting on this faulty intelligence, he immediately began to realign his army to take care of a major potential problem.[6]

Johnston basically unfolded another wing of his army out on the right flank. He recalled two brigades that were advancing on the right of the major attack at the Crossroads and sent them to the extreme new right of the army while also sending two-thirds (two brigades) of the reserve corps to the area. The result was four brigades unfolded into line on the eastern third of the battlefield. These four units moved in an area far to the east of the Hornets' Nest. The two major wings of the Confederate army were thus moving away from each other along the lines of an obtuse angle. That left relatively few Confederate troops in the center third of the battlefield.[7]

The Hornets' Nest, therefore, formed inside a vacuum left by the Confederate movements. And it was a good thing early on, for the Union position was not as strong during the initial actions in the area as it would become later in the day. Two regiments of Colonel Thomas W. Sweeny's brigade had deployed on the right of the Corinth Road, but because there was little room left between them and McClernand's brigades, the other four regiments remained in the rear as a reserve. Colonel James M. Tuttle's brigade of four Iowa regiments extended the line along an old road, with the Second Iowa (which connected with Sweeny's brigade on the road), Seventh Iowa, and the right of the Twelfth Iowa fronting Duncan Field from behind a split-rail fence. The left of the Twelfth Iowa and the Fourteenth Iowa faced a dense area of undergrowth along the Eastern Corinth Road, probably where a field had once been. But the Fourteenth Iowa did not connect with anything. It was several yards between its left and the next units in line—Prentiss's division, and they were not terribly stable since the trashing they had taken earlier that morning. Helping small portions of the Eighteenth and Twenty-fifth Missouri, Eighteenth Wisconsin, and Twelfth Michigan hold the line was the Twenty-third Missouri, which arrived as the line was reforming and almost doubled Prentiss's command to around eleven hundred. It was Prentiss's command that ultimately connected with Hurlbut's units near the Peach Orchard. In addition, all or portions of six artillery batteries (Stone's, Welker's Richardson's, Powell's, Munch's, and Hickenlooper's) studded the Federal line at various points. Still, a gap existed between Tuttle and Prentiss, and the Iowans on Tuttle's left went through several convoluted manual moves to try to shore up their flank.[8]

Within the context of the diverging wings of the Confederate army and the incomplete line of the Hornets' Nest early in the fight, gap and all, the first Confederate contact with the Hornets' Nest came around 10:30 A.M. when the extreme right of the major Crossroads attack stumbled into Duncan

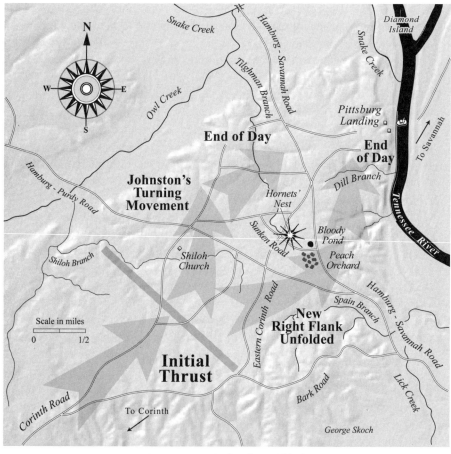

Map 3. How the battle unfolded.

Field and quickly learned a strong enemy force was there. Colonel Robert Shaver's Arkansas brigade was moving on the extreme right flank of the eight-brigade mass attack (with an additional brigade in reserve) on McClernand and Sherman at the Crossroads. His attempt to flank McClernand's left brought him into Joseph Duncan's Cotton Field, on the other side of which lay W. H. L. Wallace's men along the old farm lane later termed the Sunken Road. As Shaver's boys, particularly the right-flank regiment—the Third Confederate Infantry, entered Duncan Field around 10:30 A.M., Tuttle's Iowa soldiers were waiting for them. Enfields made gruesome wounds in the Confederate infantrymen, who (all that could) quickly took cover in the woods to the rear. Shaver withdrew a short distance and reformed. The first shots in defense of the Hornets' Nest had been fired.[9]

While the Confederate units were forming, one Confederate brigade attacked of its own volition, marking the first actual assault on the Hornets' Nest itself. Confederate second-in-command, General P. G. T. Beauregard, had sent Colonel William H. Stephens's small brigade to the right of the army; Beauregard told them to find the heaviest fighting and jump in. Stephens's division commander, Major General Benjamin F. Cheatham, took the brigade to the right of the Confederate assault, which was Shaver's brigade, and no doubt learned from them the presence of the enemy to the front. Cheatham deployed Smith's Mississippi battery and sent Stephens against the Hornets' Nest. About 11:00 A.M., Stephens led his troops into the teeth of the Federal line.[10]

Stephens's brigade was not in the best of shape even before the attack. A portion of it, along with the brigade's normal commander, Colonel George Maney, was away guarding the bridge over Lick Creek. Stephens thus had a small brigade, less than a thousand muskets total. And Stephens himself was having a bad day. He had been sick and was extremely weak but had risen from his sick bed and accompanied his command into battle. Just before the assault, his horse took a shot and threw Stephens, causing further problems for the weak colonel. Under cover of the artillery, however, Stephens urged his men on, but there was no chance the small brigade would break the Federal line. The Tennesseans and Kentuckians met the massed volleys of the Twelfth and Fourteenth Iowa as well as direct blasts from supporting artillery. One Federal officer remembered, "He made a bold attack on us, but met with a warm reception." At least some of the assault was made through Duncan Field on the left, which caused even more problems for the units on the flank who had to charge through open territory. Cheatham described the results: "The enemy opened upon us from his entire front a terrific fire of artillery and musketry . . . when another part of the enemy's force concealed and protected by the fence and thicket on our left, opened a murderous cross-fire upon our lines." The Federal fire was way too much, and the battered brigade withdrew to safety shortly after launching its assault. Some veterans later claimed that they launched a second assault, but no documentary evidence has surfaced to support that assertion.[11]

Both figuratively and literally blown away by the ferocity of the Federal defense, Stephens soon withdrew his now even-smaller brigade and moved it to the right to connect with Breckinridge's new right wing, which he could see in the distance. He did not want a gap between his right and Breckinridge's left, but he also did not want to encounter the Federal line in the Hornets' Nest again. His troops moved to the right and connected with Breckinridge's brigades in front of a large old cotton field. On the other side was a peach orchard in full bloom.[12]

At some point around 11:00 A.M. and Stephens's attack, the staunch defenders of the Hornets' Nest received a visit from their commander, Ulysses S. Grant. After arriving on the field, Grant made his way to the front lines and spoke to each division commander. Prentiss remembered Grant giving him the last orders he would receive—to hold his position "at all hazards." Prentiss would take the order literally, setting the stage for the future dramatic events that would occur that day.[13]

About the same time as Grant's visit, another group of Confederate officers were also growing concerned about the obviously strong position on the east side of Duncan Field. Shaver had just received its full force, and the racket made by Stephens's assault likely confirmed the suspicion in Confederate officers' minds. This led the ranking Confederate commander in the area just west of Duncan Field to pause from his advance to the northwest, in concert with Johnston's push to destroy the Federal army in the swamps, and focus his attention for a limited time on the Hornets' Nest line.[14]

With the wounding of the ranking Confederate in the area, Major General Thomas C. Hindman, Brigadier General Alexander Stewart became the commanding officer in the sector. He had commanded only a brigade that morning, but his own division commander (Brigadier General Charles Clark) was recently wounded, which placed him in command of that unit. Likewise, Shaver's division commander Hindman was down, and Stewart received orders to take command of both units and attack the enemy. Leading Shaver's brigade as well as one regiment of his own brigade and small elements of brigadier generals Patrick Cleburne's and S. A. M. Wood's brigades that had broken off their parent units and wandered into the area, Stewart managed to compile the largest order of battle that would assault the Hornets' Nest that day. Numbering thirty-seven hundred men combined and supported by Swett's Mississippi battery alongside Smith's artillery, the conglomerate of portions of four Confederate brigades trudged into Duncan Field around 11:30 A.M. They soon realized the folly of such a move.[15]

Stewart's command stretched from the main Corinth Road all the way across Duncan Field to the Eastern Corinth Road. The Twenty-third Tennessee and Sixth Mississippi, lost from Cleburne's brigade, manned the left with Stewart's Fourth Tennessee next in line to the right. Next came the bulk of Shaver's brigade, with the two lost units of Wood's brigade, the Sixteenth Alabama and Fifty-fifth Tennessee, manning the right of the line. The term *assault* is a misnomer; Stewart himself reported that his command merely "engaged" the enemy until Shaver sent word that his brigade was out of ammunition and was withdrawing. That, of course, effectively took any steam out of the attack, as Shaver's was the only full brigade participating. The other units soon also withdrew, some falling back for ammunition and others moving back over to the west, where the main effort was supposed to be occurring anyway. Shaver's brigade would take literally hours to rest and resupply its ammunition, taking it out of the effective ranks for that time period.[16]

Although Stephens and Stewart failed in their isolated assaults, the general Confederate advance against McClernand's Crossroads line to the west was very successful but to different degrees depending on where it was along the line. Generally, the Confederate assault was more successful the farther west one traveled, due to many factors such as terrain, shattered defending commands, and the weight of Confederate mass on the extreme-left flank. The result was that the Federals were driven toward Pittsburg Landing rather than away from it. The farther east along this line one traveled, the Confederate success became much less defined, with Shaver's right making no headway at all against Tuttle's Iowans and Stephens and Stewart being stopped in their tracks in Duncan Field and along the Eastern Corinth Road. The stiff resistance around Duncan Field thus alerted Confederate commanders of a new force that needed to be dealt with. Enter Braxton Bragg.[17]

The hard-luck commander of the Confederate second corps was the unfortunate recipient of a bungled operation at Shiloh. The original Confederate plan had called for an unwieldy attack order that soon broke down into chaos, with command and control rapidly deteriorating. The Confederate corps commanders thus acted on their own and divided up the line into sectors, with William J. Hardee taking the left, Leonidas Polk the center, and Bragg the right. (The fourth corps commander, John C. Breckinridge, was even then unfolding the new right, making Bragg's command the right center.) Bragg happened to get the area with the fewest Confederate troops in it. The bulk of the army had passed far to the west around the Crossroads, while Breckinridge was unfolding a new flank far to the east around Peach Orchard.[18]

Bragg's center third of the battlefield had only three brigades on it, and one of those (Adley Gladden's) was so badly mauled that it was essentially out of action for six hours while another (Shaver's) was resupplying its ammunition and resting from what had already been hours of intense combat. Neither brigade would be a factor again until later in the afternoon. That left Bragg with one effective brigade in the area: Colonel Randall Gibson's. By this time, seven (and one more in reserve) brigades were off to the west while five (including Stephen's) were to the east. With few numbers and long odds, Bragg finally arrived in the area around noon and began his part in the famous operations against the Union Hornets' Nest.[19]

It was a good thing the initial Confederate assaults were either short on numbers in Shaver's and Stephens's cases or were logistically uncoordinated as in Stewart's case, because the yawning gap between Tuttle and Prentiss could potentially have caused problems for the position early in the day. Seeing the need to fill the gap, Prentiss asked for help, and Sweeny sent one of his reserve regiments up to the main line. The Eighth Iowa thus took position and soon was heavily engaged. Colonel James Geddes of the Eighth Iowa reported he "immediately engaged a battalion of the enemy."[20]

The battalion described by Geddes was actually Gibson's Louisiana brigade. The result was a lot of dead and wounded Louisianans. Gibson himself described the attack: "The brigade moved forward in fine style, marching through an open [Davis wheat] field under a heavy fire and half way up an elevation covered with an almost impenetrable thicket, upon which the enemy was posted." Colonel William T. Shaw of the Fourteenth Iowa reported that he ordered his men to lie down and wait until the enemy was within thirty paces before firing: "The enemy's first line was completely destroyed." The Louisianans and Arkansans could attest to his memory, one Confederate reporting that they were repulsed easily by "a battery . . . that raked our flank, while a steady fire of musketry extended along the entire front." Although regimental reports mentioned only three charges, Gibson reported the brigade fell back, reformed, and charged a total of four times. No matter how many times they assaulted the position, it was, in the words of one soldier, "impregnable to infantry alone." The jubilant Federals agreed. Colonel Joseph Woods of the Twelfth Iowa reported, "Again and again repeatedly did he attack us, trying vainly to drive us from our position. He failed to move us one inch." Part of the reason for the Confederate failure was that the artillery battery attached to Gibson's brigade had been left in Corinth to help garrison the town while the army was fighting at Pittsburg Landing. With only long range support from Swett and Smith, with an occasional fire from Robertson's Alabama battery down the Eastern Corinth Road, Gibson's brigade made those futile assaults into the teeth of the Hornets' Nest, losing more and more men as it charged time after time. For two hours, they fought, but Gibson finally admitted, "We were repulsed." To make the defeats even worse, the Federals counterattacked on a couple of occasions, driving the fleeing Confederates before returning to their original lines.[21]

Just as Gibson's fought-out brigade was falling back from which position they ultimately moved to the right, Shaver's resupplied and replenished brigade came forward ready for action. Bragg, with Gibson's men incapable of making another attack, sent Shaver to the front once again. The Arkansas units strode into the teeth of the Hornets' Nest around 2:30 P.M., but the result was another failure.[22]

Shaver reported that Bragg ordered him to take the Federal line "posted in considerable force in a dense undergrowth in a heavy woods." Shaver's line moved forward until within fifty or sixty yards of the enemy line when "a terrific and murderous fire was poured in upon me from their lines and battery. It was impossible to charge through the dense undergrowth." An amazed Tuttle, by now counting attack after attack, remembered that the enemy was "each time baffled and completely routed." Shaver wisely concluded that his fire was doing no harm to the enemy, and he "had nothing left me but to retire or have my men all shot down." Shaver withdrew, and a disgusted Bragg ordered him to reform and resupply in the rear.[23]

Not only were the Iowa Federals in front pouring heavy fire into the oncoming Confederates but so, too, were units on the flanks. With all the commotion along the Eastern Corinth Road, the portion of Sweeny's brigade that was on line in the northern part of Duncan Field shifted in order to take the Confederates moving along that route in flank. The Seventh and Fifty-eighth Illinois turned their lines to the left and occupied a position around Duncan's log cabin and a few cotton bales he had piled nearby. As the Confederates moved across their front, the Illinois soldiers poured a heavy fire into their exposed left flank. "The enemy's ranks were visibly thinned by the steady and rapid firing which the men with the utmost coolness poured into them," remembered one Illinois officer in Duncan Field.[24]

The next Confederate brigade to go in was Patton Anderson's, which had seen severe fighting on the Confederate left all day. He had heard the severe contest to his right and, acting on orders from one of Bragg's staff officers to go to the sound of the firing, had led his men to the right. He met Colonel Marshall Smith of the Crescent Regiment, and they decided to attack. Smith was to go in on the left while Anderson led his men farther around to the right. He ultimately went in along the Eastern Corinth Road—precisely where Gibson and Shaver had assaulted before. As his brigade was moving forward through what Anderson described as "thick underbrush," they met survivors of the Thirteenth Louisiana of Gibson's brigade, who told them they "could not get through the brush." Anderson nevertheless tried, crossing the small hollow and beginning his "ascent of the opposite slope, when a galling fire from infantry and canister from howitzers swept through my ranks with deadly affect." Anderson remembered, "The thicket was so dense that it was impossible for a company officer to be seen at platoon distance." His brigade fell back under the brow of a hill, where several commanders reported "their men unable to make another charge by reason of the complete state of exhaustion they were in." The only success had been on the far left where the Crescent Regiment, apparently aided by portions of A. P. Stewart's brigade, dislodged the Illinois boys of Sweeny's brigade from their flanking position along the main Corinth road.[25]

By this time, around 4:30 P.M., the battle was beginning to simmer down to the Hornets' Nest alone. Indeed, the defenders were beginning to think something momentous was going on. "We held our position about six hours," one Federal remembered in amazement. But the Union line was not so secure on other parts of the battlefield, prompting Sweeny to send all three of his reserve regiments to those threatened areas. Sherman and McClernand had fallen back behind Tilghman Branch on the western side of the battlefield. Rather than follow and attack those units, most of the eight Confederate brigades on the western third of the battlefield wheeled to the right (according to the custom of moving to the sound of the guns) and moved on the flank and rear of the right of the Hornets' Nest. Similarly, Hurlbut's division had fallen back from the Peach Orchard, and those five Confederate brigades on the eastern third of the battlefield began to flank the left of the Hornets' Nest. More units arrived in front of the position as well, such as Wood's brigade that massed alongside Shaver's men. Attending much of the Confederate infantry's move to the center was the accompanying artillery, which was put to good effect in a massed position later called Ruggles's Battery. By 5:15, the converging Confederate units had almost encircled the Federal center and were pouring the enemy lines with massed artillery along the western side of Duncan Field. In fact, the supporting Union batteries had fallen back and gone into Grant's next line of defense, leaving the infantry to hold the line alone. By then, the Hornets' Nest was becoming untenable even for them as several rounds per second from Ruggles's massed guns fell in proximity.[26]

But Grant was not giving up; he was busy forming another line to the rear. While McClernand, Sherman, Hurlbut, Prentiss, and Wallace held out, Grant had his chief of staff Colonel Joseph D. Webster forming all available units back near the landing. Beginning around 2:30 P.M., Webster located a battery of siege guns intended for use in a siege at Corinth and used them and their psychological advantage to stud a new Federal line. Webster also had no less than three other previously unengaged batteries to put into the line by midafternoon. And these overlooked huge, gaping ravines to their front—making their defensive line that much stronger. Two gunboats in the river on the left flank added to the initial strength of this new line. So, the famous last line of defense was already very strong by 3:00 P.M. and became that much stronger as unit after unit fell back from the forward lines. For example, the Federal artillery that pulled out of the Hornets' Nest around 4:00 P.M. went into the line. By 4:30 P.M., the time Hurlbut, McClernand, and Sherman began their withdrawals into the last line, that line was already very strong. Prentiss and Wallace could have pulled out then and gone into the final line and held it all night long.[27]

But Prentiss and Wallace did not fall back. They interpreted Grant's orders to "hold at all hazards" differently than Hurlbut, McClernand, and Sherman had. The Hornets' Nest defenders literally held until they were surrounded and captured. After Hurlbut fell back on the left, Prentiss bent his flank back to the north to cover the area. Meanwhile, on the far right, several of Sweeny's and even Tuttle's regiments were almost magnetically drawn to the rear by McClernand's departure. That left Prentiss in his flank position and Tuttle's Twelfth and Fourteenth Iowa, plus the Eighth Iowa smudged in between, holding the line.[28]

Soon, even Prentiss and Wallace saw the need to withdraw, but it was too late. Wallace was mortally wounded trying to run the gauntlet of Confederate wings as they clamped shut on the Federal position. Prentiss could do nothing else but surrender himself and the twenty-two hundred men who had held out. They were now prisoners of war, but their step was somewhat lightened by the idea that they had hopefully given Grant enough time to build his next line of defense. So was born the thesis that Prentiss had saved the day at Shiloh, and it would get more and more attention as the years passed and the label *Hornets' Nest* became a household name.[29]

Modern Analysis

But was all this action really that important? Did the stand made there that day save the Federal army? Were Prentiss and Wallace sacrificial lambs, offered to the Confederates so that the rest of the Federal army could survive? There is quite a bit of evidence that argues against the idea that the Hornets' Nest was the most vicious, focal, and important sector at Shiloh. Troop positions, unit casualties, contemporary veteran testimony, placement of burials on the battlefield, and battle context all paint a different picture than that of the icon established through the years after the war. It hints that the Hornets' Nest was not the line that saved the day for Grant.

Union troop positions show that the Hornets' Nest was not the most critical area on the field for much of the day. When they went into action, Colonel Sweeny's Union brigade of six regiments, positioned in Duncan Field north of Corinth Road, did not have ample room to deploy. As a result, only two regiments went on line; Sweeny held the other four in reserve. Once the Union line began to fall apart on either side of the Hornets' Nest, Sweeny began to send his reserve regiments as reinforcements for the other more critical areas. He sent two Illinois regiments to the Peach Orchard sector and one to the north to aid McClernand. Only one regiment went to aid the Hornets' Nest. Had the Hornets' Nest been the critical point with the most-desperate and severe fighting, Sweeny certainly would not have sent his regiments away from the area.[30]

Casualty figures for the units engaged in the Hornets' Nest likewise do not point toward the most-vicious fighting taking place there. Union Colonel Tuttle's brigade of four Iowa regiments, which held the Hornets' Nest and the Sunken Road in front of Duncan Field, sustained a total of 207 killed and wounded in the battle—a number far less than some individual regiments like the Ninth Illinois (366) and the Sixth Mississippi (300) sustained on other parts of the battlefield. On the Confederate side, casualties for brigades that attacked the Hornets' Nest were actually smaller than those of other brigades that came nowhere near the position during the day. The four Confederate brigades with the highest casualties were Pat Cleburne's (1,043), Adley Gladden's (829), Winfield Statham's (809), and Robert Trabue's (800), none of which attacked the Hornets' Nest en masse. For those brigades that did attack the area, their casualties stood somewhere in the middle of the Confederate army's casualties: Gibson's brigade, with so many charges into the Hornets' Nest, ranked as eighth (of sixteen) among Confederate brigade losses, with William Stephens's and Patton Anderson's brigades ranking fourteenth and sixteenth respectively. Wood's and Shaver's brigades ranked as fifth and seventh, but as part of the first wave of attack (Hardee's Corps), they had seen heavy fighting earlier in the day as well. Perhaps Colonel Henry W. Allen of the Fourth Louisiana of Randall Gibson's brigade stated the case most clearly in his report made on April 10, 1862. After he had led his Louisiana boys into the teeth of the Hornets' Nest at least three and maybe four times, he wrote of another encounter as being the worst of the day for his men: "While drawn up in line of battle and awaiting orders[,] a Tennessee regiment immediately in our rear fired into us by mistake, killing and wounding a large number of my men." The future governor of Louisiana went on to say, "This was a terrible blow to the regiment; far more terrible than any inflicted by the enemy."[31]

The number of dead in the area also demonstrates that the Hornets' Nest did not see the heaviest fighting at Shiloh. The Federal soldiers burying the dead on April 8 almost always buried the bodies of both sides at or near where they fell. With some thirty-five-hundred bodies as well as hundreds or dead horses scattered throughout their campsite, they had neither the time nor the desire to haul the bodies any distance. An 1866 document produced by Captain E. B. Whitman, who was in charge of the laborers locating bodies on the battlefield for the new national cemetery, stated that the dead "marks most distinctly the progress of the fight, and the points where each party suffered most severely." Whitman reported the heaviest concentrations of dead lay on the eastern and western sectors of the battlefield and that the dead were fairly light in the center, where the Hornets' Nest was located. "In the center there seems to have been less fighting as fewer graves are found," Whitman testified.[32]

Moreover, placing the Hornets' Nest into the overall context of the battle shows that the center of the battlefield was the least fought-over area for most of the day. Eight out of sixteen Confederate brigades can be documented as being located on the western third of the battlefield for the majority of the time between 10:00 A.M. and 5:00 P.M. Likewise, five out of sixteen Confederate brigades can be documented on the eastern third of the battlefield for the majority of those times. With Gladden's and Shaver's brigades out of action for several hours, this leaves only one lone brigade for the center third, Randall Gibson's, supported at various times by brigades that came and went quickly, such as Stephens's Tennessee brigade and Shaver's Arkansas brigade. For the majority of the time, Bragg had no mass of Confederate forces in the center to hurl at the Union line.[33]

Even more telling, what was happening to the rear of the Hornets' Nest supports the idea that Grant did not need Wallace and Prentiss to hold out and sacrifice themselves in order to save his army. The commanding general began establishing his final line of defense around 2:30 in the afternoon. Already formidable with two gunboats, three field batteries, five siege guns, and highly defensible terrain, the position became even stronger as units fled from the battlefield and were fed into line. Thus, by the time McClernand, Sherman, and Hurlbut fell back from the flanks of the Hornets' Nest around 4:30 P.M., Grant already had had two hours to establish a very solid line, on very defensible ground, that was augmented by the withdrawing divisions. While Prentiss's eventual stand in the Hornets' Nest did cause the Confederates to focus nearly their undivided attention on that position late in the day, had the center fallen back with the rest of the army, they most likely would have gone into that last line and made it even stronger. it is known that at least twenty-two-hundred soldiers eventually surrendered, and most of these would have been available to man that last line, which due to the terrain and strength would have no doubt held as easily at 5:00 P.M. as it did an hour later. Grant himself seemed to take this point of view, writing somewhat beratingly in his memoirs, "In one of the backward moves, on the 6th, the division commanded by General Prentiss did not fall back with the others. This left his flanks exposed and enabled the enemy to capture him with about 2,200 of his officers and men."[34]

Thus, the evidence points to the fact that the Hornets' Nest was not the most vicious, important, or decisive engagement at Shiloh. The soldiers themselves stated as much, the positions of troops do not support the idea, and the casualties and burials firmly argue against such a notion. Most important, the Hornets' Nest, when viewed within the context of the battle as a whole, does not stand out as the dominant engagement at Shiloh.

Hornets' Nest Historiography

Such evidence, then, leads to the question of why the Hornets' Nest has become so famous and important in Shiloh historiography. It was not always so. No one fighting in the Hornets' Nest knew it by that name. But then, no one participating in Pickett's Charge knew that it would be so named years later; no one fighting at Antietam knew the road sunken into the earth would one day be called the Bloody Lane. The Confederates apparently called the Union position as such that day because the enemy bullets zipping past their ears sounded like swarms of angry hornets. Such an expression was a common phrase at the time, however, but few if anyone used the term in reference to the position at Shiloh immediately after the battle. A diligent search has not yet turned up any mention of the name in contemporary literature; a search of all well-known and obscure Civil War newspapers, letters, and diaries might turn up a mention or two of the name but as of now nothing has surfaced.[35]

The Hornets' Nest is not the only later-named position. No soldiers knew they were drinking from the Bloody Pond; no defenders knew they were holding Grant's Last Line. The only two proper place names that consistently appear on contemporary maps are Pittsburg Landing and Shiloh Church. The rest are postwar names, and it is difficult to date the origin of these famous labels.[36]

The name *Hornet Nest* appears on a tantalizingly undatable map in the Library of Congress, but it can be proven that the map is of 1862 vintage. The map maker, Leon J. Fremaux, created several versions of his map (this is known because of several modifications), but it is not known when he drew the version that bears the famous name. The only known time and space connection that brings Shiloh and the term *Hornets' Nest* together during the war is an 1864 letter from a sailor aboard the USS *Tawah*, a wooden gunboat plying the Tennessee River. He remarked that his gunboat shelled the "historic Pittsburg Landing" but "failed in our object—that of stirring up a Rebel hornet's nest." And, it would seem that another battle has as much claim to the historic name as Shiloh: a Confederate colonel in 1863 labeled a section of the line at Vicksburg as "a hornet's nest of lines and works, bristling with cannon and bayonets and crammed with soldiers."[37]

The term *Hornets' Nest* apparently did not surface in print, and as such in the major public's knowledge, until the late 1870s. William Preston Johnston, writing about his father's role at the Battle of Shiloh in *The Life of General Albert Sidney Johnston* (1879), remarked that the Union position "was nicknamed by the Confederates, by a very mild metaphor, 'The Hornets' Nest.'" Of course, Johnston would have been in a position after the war to hear tales of the story. Johnston's name for the Federal defense caught on somewhat. Other authors of the era also mentioned the Hornets' Nest, such as Manning Force in *From Fort Henry to Corinth* (1881). He first broached the idea that the country road on which the Federal regiments aligned was "sunk"; more important, he also mentioned the Hornets' Nest. P. G. T. Beauregard did not mention the name in his 1883 authorized biography by Alfred Roman, *The Military Campaigns of General Beauregard*. Neither did Ulysses S. Grant in his *Personal Memoirs of U. S. Grant*, published in 1885. Although the literature of the early 1880s began to mention the name, it clearly had not stuck.[38]

In 1885 came the first of a series of media productions that would forever make the name lodge in the minds of Americans and definitely sway the way people today look at the Battle of Shiloh. Under the direction of A. T. Andreas of the Western Art Association, the artist Theophile Poilpot and twelve assistants produced in Chicago what must have been a remarkable panorama painting along the lines of the cycloramas for Gettysburg and Atlanta. While Poilpot had the entire battle as inspiration for scenes, including the legendary names of Shiloh Church and Pittsburg Landing, he chose to paint the action in the Hornets' Nest. "The name of 'Hornets' Nest' was given to our position by the rebels themselves," Hornets' Nest brigade commander James Tuttle remembered, "and the identification was made complete by some rebel officers in the fall of 1884, while making a survey for the picture at Chicago. . . . These soldiers had been in some of the charges made against our lines, and their decision in the matter is not disputed." Thus, this panorama, with lectures at times by none other than Benjamin Prentiss himself, solidly fixed the term *Hornets' Nest* in the American mind. An accompanying publication, *Manual of the Panorama of the Battle of Shiloh*, increased the attention given to that part of the battlefield, testifying, "The Thermopylae of modern times, was the 'Hornets' Nest' at Shiloh" and "for some hours it was the turning point in the battle, and beyond doubt saved what was finally saved of the first day's wreck at Shiloh." The inclusion of several panels in the widely distributed *Century* magazine articles (now known collectively as the four-volume *Battles and Leaders of the Civil War*) took the name to more and more Americans, while Thure de Thulstrup's 1888 L. Prang and Company lithograph centering on the Hornets' Nest brought even more attention to Prentiss and his stand.[39]

The growing body of literature mentioning and illustrating the Hornets' Nest and the massive boost given the term by the panorama convinced the

Union veterans of the worth of the name. Veterans of the Iowa regiments that had defended that section of line (the Second, Seventh, Eighth, Twelfth, and Fourteenth Iowa) began talking of a veterans' organization of the defenders of the Hornets' Nest as early as 1884, during a visit to the battlefield. In 1887, the dream became a reality with the first meeting of the "Iowa Hornets' Nest Brigade." The veterans themselves, this time Union soldiers, carried on the by-now common name, and they also continued the argument that the "Hornets' Nest Brigade saved the day at Shiloh."[40]

Several "Iowa Hornets' Nest Brigade" reunions took place over the following years. The critical development in this veterans' association was not so much what they called themselves, although that in itself illustrated the growing usage of the term, but more important in whom they produced. The Twelfth Iowa veterans, back at their first meeting in 1880, had elected themselves a historian. His name was David W. Reed. Historian Reed would also become a factor in the Hornets' Nest Brigade reunions and would ultimately take the growing fame of the Hornets' Nest and make it a household name.[41]

By the mid-1890s, Reed was ready to take the idea of the Hornets' Nest one step further, and he was possibly the only man in the United States who was in a position to do so. Congress has passed legislation to create a national military park out of the battlefield of Shiloh in 1894. The congressman who sponsored the legislation was another Twelfth Iowa veteran, David B. Henderson—soon to be speaker of the House of Representatives. Once the bill was passed and the war department began to make appointments to the governing commission, Henderson prevailed on Secretary of War Daniel S. Lamont to appoint Henderson's close friend David W. Reed to be historian. (He also got other friends hired as well.) Reed thus began the historical work at Shiloh with a golden opportunity to shape how the battle was interpreted both in the creation of the physical battlefield and in the written version of the battle, neither of which had been fully done before.[42]

Not only did Reed produce a battlefield thoroughly marked with monuments and tablets that told the story of the Hornets' Nest as well as other positions on the field but he also produced major media publications that gave the story even more prominence. Prior to Reed and his comrades' reunions, none of the major publications mentioning the battle had dwelt on the Hornets' Nest as the key to Union victory. In the *Century* articles, for example, the writers did not dwell on that aspect of the battle or make grand arguments that the Federal stand there saved the day. It was Reed and his comrades who did.[43]

In *The Battle of Shiloh and the Organizations Engaged*, Reed subtly described the Hornets' Nest's role in the battle as one of extreme importance.

He described in vivid detail how the units there defeated numerous charges upon the Union line, even counterattacking on a couple of occasions. He also made it clear that the entire Confederate army was involved in the capture of the Hornets' Nest defenders; at one point he made the correct assertion that adjoining Federal regiments surrendered to the two different extreme flanks of the Confederate army, which had overlapped in rear of the Union line. He also argued that the Confederate army had to "reorganize . . . for an attack upon the Union line in position near the Landing." In Reed's government-published book, he never came out and blatantly said he and his comrades had won the battle, but he hinted that their stand had allowed the Federals to build another line in rear—one that held and ultimately secured the victory.[44]

The Iowa historian was not so subtle in his regimental history *Campaigns and Battles of the Twelfth Regiment Iowa Veteran Volunteer Infantry*, produced a decade earlier but only published one year later in 1903. There, he was able to tell what he and his comrades believed to be the real story of Shiloh—that the Hornets' Nest had been the pivotal action of the day by allowing the beaten fragments of Grant's army time to build another line of defense. Reed tantalizingly told his readers, "It has been claimed that the delay caused by the stubborn resistance of parts of five regiments at the 'Hornets' Nest,' even after the other troops had fallen back, saved Grant's army; and there is at least good reason for the claim." Reed then gave detail after detail from report after report on how the Hornets' Nest was the key event at Shiloh. At the end, Reed drove home the point: "To those comrades who survived that desperate struggle, and to the friends who still mourn those who fell on that glorious field, there is the consolation of knowing that, after years of waiting, the final summing up of the evidence will convince any unprejudiced searcher after the truth that the valor of the troops at the 'Hornets' Nest' *saved the day at Shiloh*" (italics his).[45]

For years, Reed's work on Shiloh was just about all that was produced on the battle, and his words convinced visitors and readers. With the Hornets' Nest growing into almost-legendary status, however, one final media presentation made it the icon known today. The National Park Service took over Shiloh National Military Park in 1933. Its historians began working on interpretive publications and services that would provide insight on the battle to a growing nonveteran clientele. By far, the best-known and most important of these publications and presentations was the park's introductory movie, *Shiloh: Portrait of a Battle*. Written by park historian Charles E. Shedd Jr. and narrated by park superintendent Ira B. Lykes, the film was an overview of the battle with the Hornets' Nest as the central theme. Shedd had little more than Reed's books and the interpretation handed down from him through the years on which to base his narrative. No wonder he placed such high importance on the Hornets' Nest.[46]

The film, shot between 1954 and 1956, was the first narrative-style motion picture shown at a national park site. That in itself, even the fact that the movie firmly placed the Hornets' Nest as the key event at Shiloh, was not what made the movie so critical in the growth of the Hornets' Nest legend. Rather, that the movie is still being shown today, fifty years later, makes it remarkable for its longevity; it is by far the longest-running National Park Service film in existence. In that longevity comes the importance to the Hornets' Nest story; literally millions of people have watched the film over the course of its fifty-year career, and they soaked up the story of the Hornets' Nest's importance at Shiloh.[47]

Thus, the Hornets' Nest was the result of the veterans' interpretation of the facts, not the facts themselves. And that interpretation, added to and strengthened through the years, has dominated Shiloh historiography to the point that the Hornets' Nest has become an icon. But a thorough examination of the historiography as well as battle accounts leads to a different conclusion, one that is very revisionist in nature and sure to cause some argument. But in seeking to find the objective truth, the historian must wade through decades of interpretations and test them for validity. Such an activity points to the importance of the future study of Civil War memory.

The traditional view of the Battle of Shiloh is that the Hornets' Nest was the rock against which the Confederate tide crashed time after time, ultimately splitting itself and going around the flanks. The reality is that the center had so few Confederate troops in it that the strength of the Hornets' Nest was less because of the inherent power of the Federal line and more a result of the lack of numbers sent against it. The Confederates did not split their army on the immovable rock; the determined stand in the Hornets' Nest was the result of the split already occurring in the Confederate army. With major portions of Johnston's troops already going around the Hornets' Nest, that Federal position was bound to hold against the relatively minor forces thrown against it. The defenders of the Hornets' Nest actually saw less fighting than their comrades in arms; they just did a better job of getting their story out, thus creating the icon that today is the Hornets' Nest at Shiloh.

Notes

1. David W. Reed, *Campaigns and Battles of the Twelfth Regiment Iowa Veteran Volunteer Infantry: From Organization, September, 1861, to Muster-Out, January 20, 1866* (n.p., 1903), 48–50, 53, 250.

2. David W. Reed, *The Battle of Shiloh and the Organizations Engaged* (Washington, DC: GPO, 1902).

3. Reed, *Battle of Shiloh*, 15.

4. Larry J. Daniel, *Shiloh: The Battle That Changed the Civil War* (New York: Simon and Shuster, 1997), 197.

5. Reed, *Battle of Shiloh*, 16.

6. U.S. War Department, *The War of the Rebellion: A Compilation of the Official Records of the Union and Confederate Armies*, ed. Robert N. Scott, 128 vols. (Washington, DC: GPO, 1884), 10.1:404. (This source is hereafter referred to as "*OR*." All references are to series 1 unless otherwise noted.)

7. *OR*, 10.1:404.

8. *OR*, 10.1:151, 153, 291. For more about the plants of the area, see Ray H. Mattison, "The Vegetative Cover of the Hornets' Nest Area during the Battle of Shiloh," Vertical Files, Shiloh National Military Park.

9. Reed, *Battle of Shiloh*, 70.

10. *OR*, 10.1:438.

11. Reed, *Battle of Shiloh*, 84–85; *OR*, 10.1:151, 438, 453. For the claim of a second Stephens assault, see Troop Position Tablet # 337, Shiloh National Military Park.

12. *OR*, 10.1:438–39.

13. *OR*, 10.1:178, 279.

14. *OR*, 10.1:428.

15. Reed, *Battle of Shiloh*, 17.

16. *OR*, 10.1:428

17. *OR*, 10.1:466; Reed, *Battle of Shiloh*, 45.

18. *OR*, 10.1:408.

19. *OR*, 10.1:574; Reed, *Battle of Shiloh*, 70, 73.

20. *OR*, 10.1:165–166, 278.

21. *OR*, 10.1:151, 153, 480, 488, 491.

22. Reed, *Battle of Shiloh*, 70.

23. *OR*, 10.1:149, 574.

24. *OR*, 10.1:162–64.

25. *OR*, 10.1:162–164, 498; Reed, *Battle of Shiloh*, 18.

26. Reed, *Battle of Shiloh*, 18–19, 50; *OR*, 10.1:149.

27. Reed, *Battle of Shiloh*, 19, 61.

28. *OR*, 10.1:179.

29. *OR*, 10.1:279.

30. Reed, *Battle of Shiloh*, 50; Tony Horwitz, *Confederates in the Attic: Dispatches from the Unfinished Civil War* (New York: Vintage, 1998), 177–79.

31. *OR*, 10.1:101, 395, 489.

32. E. B. Whitman to J. L. Donelson, April 29, 1866, RG 92, E 576, Box 53; National Archives and Records Administration, Washington, D.C.

33. Stacy D. Allen, "Shiloh!: The Campaign and First Day's Battle," *Blue and Gray* 14, no. 3 (Winter 1997): 47.

34. Ulysses S. Grant, *Personal Memoirs of U. S. Grant*, 2 vols. (New York: Webster, 1885–86), 1:201.

35. Carol Reardon, *Pickett's Charge in History and Memory* (Chapel Hill: University of North Carolina Press, 1997).

36. See George B. Davis, Leslie J. Perry, and Joseph W. Kirkley, *The Official Military Atlas of the Civil War* (Washington, DC: GPO, 1891–1895), plates 10, 12, 13, and 14 for various contemporary maps of the battlefield of Shiloh.

37. Leon J. Fremaux, "Map of the Battlefield of Shiloh, April 6 & 7, 1862," Geography and Map Division, Library of Congress; William T. Ross to "Lizzie," October 31, 1864, William T. Roass Letter, Vertical Files, Shiloh National Military Park; *OR*, 24.2:33. See various Fremaux maps on file at Shiloh National Military Park and in Davis, *The Official Military Atlas of the Civil War*, for variations of his maps.

38. William Preston Johnston, *The Life of Gen. Albert Sidney Johnston, Embracing His Services in the Armies of the United States, the Republic of Texas, and the Confederate States* (New York: Appleton, 1879), 604; Manning F. Force, *From Fort Henry to Corinth* (New York: Scribner's Sons, 1881), 142, 144; Alfred Roman, *The Military Operations of General Beauregard in the War Between the States, 1861 to 1865: Including a Brief Personal Sketch of His Services in the War with Mexico, 1846–8*, 2 vols. (New York: Harper, 1883); Grant, *Personal Memoirs*, 2 vols. (New York: Webster, 1885–1886); William K. Kay, "The Sunken Road," internal report, Vertical Files, Shiloh National Military Park, 4.

39. David G. Martin, *The Campaign of Shiloh, March–April, 1862* (New York: Fairfax, 1987), 105; David Nevin, *The Road to Shiloh: Early Battles in the West* (Alexandria, VA: Time-Life Books, 1983), 130–35; "First Reunion of Iowa Hornets' Nest Brigade," October 12–13, 1887, series 3, box 4, folder 216, Shiloh National Military Park, 12; *Manual of the Panorama of the Battle of Shiloh* (Chicago: Andreas, 1885), 5, 14; Don Carlos Buell, "Shiloh Reviewed," in *Battles and Leaders of the Civil War*, ed. Robert V. Johnson and Clarence C. Buel, 4 vols. (New York: Century, 1884–87), 1:504–5, 510–11; Thure de Thulstrup, *Battle of Shiloh Lithograph* (Prang, 1888); Kay, "Sunken Road," 5.

40. "First Reunion of Iowa Hornets' Nest Brigade," 30.

41. Reed, *Campaigns and Battles*, 1. For Reed's participation at the Hornets' Nest Brigade reunions, see "First Reunion of Iowa Hornets' Nest Brigade," and "Third Reunion of Iowa Hornets' Nest Brigade, August 21–22, 1895," both in series 3, box 4, folder 216, Shiloh National Military Park.

42. Timothy B. Smith, *This Great Battlefield of Shiloh: History, Memory, and the Establishment of a Civil War National Military Park* (Knoxville: University of Tennessee Press, 2004); Timothy B. Smith, "David Wilson Reed: The Father of Shiloh National Military Park," *Annals of Iowa* 62, no. 3 (Summer 2003): 333–59.

43. T. B. Smith, *This Great Battlefield of Shiloh*; "Historians and the Battle of Shiloh: One Hundred and Forty Years of Controversy," *Tennessee Historical Quarterly* 63, no. 4 (Winter 2003): 338–39.

44. Reed, *Battle of Shiloh*, 18–20.

45. Reed, *Campaigns and Battles*, 54, 61.

46. T. B. Smith, *This Great Battlefield of Shiloh*, 126–27.

47. T. B. Smith, "Shiloh: Portrait of a Battle: Fifty Years Later," *Tennessee Historical Quarterly* 65, no. 2 (Summer 2006): 147–61; James Lee McDonough, *Shiloh: In Hell before Night* (Knoxville: University of Tennessee Press, 1977). The movie also influenced a young historian writing about the battle, James Lee McDonough, whose first academic book on the battle, *Shiloh: In Hell before Night*, became the academic standard for decades. Apparently, McDonough was also heavily influenced by an internal National Park Service study by Donald F. Dosch entitled "The Hornets' Nest at Shiloh," which can be found in the Vertical Files, Shiloh National Military Park.

4

INTOLERABLY SLOW

LEW WALLACE'S MARCH TO THE BATTLEFIELD

Steven E. Woodworth

T he Battle of Shiloh had been raging for five hours, and the sun was nearing its zenith. Ulysses S. Grant, together with several of his staff officers, was inspecting the lines near the right wing of his hard-pressed army. Seeing a body of Union troops moving up in support of the line, Grant exclaimed, "Now we are all right, all right. There's Wallace." But the troops Grant had spotted did not belong to Brigadier General Lew Wallace's Third Division but rather to one of the other divisions already on the field, as Grant soon discovered.[1] For more than an hour, Grant had been expecting the arrival of Wallace's troops, expecting that the Third Division would turn the tide of battle that had been against his outnumbered troops all morning.[2] He was to continue waiting—in vain—for Wallace's appearance throughout the afternoon. Not until after nightfall—and after the firing had stopped for the day—did the Third Division reach the battlefield, despite that it had been camped that morning barely five miles away.

Wallace's late arrival at Shiloh has remained one of the most bitter and enduring controversies of the battle. It poisoned the relationship between Grant and Wallace, blighting the career of the young Hoosier general who had, up until that time, seemed to be one of the most rapidly rising stars among the nonprofessional generals in the Union armies. Even after the lapse of nearly a century and a half, historians still differ about the events that transpired between Pittsburg Landing and Crump's Landing on April 6, 1862. The key questions remain, why was Wallace late, and why did Grant blame him for the delay?

When what was soon to be called the Army of the Tennessee moved up the river of that name in mid-March and arrived in the vicinity of Savannah, Tennessee, Brigadier General Charles Ferguson Smith, who commanded the expedition, had, in keeping with the instructions of Major General Henry

W. Halleck, dispatched expeditions to break the railroads that converged at Corinth. He sent Wallace's Third Division to Crump's Landing, whence it marched fifteen miles west to reach the Mobile & Ohio Railroad at Purdy, Tennessee. Wallace's men tore up about a half mile of track and then marched back to Crump's Landing. Smith dispatched General William Tecumseh Sherman's Fifth Division to a point on the river above Pittsburg Landing and below Eastport, Mississippi, but torrential rains and a flooded landscape prevented the division from reaching and breaking the Memphis & Charleston Railroad east of Corinth.[3]

Sherman's division, along with Brigadier General Stephen A. Hurlbut's Fourth, and Smith's own Second encamped at Pittsburg Landing and within the next fortnight were joined by Major General John A. McClernand's First, which had moved up from Savannah, ten miles downstream. Also joining them were the elements of what was to become Prentiss's Sixth Division, which organized at Pittsburg Landing. Grant resumed command of the army in late March. The only elements of the army that did not take position at Pittsburg Landing were Wallace's division, still at Crump's, and Grant's own headquarters, which he kept at Savannah in hopes of making early contact with General Don Carlos Buell. This dispersed arrangement of Grant and Wallace was at the heart of the Third Division's late arrival for the Battle of Shiloh.

On Monday, March 31, Wallace moved one of his three brigades, Colonel Charles Whittlesey's Third, initially commanded by Colonel Charles Woods, five miles inland on the Purdy road at the tiny settlement of Adamsville, Tennessee. He placed another of his brigades, Colonel John M. Thayer's Second, halfway between Adamsville and Crump's at a crossroads known as Stony Lonesome. The next morning, a patrol from Woods's brigade clashed inconclusively with Confederate cavalry between Adamsville and Purdy.[4]

On the evening of Thursday, April 3, two of Wallace's scouts, who had been acting independently of each other, brought him word that the Rebel army was advancing from Corinth and aiming to strike the force at Pittsburg Landing—not, as Union commanders had previously half expected, toward Wallace's isolated force at Crump's. In his memoir, Wallace claimed that the scouts' reports were detailed and fairly accurate. They correctly noted that the entire Confederate force was on its way, artillery included, and that it was commanded by Albert Sidney Johnston and divided into four corps commanded by Generals William J. Hardee, Braxton Bragg, Leonidas Polk, and John C. Breckinridge in that order—precisely the order in which they attacked on April 6. The scouts overestimated the Confederate total strength somewhat at fifty thousand men. But Wallace's claim of uncanny accuracy leads one to suspect that Wallace's memory had enhanced his scouts' perceptions. Still, it is possible that the scouts did bring in a significant intelligence bonanza. Johnston's army had marched out of Corinth that morning, twenty-five miles south of Wallace's headquarters at Crump's Landing, and if, as the scouts claimed, they actually did converse with members of the Confederate army, they could have learned its intended destination.[5]

In response to the reports of his scouts, Wallace sent notice to his brigade commanders. He then sat down in his tent and by candlelight wrote a note to Grant conveying what he had just learned. During early April, Grant was spending his days at Pittsburg Landing and returning by steamboat to his headquarters at Savannah for the night. Wallace had not seen Grant's boat, the *Tigress*, pass Crump's on its way down to Savannah that evening, and so he surmised that the commanding general might be spending the night at Pittsburg Landing. Wallace sealed the note in an envelope and directed his orderly, Thomas W. Simpson, to ride to Pittsburg Landing and place the envelope in Grant's hand, if he was still there, or, if not, to entrust it to the postmaster at Pittsburg Landing for transmission to Grant. As it turned out, Simpson missed Grant, and the note never reached him.[6]

The following day, Friday, April 4, Wallace was concerned enough about the prospect of an imminent attack, either on his own division or on Pittsburg Landing, that he ordered his subordinates to issue three days' rations to the troops, part of the standard preparation for impending battle or other active operations. That day, the information Wallace received indicated that a heavy force of Confederate infantry, artillery, and cavalry was at Purdy, posing a dire threat to Woods's Third Brigade at Adamsville. That night, while Sherman's division was fending off a Confederate skirmish probe near Shiloh Church, Wallace marched his First and Second brigades to Adamsville to reinforce Woods. On arriving there, however, Wallace learned that the supposed threat had really amounted to nothing more than a sighting of a small force of Rebel cavalry. The gray horsemen had since disappeared, and no trouble was expected in the vicinity. So after giving his men the morning of Saturday, April 5, to rest from their nocturnal tramp, Wallace had the First and Second brigades march back to their respective posts that afternoon.[7]

Grant continued to be concerned about the possibility of a Confederate strike against Crump's Landing. He was apparently aware of the same reports that had alarmed Wallace on Friday, for on that same day, Grant sent the Third Division commander a note directing him to confer with Brigadier General William H. L. Wallace (no relation), who had just taken over command of the Second Division in place of the ailing Smith. Grant wanted the Wallaces to work out the best routes between their positions with a view to rapid reinforcement. To William, Grant wrote, "It is believed that the enemy are re-enforcing at Purdy, and it may be necessary to re-enforce General Wallace to avoid his being attacked by a superior force. Should you find danger of this sort, re-enforce him at once with your entire division."[8] The Second Division was encamped closest to Pittsburg Landing and was the army's reserve. If the Rebels attacked the force at Crump's Landing, the Second Division would be the first to go to its aid.

William wrote to Lew Wallace, who replied the next day, Saturday, April 5. Writing from the camp of his most advanced brigade in Adamsville, he explained that his cavalry had gone over the road from Adamsville to the camps of the Second Division at Pittsburg Landing several times. The route in question was known as the River Road (also called Hamburg-Savannah Road) because it closely paralleled the Tennessee River. The recent high water of the river had blocked the road, but the Tennessee had now receded sufficiently to leave the River Road passable but muddy and difficult. Lew promised to send a cavalry officer over to the Second Division the next day to familiarize William's cavalry with the route.[9]

Sunday morning, April 6, Lew Wallace was awakened in the gray morning twilight by a sentry who stuck his head in at the tent flap to announce, "I hear guns up the river." Within a short time, Wallace had joined the sentry outside, listening to the sounds from the south. His staff soon joined him, and all agreed that the sound, including both the rattle of musketry and the deep boom of cannon, was a battle in progress. Wallace wrote after the war that this was at about 6 A.M., which would have been about half an hour before sunrise. He decided to concentrate his division at Stony Lonesome, with the Third Brigade marching east from Adamsville and the First Brigade marching west from Crump's Landing. He sent a staff officer galloping off with orders to the brigade commanders to assemble at Stony Lonesome and to hold their troops in readiness for immediate movement from that point.

Stony Lonesome was a particularly good place for Lew Wallace to hold his division pending orders, because from there, roads led both directly to Pittsburg Landing (the River Road, or Hamburg-Savannah Road) and to the right wing of Sherman's division at the southwestern edge of the Union encampment near Shiloh Church, which was three miles from Pittsburg Landing. The latter road was known as the Shunpike. Wallace would thus be able to travel directly to either Pittsburg Landing or the church.[10]

Lew Wallace himself remained at Crump's Landing with his staff on a steamboat, the *Jesse K. Bell*, that was tied up there. From its deck, Wallace felt he could hear more clearly the sounds of battle from upriver, and he would be in a position to see Grant's steamer, *Tigress*, heading up the river from Savannah on its way to the scene of the fighting. Wallace figured that

Grant would stop to give him orders. It was not until about 8:30 A.M. that the *Tigress* came into view and soon tied up alongside Wallace's boat.[11]

"Have you heard the firing?" Grant asked, Wallace recalled in his memoirs.

"Yes, sir, since daybreak," Wallace replied.

Grant asked what Wallace thought of it, and the latter replied that it was "undoubtedly a general engagement."

Grant's response was to order Wallace to "hold yourself in readiness to march upon orders received."

As Wallace reported the incident in his memoirs, he replied, "But, general, I ordered a concentration about six o'clock. The division must be at Stony Lonesome. I am ready now." Grant's volunteer aide, Douglas Putnam, describing the event years later, recorded a simpler response: "My division is in line, waiting for orders."

"Very well," Grant replied. "Hold the division ready to march in any direction." Putnam recalled Grant adding "that as soon as he got to Pittsburg Landing and learned where the attack was, he would send him orders." With that, the *Tigress* continued upstream on the north-flowing Tennessee River toward Pittsburg Landing.[12]

With the advantage of hindsight—and full knowledge of what was really underway around Shiloh Church at that time—it is clear that Grant should have ordered Wallace to march at once. Grant can hardly be blamed for failing to act on information he did not have, but the situation points up the awkwardness of the arrangement that had Grant's headquarters five miles from Wallace's division and ten from the rest of his army. It is quite possible that the sounds of the battle around Shiloh Church were audible at Crump's Landing some time before they could be heard at Savannah, and Grant may not have known that a battle was in progress until it had developed to a very impressive crescendo of sound—all the more so because Grant and his staff members were residing in a brick house while Lew Wallace and his men were sleeping under canvas.

As soon as Grant heard the sound of the guns from the south, he had abandoned the breakfast to which he had just seated himself and ordered his staff to go to Pittsburg Landing at once. Putnam noted that the *Tigress* did not have steam up at the time and that they started out "as soon as steam could be raised." This would have entailed a delay of at least half an hour. Then the *Tigress* would have had to fight the strong current of the Tennessee River, swelled as it still was at that time from heavy spring rains. It might have taken an hour to steam from Savannah to Crump's landing. This accounts for an hour and a half of the two-and-a-half-hour lapse between the time the men at Crump's first heard sounds of battle and the time Grant arrived.

The other hour probably represents the difference between the initial flare up of fighting in front of Prentiss's camps, which was, perhaps, just audible at Crump's Landing around 6 A.M., and the opening of the much larger and even more intense clash in front of Sherman's division in the Shiloh Church sector around 7 A.M., which may well have been the first sounds of battle to reach Savannah.

Yet, even when he spoke with Lew Wallace from the deck of the *Tigress*, Grant still did not know what was afoot near Pittsburg Landing. A skirmish there Friday evening had brought him racing up the river only to find that all had subsided before his arrival. Unwilling to be stampeded, Grant at 8:30 that morning was not yet ready to order Wallace to march for the battlefield. The inescapable conclusion, again with the wisdom of hindsight, is that Grant should have established his headquarters in a tent at Pittsburg Landing, as he had already made plans to do later that day. The first two hours, at least, of the delay in the Third Division's arrival on the battlefield was attributable to the inappropriate location in Savannah of Grant's headquarters.

Any serious student of a Civil War battle (or any other battle, for that matter) will quickly discover the customary muddle that surrounds questions of time during a battle. Men guessed at time by the position of the sun or simply guessed by their internal sense of the passage of time—something a battle was sure to throw off kilter. If they had watches, there was no particular reason those watches would be set to the same time or that men would remember the times those watches had shown when key events took place. Hence, once a man became embroiled in the swirl of battle, his reports about what time a given event took place should generally be considered as accurate, at most, only to within plus or minus two hours. Still, the confusion of times in connection with Lew Wallace's march to the battlefield is unusually vexatious.

Tigress continued to fight the strong current of the Tennessee from Crump's to Pittsburg Landing. In that stretch of river, they encountered the steamer *Warner*, racing downstream on orders from William Wallace to inform Grant that a general engagement was in progress. With this news, Grant could, theoretically, have made his decision to bring up Lew Wallace and might have entrusted such a message to those aboard *Warner*. Unconvinced as yet, Grant proceeded, and *Warner* came about and followed *Tigress* back to Pittsburg Landing, where they probably arrived between 9 and 9:30 A.M. As soon as Grant's horse and those of his staff could be brought down the gangplank, they rode inland to investigate. Other witnesses testified that the sound of battle could be heard much more clearly from the top of the bluff above the landing, and it would by this time have been an unbroken roar.[13]

About half a mile from the landing—perhaps ten minutes' ride, including the climb up the steep bluff—they encountered William Wallace, who assured Grant that the army was under attack along its entire front. Convinced at last, Grant turned to his most-trusted aide, Colonel John A. Rawlins, and ordered him to ride back to the river and dispatch the army's chief quartermaster, Captain A. S. Baxter, to summon Lew Wallace to the battlefield at once. Rawlins did as Grant directed, found Baxter, and gave him the order—orally, as Grant had given it to him. Baxter was not comfortable with this and asked to have the order in writing. The two officers hurried aboard *Tigress* and sought writing materials in the cabin. On the floor, they found a piece of paper—half a sheet of foolscap, ruled, tobacco-stained, and marked by the heels of boots. It would do. They could find no pen, so Baxter scratched out the order with a pencil as Rawlins dictated. Then Rawlins hurried ashore and set out to catch up with Grant, while *Tigress* backed out into the channel and set out once more, this time carrying Baxter and his piece of foolscap downstream toward Crump's. The time could hardly have been later than ten o'clock—Rawlins thought it was nine but his times seem to be consistently an hour earlier than those reported by Lew Wallace and the officers of the Third Division. *Tigress* must have reached Crump's before 10:30.[14]

Almost a full hour later, Lew Wallace and his division were still waiting impatiently for orders from Grant. Wallace had taken his staff to await orders at Stony Lonesome, where the division was concentrating, and he had left a saddled horse tied at the landing as ready transportation for whatever courier Grant might send via steamboat. For some reason, the Third Brigade had not yet come up from Adamsville, and Wallace dispatched a staff officer to hurry it along. Shortly after eleven o'clock Wallace dispatched Lieutenant John W. Ross to ride back to Crump's and see what he could find out there. Around 11:30, Ross returned at a gallop along with Baxter.[15]

A reasonably fast ride from the landing to Stony Lonesome might account for some fifteen minutes at most, but the rest of the hour—at least—between Baxter's probable landing at Crump's before 10:30 and his arrival at Lew Wallace's new headquarters remains a mystery. The most probable explanation is that Baxter remained at Crump's during that time, bewildered and unable to find Wallace or his division. Here the fault is Wallace's. He had last met with Grant at Crump's and had given his commander no notice of his intent to move to Stony Lonesome. Allowing that Stony Lonesome was the best place to hold the division in readiness to march and that Wallace needed to be with his troops, he ought to have left a staff officer at the landing to direct a messenger of Grant's. The saddled horse was a nice touch, but it could not tell Baxter where Wallace had gone.

The content of the order Baxter handed Wallace at 11:30 became the center of much controversy after the battle. Wallace claimed it read "almost, if not quite, verbatim," as follows: "You will leave a sufficient force at Crump's Landing to guard the public property there; with the rest of the division march and form junction with the right of the army. Form line of battle at right angle with the river, and be governed by circumstances."[16] This agrees substantially with what Wallace gave as the substance of the dispatch in his report of the battle, written April 12, 1862. The order, he said, directed him "to come up and take position on the right of the army and form my line of battle at a right angle with the river."[17]

Rawlins remembered the order quite a bit differently. In his version, the paper read, "You will move forward your division from Crump's Landing, leaving a sufficient force to protect the public property at that place, to Pittsburg Landing, on the road nearest to and parallel with the river, and form in line at right angles with the river, immediately in rear of the camp of Maj. Gen. C. F. Smith's division [the Second Division, now commanded by W. H. L. Wallace] on our right, and there await further orders."[18] No one can now refer to the written order to settle the dispute. Lew Wallace handed it to staff officer Frederick Knefler, who lost it that same day.[19]

"The road nearest to and parallel with the river" would obviously have been the River Road, or Hamburg-Savannah Road, but the shortest route "to form a junction with the right of the army," as it had been deployed at dawn that morning, would have been the Shunpike. Grant probably had no knowledge of the Shunpike's existence and definitely expected Lew Wallace to use the River Road. Wallace chose the Shunpike. The question—and one that will likely never be answered—is whether the order read as Wallace claimed and thus all but required the choice he made or whether it read as Rawlins maintained, and Wallace decided to disobey its letter in order to achieve more effectively what he took to be its intended result. By marching on the Shunpike, he would have reasoned, he would move directly to a position on the right flank of the embattled fighting line, and his division would be able to make the earliest possible impact on the battle.

At Fort Donelson, seven weeks before, Lew Wallace, in marked contrast to the old Regular C. F. Smith, had disobeyed the letter of Grant's order not to move his forces and had sent help to the hard-pressed McClernand, thus making an important contribution to Union victory. The Army of the Tennessee, throughout its uniquely successful career, was to be characterized by inspired improvisation on the part of capable nonprofessional officers. Wallace's case was to be a lesson, however, in how badly such improvisation could turn out for both the improviser and the army in the presence of sketchy information and poor communication on a day when nothing was going right for the Army of the Tennessee—nothing but the courage and tenacity of the men in its ranks.

Before setting out to return to Crump's Landing and the waiting *Tigress*, Baxter gave Lew Wallace another piece of information that may well have influenced the decision to take the Shunpike. "How is the battle going?" Wallace asked. To which Baxter replied, "We are repulsing the enemy."[20] Naturally, Baxter's assessment was based only on what news had filtered back to the landing from the fighting lines two to three miles away prior to his departure around ten o'clock. He probably had not heard of the fall of Prentiss's camps, which probably occurred somewhat less than an hour before, and he could not have heard of the loss of Sherman's camps, which must have occurred almost simultaneous with if not somewhat after his departure from Pittsburg Landing. Another feature that was to characterize the Army of the Tennessee was an unthinking, almost instinctive assumption on the part of its men, in almost every one of its battles, that its forces would drive the enemy as a matter of course. Baxter had made the natural assumption and had seen nothing to refute it. The result, however, was to lead Wallace to believe that he would find the army, and in particular its right flank, where it had been the night before.

Wallace's choice of the Shunpike was to be very costly in terms of time, the largest single factor that was to keep the Third Division out of combat on April 6. Where the fault for that decision lies depends primarily on the wording of the written order and secondarily on Baxter's understandable misconception of how the battle was going. Yet, the division might have arrived on the battlefield a little earlier than it finally did, and in the end, it was these additional delays, small though they were, that probably weighed most heavily against Wallace in Grant's eyes and thus did the most to ruin the Hoosier general's career.

The first additional delay was immediate. Having received Grant's order at 11:30, Wallace, by his own account, gave his troops half an hour, as he put it, "for dinner."[21] With their comrades fighting for their lives and dying in numbers unprecedented in the history of the republic, Wallace's troops might have been expected to munch their hardtack while they marched. Of course, Wallace did not know how poorly the battle was going, but with any battle in progress, he might have been expected to dispense with such niceties as a lunch break for troops that had already been lounging about idly for several hours.

Grant, meanwhile, was growing impatient. Partially, this impatience was simply the result of his desperate need. Sherman recalled in his memoirs that

Grant had visited him on the battlefield around ten o'clock that morning and expressed "great satisfaction" at the stand Sherman was making. Grant also explained that "things did not look as well over on the left," but he also gave him the encouraging news that Wallace's division would soon be arriving.[22] Because watches in Grant's entourage apparently read about one hour earlier than those of Third Division officers, the time of this exchange may have been as much as an hour and a half after Grant had ordered Rawlins to send the summons to Lew Wallace.[23] Assuming, as Grant did, that Wallace had his division massed at Crump's Landing, that he would march by the River Road, march at once and very hard, the Third Division at the time of Grant's conversation with Sherman still would have been an hour's march north of Pittsburg Landing and after arriving there would have needed thirty minutes to an hour, at least, to come up to the firing line. In the heat of battle, Grant seems to have become a bit overoptimistic about Wallace's time of arrival, even by his own assumptions. The most likely explanation is the well known and entirely understandable tendency of intense combat to fog a man's sense of the passage of time.

It was apparently about this time—10 A.M. by the watches of those with Grant, probably 11 A.M. by those with the Third Division—that Grant dispatched a young lieutenant of the Second Illinois Cavalry to ride to Lew Wallace and urge him to come on as rapidly as possible. According to Rawlins, it was about one hour after Baxter had left Pittsburg Landing on *Tigress*, and Rawlins placed that event as "not later than nine o'clock."[24]

The lieutenant would have ridden via the River Road, because Lew Wallace was expected to be traveling on it. The distance to Stony Lonesome via the River Road and Crump's Landing would have been eight and a half or nine miles, depending on the point on the battlefield whence Grant dispatched the officer. Allowing a brief period of walking through the Snake Creek swamps and a brisk trot the rest of the way, the lieutenant might have made the trip in an hour and ten minutes. This is consistent with the lieutenant's report that his return ride took him "more than one hour." It would have had him reaching Stony Lonesome at 11:10 A.M. "Grant-time" or 12:10 P.M. "Wallace-time." Rawlins then relates that the lieutenant returned to Grant, joining him on the battlefield "between 12 o'clock m. [noon] and 1 o'clock P.M."[25]

This allows for a complete round trip of between two and three hours—time enough to cover the distance to Stony Lonesome and back at the rather ambitious pace supposed here, along with what was by all accounts the shortest of exchanges with Wallace. If his return had been at almost 1 P.M., he might have had time to have trotted a couple of miles south of Stony Lonesome on the Shunpike, but he could hardly have gone farther and returned by 1 P.M. unless he had galloped a substantial portion of the way on rough and muddy roads.

This makes it very difficult to reconcile the accounts of Rawlins and Wallace, even allowing for the one-hour time offset. Rawlins reported that the lieutenant found Wallace and his division "all ready to move" but apparently not yet having moved from Stony Lonesome. According to the lieutenant's account, as related by Rawlins, Wallace asked if he had written orders and when told that he did not, refused to move until he should receive them. If this account is true, it would have meant that the lieutenant made slightly faster time than estimated above or that Wallace did not, as he claimed, march at precisely noon but rather was still at Stony Lonesome as late as 12:10 P.M. And what of the exchange about a written order and the lack thereof? Was Wallace demanding a written order before he would cut short his lunch break? Or had the lieutenant misunderstood the implication of Wallace's query as to whether he carried a written order?[26]

Wallace, for his part, denied that he demanded a written order as a prerequisite to putting his division in motion and gave an entirely different story of the meeting with the lieutenant. In Wallace's account, it was one o'clock, and the division had been marching for an hour and a half, and its rear guard had just crossed Clear Creek when the lieutenant overtook him. The cavalryman's horse had obviously been ridden hard and was heavily splattered with mud. "General Grant sends his compliments," the lieutenant said. "He would like you to hurry up."

"My compliments to General Grant," replied Wallace, "and tell him I am making good time, and will be up shortly." With that the courier departed, riding toward the rear, not the front, as would have been expected if Wallace was truly on the shortest route to the rest of the army.[27]

The Third Division certainly was making good time if Wallace's account is accurate. Clear Creek was five miles from Stony Lonesome, and if the rear guard was across the creek, the van must have been a mile or so farther on, approaching the junction of the Shunpike and the Hamburg-Purdy Road, only about two miles from the edge of the battlefield. The lead regiment, the Twenty-fourth Indiana would have covered six miles in an hour and a half, a very impressive four-mile-per-hour pace. The courier, too, would have been making excellent time, having covered thirteen and a half miles in something under an hour and a half, a pace in excess of nine miles per hour—nearly eleven miles per hour if he made the trip in the hour and fifteen minutes that would place his absence in the middle of the range given by Rawlins. To complicate matters further, Wallace gave a slightly different account in a letter he sent to General Henry Halleck, almost a year after the battle, defending his performance. In that letter, he claimed that his entire march along the Shunpike took him only four and a half miles from Stony Lonesome and that the division did not cross Snake Creek, much less the more distant Clear Creek. This version obviously allows for much more reasonable speeds both for Wallace's marching troops and for the cavalry lieutenant.[28]

Both of Wallace's accounts, as well as Rawlins's, are internally consistent, and neither contains any outright impossibilities. The two men's accounts simply cannot be reconciled with each other. The conclusion is hard to escape that someone was not being entirely candid about the events of that day.

When the cavalry lieutenant returned to Grant with the report that Lew Wallace had refused to move without written orders, Grant turned to Captain William R. Rowley of his staff and directed him to ride to Wallace and get him moving, providing written orders in Grant's name if necessary. Rowley was to take the cavalry lieutenant and two orderlies, and, Grant added, "See that you do not spare horse flesh." Rawlins recorded that Rowley set out no later than one o'clock—Grant-time, of course. Rowley thought it was more like 12:30.[29] Wallace reported Rowley's arrival "a few minutes after two o'clock."

"I've had a devil of a time in finding you," blurted Rowley, who like the cavalry officer before him had ridden all the way down the River Road and then roundabout through Stony Lonesome. He explained that he had been sent to hurry Wallace up, and the general replied that this was the second such message and that he did not understand why. Rowley also mentioned the report that Wallace had demanded written orders before moving. This Wallace denounced in strong language as a lie. "You see me on the road," he continued in proof of his willingness to march.

Rowley somewhat dryly observed the Wallace was indeed on a road but he hardly thought it was the road to Pittsburg Landing. It certainly was not the road Rowley had come on, and he had traveled farther since leaving Wallace's camps than he had traveled from the battlefield to the camps. Wallace replied, somewhat lamely, that it was the road his cavalry had shown him and the only one he knew anything about. This was a strange statement in view of Wallace's note to William Wallace the day before. Obviously, Lew Wallace was aware of the River Road. Perhaps Rowley misunderstood. In any case, he asked Wallace just where he thought he was going on this road.

"To join Sherman," Wallace explained.

Rowley excitedly explained that Sherman no longer held the position at the south end of the Shunpike. "Don't you know Sherman has been driven back?" he exclaimed. "Why, the whole army is within half a mile of the river, and it's a question if we are not all going to be driven into it."

Wallace was thunderstruck. He asked what Grant's orders were, and Rowley replied that Grant wanted Wallace and his division at Pittsburg Landing. Did Rowley know of a crossroad that would take the division over to the River Road? He did not. So Wallace dispatched two orderlies to ride back up the Shunpike and procure a resident civilian, voluntarily if possible, at gunpoint if necessary, who could serve as a guide to the local road net. They shortly procured one and from him learned of such a road, of very poor quality, some miles behind the head of the column. It would be necessary, therefore, to backtrack.

Wallace had available to him two different methods of doing this. He could simply face his column to the rear and march off in that direction, or he could countermarch, having the lead unit double the length of the column, followed in turn by each of the other units of the division in succession, so that the column would remain in the same sequence as before. This was the method Wallace chose. It entailed an extra twenty to thirty minutes' delay, but Wallace wanted to keep his favorite fighting units at the front of the column in case, as he now began to fear, the division had to fight its way into Pittsburg Landing.[30]

So the Third Division laboriously countermarched and proceeded over the road it had come, more than half way back to Stony Lonesome, still led by the Twenty-fourth Indiana, followed by Morgan Smith's First Brigade. The Third Brigade, now under the command of Whittlesey, had gotten a late start from Adamsville and was still trying to catch up. At the crossroad, Lew Wallace had Morgan Smith's brigade take the lead. It had been his own and included the Eleventh Indiana, the Zouave regiment he had brought down from the Hoosier state himself, as well as the Eighth Missouri, Morgan Smith's own. Smith himself was one of the best officers in the army and had led the brigade to impressive exploits at Donelson. Wallace definitely wanted these regiments near the front if the division was marching to a fight. The Twenty-fourth Indiana, however, continued to serve as advance guard, immediately behind the cavalry. Thayer's brigade followed, and Whittlesey brought up the rear. Rowley rode along with Wallace, who had insisted that the staff officer remain with him to act as a guide on the River Road.[31]

Wallace himself had to admit that progress on the crossroad was "toilsome and intolerably slow." The head of the column was more than halfway over to the junction with the River Road, perhaps four or four and a half miles from the battlefield, when Major Rawlins and Lieutenant Colonel James B. McPherson overtook Wallace from the rear. Grant had dispatched them around 2 P.M., by Rawlins's watch, and over the next hour and a half, they had ridden all the way up the River Road, over to Stony Lonesome, down the

Shunpike, and over the crossroad. Wallace later described Rawlins upon his arrival as "terribly excited."[32]

He was, indeed, and his mood was not improved by the fact that Wallace had called a halt to the march to rest his men and allow the column to close up and then had dismounted and seated himself placidly on a log by the side of the road. To a man such as Rawlins who had just come from the terrible intensity of battle and knew that the army was fighting for its life with its back to the river, this scene was almost unbearable. Rawlins asked about the report that Wallace had refused to advance without written orders, and Wallace hotly denied it. Rawlins urged that the advance be resumed at once and with greater speed, but Wallace demurred. The division was doing its best, he maintained. He also expressed doubt as to whether they were really on the right road to reach the River Road. McPherson took care of that problem by going to a nearby house and asking. Their road was indeed the correct one.

Rawlins suggested leaving the artillery behind to follow along as best it could on the rutted and muddy roads and pressing ahead with the infantry. Wallace refused. What about sending each infantry regiment forward at its best pace as soon as it reached the more easily traveled River Road? Again Wallace refused. "There should be no piecemeal in the business," Wallace argued. "To make an impression the division must go as a unit." He added that Grant "wanted the division, not part of it." The idea of Wallace instructing Grant's two most trusted staff officers, who had just come from his presence, about just what it was that Grant really wanted may well have rendered Rawlins even more "excited." The major suggested to McPherson, in Wallace's hearing, that they ought to arrest him. The quiet, mannerly McPherson "did not encourage the idea," as Wallace recalled. He did, however, suggest that for the fastest possible marching, the artillery should not be sandwiched into the column as Wallace had it but should instead follow at the rear. To this Wallace agreed, but somehow the maneuver of passing the batteries to the rear took up another half hour, by Rawlins's estimate, driving that staff officer nearly to distraction.[33]

Finally, the column moved forward. The troops struggled through the execrable crossroad and into the more commodious River Road. Progress was better—for a time. Then, the road led downhill into the broad, swampy bottoms of Snake Creek. The road became soft under foot and wheel and replete with mud holes. "It was out of one hole into another," Wallace recalled. Then came a stretch where the road was visible only as an open path through the trees, its bed invisible beneath a sheet of yellow water. The column splashed and struggled onward.[34]

They encountered some civilians who reported that the Rebels held the bridge over Snake Creek, and Wallace halted the column and sent his cavalry detachment forward to scout. The horsemen trotted forward, accompanied by McPherson and Rowley, while Rawlins waited with Wallace. In a few minutes, they returned with word that the bridge was open. Yet, Wallace kept the column halted—another chance for the men to rest and the column to close up. From the south, the thunder of artillery rose to a noticeable new crescendo, louder, deeper, and closer than it had been before. Rawlins and McPherson recognized in the thunder the reports of the army's siege guns, heavy weapons that had been arrayed on that last ridge south of Pittsburg Landing as part of a final line of defense. If the heavy guns were in action now, it meant that Grant was making his last stand. The staff officers looked at each other grimly, but there was almost nothing more they could do to accelerate Wallace's march.[35]

Rawlins did suggest that it might be a good idea to send forward a brigade to hold the Snake Creek Bridge and make sure the Rebels did not get to it before the rest of the column could come up. To this Wallace acceded, dispatching Morgan's Smith brigade to cross the bridge, form up on the far side, and there await further orders. The brigade moved out, and Wallace, finding another convenient log beside the road, sat down to wait until he felt his division was sufficiently rested and closed up to justify proceeding. Rawlins road on ahead and joined McPherson and Smith's brigade at the bridge. To his fellow staff officer, Rawlins suggested that they direct Smith, by order of General Grant, to proceed immediately with his brigade to join the rest of the army, but McPherson again hesitated to take drastic action. Darkness was gathering, and the firing had largely ceased.[36]

Eventually, the Third Division moved on. Night had fallen by the time the Twenty-fourth Indiana, still in the lead, entered the area of the day's fighting, uncertain as to what they would find. Out of the darkness ahead came the challenge: "Who comes there?"

"Hoosiers!" replied Colonel Alvin P. Hovey.

"Welcome, Hoosiers!" answered the voice in the darkness. They had made contact with the Sixty-sixth Illinois, Birge's Western Sharpshooters, assigned to picket the northern fringe of Grant's army. Wallace's march to the battlefield, covering a distance of at least sixteen miles in seven or eight hours, was finally complete.[37]

Its repercussions, however, were to last for the rest of the war. Wallace never regained Grant's confidence, and Grant's low opinion of him crippled his career. In some ways, Grant's condemnation was unfair. In an April 1863 note to Halleck, Grant claimed that if Wallace had been relieved of command on the morning the battle opened, and command of his division had passed to Morgan Smith, Smith would have had the division on the battlefield by 10 A.M.[38] This was an obvious impossibility. Nonetheless, Wallace spent most of the war without an active command, and when he did serve, it was in backwater areas.[39] His one great day of the war, other than Fort Donelson, came at the Battle of Monocacy in 1864, when he fought a crucial delaying action against the Confederate forces of Jubal A. Early and helped save Washington, D.C. Yet, he never fulfilled the bright prospects that his quick rise early in the war had suggested. Had it not been for Shiloh or for the flaws it revealed, Wallace would have been commanding a corps in the Army of the Tennessee when the war ended.

Wallace spent much effort during the war and more afterward in the attempt to clear his name, to show that he had not been mistaken in his choice of roads but had acted according to orders, at least as he understood them.[40] Yet, this was, in many respects, entirely beside the point. To the extent that anything mattered about his performance at Shiloh other than that he completely missed the first day's fight, the key factor was not his choice of roads when he thought the army was holding its own but his lack of drive to reach the battlefield after he knew the army was being driven back toward the river and disaster. A mistake could be forgiven, perhaps, but lack of zeal, energy, and loyalty could not. The high command of Army of the Tennessee might have been characterized by flexibility, improvisation, and high confidence, but it also came to be characterized by strong loyalty. This was Grant's doing, and he worked at it. Not every general in the army showed those traits, but those whom Grant saw as disloyal and self-serving, like John A. McClernand or Charles Hamilton, he purged when he was able.

Wallace's approach march at Shiloh might have been quite a natural and commendable march for a division that was not supposed to be rushing to the aid of its hard-pressed and dying comrades, but it was not at all appropriate for the situation that day—a fact that was painfully plain to men like Rowley, Rawlins, and McPherson, who had just come from the battle. Rowley summed it up by noting that Wallace's march "appeared intolerably slow, resembling more a reconnaissance in the face of an enemy than a forced march to relieve a hard-pressed army." It is noteworthy that the Third Division did its best marching of the day before Wallace heard from Rowley that all was not well at Pittsburg Landing. By his own testimony, Wallace gave the division only a single, three-minute rest break during that time, and Rowley later testified that the division was taking a rest when he arrived. After Rowley's conversation with Wallace, when the Third Division ought to have been pushing on with the same desperation with which Grant's other forces were fighting,

Wallace gave his troops several thirty-minute halts. The last several hours of the march, when he was closest and the need was most intense, were the slowest of the day.

That was not the sort of performance Grant expected from his subordinates. The kind of loyalty Grant wanted was epitomized by an incident in the Vicksburg campaign almost a year after the battle of Shiloh. When Admiral David Dixon Porter and part of the Union gunboat fleet became stranded and threatened with capture by a harassing Confederate force during an expedition up tiny Sunflower Creek, a brave African American brought word of the predicament to the nearest Union forces, a detachment of the Fifteenth Corps under William Tecumseh Sherman. Sherman at once set off personally in a canoe among the swamps to visit several of his nearby encampments and put together the best scratch force he could manage. Then he set off at their head, marched through the night, waded swamps, and arrived in time to save the fleet. That was the kind of effort Grant expected when it was necessary for soldiers to come to the aid of their comrades, and it says something about why Sherman finished the war as Grant's chief lieutenant, commander of the Military Division of the Mississippi, and Wallace never again held a command that was meant to be as important as the one he held on the morning of April 6, 1862.

Notes

1. Douglas Putnam Jr., "Reminiscences of the Battle of Shiloh," in *Papers of the Military Order of the Loyal Legion of the United States*, 56 vols. (Wilmington, NC: Broadfoot, 1994), 2:198–207. This volume is hereafter referred to as MOLLUS.

2. U.S. War Department, *The War of the Rebellion: A Compilation of the Official Records of the Union and Confederate Armies*, ed. Robert N. Scott, 128 vols. (Washington, DC: GPO, 1884), 10.1:179. (This source is hereafter referred to as "*OR*." All references are to series 1 unless otherwise noted.)

3. *OR*, 10.1:9–10, 22–23; Brooks D. Simpson and Jean V. Berlin, eds., *Sherman's Civil War: Selected Correspondence of William T. Sherman, 1860–1865* (Chapel Hill: University of North Carolina Press, 1999), 197.

4. William W. McCarty to "Dear Ellie," April 4, 1862, William W. McCarty Papers, Civil War Miscellaneous Collection, U.S. Army Military History Institute, Carlisle, PA; *OR*, 10.1:78–79.

5. Lewis Wallace, *Smoke, Sound, and Fury: The Civil War Memoirs of Major-General Lew Wallace, U.S. Volunteers*, ed. Jim Leeke (Portland, OR: Strawberry Hill, 1998), 107–9. Wallace claimed that the report of the scouts came on the evening of "Thursday, the 4th." Thursday was March 3, and I have concluded that the report took place on that day because (1) it is more likely that a man would mistake the day of the month than the day of the week, and (2) Wallace's subordinate Lieutenant Colonel George F. McGinnis, commanding the First Brigade, which was posted adjacent to Wallace's headquarters at the Landing, asserted in an article written after the war,

that Wallace "[e]arly as Thursday evening . . . had received intelligence from his most reliable scouts that the whole rebel army was in motion from Corinth to Pittsburg Landing." George F. McGinnis, "Shiloh," MOLLUS, 24:7.

6. Wallace, *Smoke, Sound, and Fury*, 107–9.

7. McGinnis, "Shiloh," 6–7.

8. *OR*, 10.2:91.

9. Louis Wallace to W. H. L. Wallace, April 5, 1862, Wallace-Dickey Family Papers, Illinois State Historical Library, Springfield, Illinois; Wallace, *Smoke, Sound, and Fury*, 111.

10. Wallace, *Smoke, Sound, and Fury*, 111; George F. McGinnis, "Shiloh," 7.

11. Wallace, *Smoke, Sound, and Fury*, 111–12; McGinnis, "Shiloh," 7–8.

12. Putnam, "Reminiscences of the Battle of Shiloh," MOLLUS, 2:198–207; Wallace, *Smoke, Sound & Fury*, 111–12.

13. *OR*, 10.1:178.

14. *OR*, 10.1:185.

15. Wallace, *Smoke, Sound, and Fury*, 112–13; Wiley Sword, *Shiloh: Bloody April* (Dayton, OH: Press of Morningside Bookshop, 1974), 216–18; O. Edward Cunningham, *Shiloh and the Western Campaign of 1862*, ed. Gary D. Joiner and Timothy B. Smith (New York: Savas, 2007), 159–60.

16. Wallace, *Smoke, Sound, and Fury*, 113.

17. *OR*, 10.1:170.

18. *OR*, 10.1:185.

19. Wallace, *Smoke, Sound, and Fury*, 115–16.

20. Ibid., 115.

21. Ibid., 116.

22. William Tecumseh Sherman, *Memoirs of General W. T. Sherman* (New York: Library of America, 1990), 266.

23. As an example of the difference in reported times, Rawlins gave the time of Grant and Wallace's steamboat conversation at 7 or 7:30 rather than 8:30 as Wallace did. *OR*, 10.1:185; *Wallace, Smoke, Sound, and Fury*, 112.

24. *OR*, 10.1:185.

25. Ibid.

26. *OR*, 10.1:185–86.

27. Wallace, *Smoke, Sound, and Fury*, 115.

28. *OR*, 10.1:177.

29. *OR*, 10.1:178–80, 186.

30. Wallace, *Smoke, Sound, and Fury*, 116–17; *OR*, 10.1:179–80.

31. The new order of march was noted by Rawlins upon his arrival. *OR*, 10.1:186–87.

32. Wallace, *Smoke, Sound, and Fury*, 117; *OR*, 10.1:187.

33. Ibid.

34. Wallace, *Smoke, Sound, and Fury*, 118.

35. *OR*, 10.1:187.

36. Ibid.

37. Alvin P. Hovey, "Pittsburg Landing," *National Tribune*, February 1, 1883, 1; Wallace, *Smoke, Sound, and Fury*, 119; McGinnis, "Shiloh," MOLLUS, 24:16.

38. *OR*, 10.1:178.

39. Stacey Allen, "If He Had Less Rank," in *Grant's Lieutenants: From Cairo to Vicksburg*, ed. Steven E. Woodworth (Lawrence: University Press of Kansas, 2001).

40. An example is Wallace's March 14, 1863, letter to Henry W. Halleck and his letter to Edwin M. Stanton, of July 18 of that year. *OR*, 10.1:174–76, 188–89.

5

SOUL-STIRRING MUSIC TO OUR EARS
GUNBOATS AT SHILOH

Gary D. Joiner

The Confederate artillerymen and their infantry guardians gazed down and to their left from the bluffs at the two black menacing shapes. The vessels pulled around the large island in the middle of the stream and halted, their wheels churning just enough to maintain steerage. Even at one thousand yards, the men could see the vessels were similar but not twins. Both had high vertical sides, very tall chimneys, and each bristled with guns. The pair did not look like normal transports or even gunboats. They appeared to be entirely encased in darkly painted wood or metal. The lead gunboat's smokestacks were amidships and the other's well forward. The boats had steamed past the bluffs recently, but no orders were given to challenge them until that day. The battery commander gave the order to fire, and one of the guns sent a round sailing over the first boat, raising a geyser of spray well astern of the lead vessel.

The gunboat in front was the USS *A. O. Tyler*. Trailing was her near-sister, the USS *Lexington*. Lieutenant William Gwin, the *Tyler*'s commander, stood on deck and examined the prominence to his front and the telltale notch in the bank that indicated a steamboat landing and road. The pair of gunboats was ordered, as they had been the previous month, to patrol the northward-flowing Tennessee River from its mouth to a point as far upstream as Gwin believed to be safely navigable. Lately, this was near the bridge at Florence, Alabama. The Tennessee River's depth fluctuated wildly with rains and the lack of them. The boats had drafts of six feet, which made them much better suited for work in shallow water than the ironclads of the Western Gunboat Flotilla. The road was the Old Corinth Road, the shortest route from the river to the major rail intersection at Corinth, Mississippi.[1]

Gwin watched as the puff of smoke rose from the cannon and noted that the ranging round flew overhead. Then he signaled his counterpart, Lieutenant James Shirk, aboard the *Lexington*. Both vessels opened fire on the artillery battery of six to eight guns and silenced them after about half an hour.[2] Both gunboats carried infantry troops aboard for shore interdiction missions. Gwin sent four small landing boats ashore with a contingent from the Thirty-second Illinois Infantry detachment.

The Confederate commander, Colonel Alfred Mouton, deployed portions of the Eighteenth Louisiana Infantry to fire upon the invaders. The Louisianans attacked the shore party and, after a sharp firefight, forced its retreat. After the Union soldiers shoved off, heading for the gunboats, the Eighteenth Louisiana opened up on them again. Gwin and Shirk returned fire, but Gwin reported that his landing boats were "perfectly riddled with balls."[3] The Eighteenth Louisiana retired to the relative safety of the heights, and the Union shore party returned to the safety of their gunboats. The *Tyler* fired 202 rounds of ammunition, and the *Lexington* fired 86 during the attack on the battery and the Louisiana infantry. The Union suffered two killed, six wounded, and three missing. A Union soldier writing his parents about the action noted that the gunboats "paid them [the Confederates] a visit one day and shelled them to atoms." [4] The date was March 1, 1862. The struggle to control that notch, known locally as Pittsburg Landing, was the opening round of what would, in early April, become the Battle of Shiloh.

The *Tyler, Lexington*, and a third vessel, the USS *Conestoga*, were the result of a rapid program to build gunboats as quickly as possible and place them on the rivers to confront Confederate fortifications, escort troop transports, and perform interdiction missions. Unlike the more famous City Class ironclads like the USS *Cairo* and her sisters, these gunboats were protected by wood rather than iron. Commander John Rodgers purchased them at Cincinnati on June 8, 1861 for naval service.[5] With all necessary changes and additions, the vessels were to cost about $34,000 each and would be ready for service before the end of June. Only wooden laminate was to be used as armor; thus, these three vessels were to be known as timberclads. These wooden warships shared a common ancestry with the City Class ironclads. The final plans for both types were created by Samuel Pook, one of the great naval architects of the nineteenth century.

The timberclads provided their share of problems because no one had ever converted river steamers of such size into men-of-war. Pook designed the changes to the three existing sidewheelers, creating the signature high-walled sides and majestically tall chimneys that became their trademarks. Laminated, five-inch oak panels, used as wooden armor, protected the crew and guns, because all iron plating was designated for the ironclads being built at Cairo and Mound City, Illinois. Timbers and beams were installed to hold the weight of the big naval guns, and steam pipes were lowered as much as possible. Pook ordered the engines and boilers to be dropped into the hold near the waterline. He knew that they would be susceptible to cannon fire there but felt he had no alternative.[6] If the machinery remained on the main deck, it would be susceptible to plunging fire from enemy forts.

In June, Rodgers obtained the services of three experienced men to assist him with his new vessels: Lieutenant Seth Ledyard Phelps, Lieutenant Roger Stembel, and Master Joshua Bishop. Stembel and Bishop were immediately sent to recruit crews for the boats, and, when the Ohio River's water level began to drop quickly, Rodgers sent Phelps to Louisville to get the boats moved to Cairo.[7] Upon arriving at Louisville, Phelps found the water already too low to bring out the boats. He also discovered that the carpenters working on the vessels had fouled the job, and he struggled to rectify the problems. The workmen had constructed the boats' ladders of soft poplar wood, which would not stand up to use. They had placed a single ladder on the *Lexington* to access the main deck and another forward on the forecastle. Because of this, anyone attempting to get to the pilothouse when the boat was under fire was in danger of being killed. Additionally, there was no access to the lookout house aft. The *Conestoga* had no permanent supports on its centerline; therefore, if the temporary supports were removed, the pilothouse and ship's bell would fall into the middle of the vessel. The vessels lacked enough staterooms for the officers, and, because the boats had not been painted, they were vulnerable to the elements.

During the remainder of the summer, the major problems on the timberclads were corrected. The guns were loaded aboard, although they were not uniform in number or type. This problem stemmed from the inability to get the proper requisitions from the army. The *Conestoga* was armed with four 32-pounder smoothbores, and the *Lexington* and *Tyler* both carried two 32-pounders and four 8-inch smoothbores.[8] The waters in the Ohio finally began to rise in early August, and Phelps herded the boats into Cairo on August 12. The three timberclads and the ironclads based in Cairo formed the original backbone of the Western Gunboat Flotilla and later the Mississippi Squadron. The timberclads provided the primary means of reconnaissance deep into Confederate-held territory. Operating much like cavalry screens, they became the eyes and ears of the army.

After Phelps brought the three timberclads to Cairo, he busied himself obtaining and training crews, preparing the boats for fighting, and carrying out missions on the Ohio and Mississippi rivers. Large pockets of Southern sympathy still existed on the south bank of the Ohio, and Confederate troops and irregulars raided sporadically. The *Conestoga*, under Phelps's command,

and the *Lexington* made runs during September up the Ohio River past Louisville and also down the Mississippi to above the Confederate-held town of Columbus, Kentucky.[9] For several months, Phelps was the face of the navy in the region, and he was indispensable to the army throughout the latter half of 1861. Phelps took the *Conestoga* up the Cumberland and Tennessee rivers at the behest of Brigadier General Charles Ferguson Smith, who commanded at Paducah, Kentucky. In a glowing report to the adjutant general in Washington, D.C., on November 8, Smith described all of the Confederate defenses that Phelps had discovered:

> SIR: In my report of the 6th instant, in relation to the forces of the enemy, I accidentally overlooked in my notes the works on the Tennessee and Cumberland rivers.
>
> The more important is Fort Henry, 71 miles up the Tennessee, just at the State line. It is a strong earthwork on the water front, but not nearly so strong on the land side. It has three 24 or 32 pounders, one or two 8-inch columbiads, and the remainder of field guns, in all, from 14 to 16; its garrison was, two weeks since, about 1,200. They have been under apprehension of attack from here for the past two weeks.
>
> Some 8 miles above Fort Henry the enemy has been for many weeks endeavoring to convert river steamers into iron-plated gunboats. This fort is an obstacle to our gunboats proceeding to look after such work.
>
> I sent an intelligent person to see what progress had been made on these gunboats, but he was captured. It is my only weak point (this river), made so by the use of gunboats.
>
> The Conestoga, gunboat, admirably commanded by Lieutenant Phelps, of the Navy, is my only security in this quarter. He is constantly moving his vessel up and down the Tennessee and Cumberland. From the latter river he came in this morning, having gone into the State of Tennessee as far as Dover, where the enemy have a work called Fort Gavock, or Fort MacGavock, or something else, usually called Fort Gavock [Fort Donelson]. He could not give me an idea of its armament.[10]

Lieutenant Phelps's discovery of the two Confederate forts on the Cumberland and Tennessee rivers was cause for alarm. General Smith at Paducah rightly believed his position was vulnerable. The Tennessee River's headwaters were in the mountains of eastern Tennessee. The river flowed southwest to Chattanooga before making a graceful arc down into Alabama and northward near Corinth, Mississippi. From there, it moved through Tennessee and joined the Ohio River just east of Paducah. After rising in the Cumberland Mountains, the Cumberland River flowed through parts of Kentucky, descended to Nashville, Tennessee, and flowed north to parallel the Tennessee River before emptying into the Ohio, east of the Tennessee. The average distance between the two streams where they flow parallel is only twelve miles. Confederate forces concentrated their defenses in this area. Given enough time, the fortifications might have been all but impregnable. Time was not on their side, and neither was the Tennessee River.

Union Major General U. S. Grant read Phelps's reconnaissance reports and General Smith's letters with interest. He knew that if both forts could be destroyed or captured, Confederate General Albert Sidney Johnston's defensive line in Kentucky would evaporate; and his headquarters at Bowling Green would be rendered useless without support. The Confederate fort at Columbus would become untenable and open the Mississippi down to another Rebel fortress at Island No. 10, about twelve river miles downstream. Taking the two forts would, in effect, destroy the Confederate's upper defense line and endanger the great rail and supply center of Nashville. If Nashville were taken, a strike down the railroad to Mobile, Alabama, would shut that vital port and split the Confederacy.

Union land forces under General Grant and naval forces under Flag Officer Andrew Hull Foote staged large-scale operations against forts Henry and Donelson culminating in the capture of both installations. The fall of Fort Henry yielded an easy victory, but the navy's ironclads received heavy damage from the Fort Donelson artillery batteries.

Soon after the fall of Fort Donelson, Foote took his damaged flotilla back to the naval facility at Mound City for extensive repairs. He knew he had a chance to disrupt Confederate activity on the Mississippi after the loss of their Cumberland and Tennessee rivers' forts. Foote took the City Class ironclads and two mortar rafts down to Columbus on February 23 but did not realize that the Rebels were withdrawing to Island No. 10 after the remaining artillery crews fired a few rounds in his direction. Foote tried to take Columbus again on March 5, this time encountering the Confederate gunboat CSS *Grampus*. The Rebel gunboat struck its colors when confronted by the ironclads but left quickly when the ironclads seemed paralyzed. The Union crew did not fire or approach. Foote gave chase only to find the boat under the shelter of the heavily fortified island. He immediately sent the gunboats to the bases at Cairo and Mound City and ordered the ironclads fully repaired, their pilothouses strengthened, and their engine rooms and boiler areas better protected. He did not want a repeat of the damage that the barrage from Fort Donelson had caused. This refurbishing and augmentation were the primary reasons that only the *Tyler* and *Lexington* were available at the Battle of Shiloh. While the ironclads were repaired at Mound City, the task of patrolling the Ohio, Cumberland, and Tennessee rivers continued. The three timberclads shouldered this responsibility. The *Tyler* and *Lexington* were assigned primary responsibility for the Tennessee River. At the same time, Grant prepared his army for a push to the next large objective near the river, Corinth, Mississippi, with it the major railroad intersection and supply depots serving the north-south Mobile & Ohio and the east-west Memphis & Charleston railroads. The decision to take Corinth increased the importance of Pittsburg Landing. Phelps's reconnaissance missions proved that this was the only steamboat landing that could handle large numbers of vessels in high or low water, and the bluffs were the only high ground upriver and south of the town of Savannah, Tennessee.[11] The landing was also the mouth of the primary road to Corinth and served as the closest point of access to the river from the town. Maintaining control of the landing and the road leading to the rail junction at Corinth became a priority for the Confederate commanders.[12]

The Tennessee was still unpredictable, rising and falling erratically as winter gave way to spring. During February and March, the gunboats patrolled the Tennessee as far as Florence, Alabama, where the river became too shallow to navigate, even for the six-foot-draft vessels.

When the *Tyler* and *Lexington* encountered the Confederate artillery battery and the Eighteenth Louisiana infantry at Pittsburg Landing that March 1, they had not just found an advance party of Rebels. What they found was the northern extent of the Confederate defenses of the approaches to Corinth, Mississippi. During the coming weeks, Gwin paid particular attention to the landing and returned often to check on it. He reported this activity to Foote, who thought it important enough to dispatch the *Cairo*, which was patrolling the Cumberland at the time and could not arrive until the end of March.[13]

The Union army generals understood that moving troops and supplies up the Tennessee without gunboat escort was foolish. Generals U. S. Grant, William Tecumseh Sherman, and John McClernand all agreed on this principle.[14] During the upcoming campaign, the Navy and the Army Quartermaster Corps used 174 vessels for convoying, ferrying, and landing fifty thousand troops, as well as performing artillery support and interdiction duties.[15]

Sherman, whose headquarters was at Pittsburg Landing, described the seemingly organized chaos of the major forward operating base. Vessels were tied up or anchored out into the river three layers deep, with the boats having to alternate unloading times at the landing while others stood out in the river waiting their turn. "The only drawback is that at this stage of water the space for landing is contracted too much for the immense fleet now here discharging."[16]

On March 13, the Army of the Tennessee began its efforts in the region in earnest. Major General Lew Wallace's division left Crump's Landing on the west side of the river and ripped up some of the Mobile & Ohio Railroad. Brigadier General Sherman raided south of the landing on the fifteenth, attempting to disrupt the Memphis & Charleston Railroad across the line in Mississippi. Sherman believed he needed gunboat support to secure his rear and to perform forward reconnaissance. Gwin volunteered the *Tyler*. [17]

The great number of vessels, particularly the Army Quartermaster Corps transports, occasionally caused logistical problems on the Tennessee River. The lack of suitable landings on the stretch north of Savannah meant that troops had to be deployed several miles upstream from Pittsburg Landing or based there. The lack of available space at the landing caused severe delays. On April 1, the *Cairo*, *Tyler*, and *Lexington* accompanied another of Sherman's raids up the Tennessee. While no Confederates were seen, the expedition was cut short because the Tennessee began to drop precipitately. The vessels only reached the small town of Hamburg, a few miles south of Pittsburg Landing.

All of the riverine raids toward Corinth ended on April 6, 1862, when the Union Army of the Tennessee was completely surprised by a full-scale Confederate attack on its steamboat landing base.[18] Johnston gambled everything on an Armageddon-like thrust into the Federal camps, and Grant and Sherman were unaware that the Rebels had amassed forces. No attempt was made to reconnoiter or to entrench the Union camps.

The *Tyler* was at Pittsburg Landing at dawn on the sixth. The *Lexington* was six miles north at Crump's Landing. Both Gwin and Shirk heard the initial attack and quickly responded. Gwin steamed the *Tyler* south about a mile to provide cover for the Seventy-first Ohio Infantry on the Union left flank, who were pinned. The *Lexington* steamed up to the landing, arriving about 10:15, but they could see nothing due to the high bluffs. Shirk took the gunboat back to Crump's Landing to provide support to General Lew Wallace's division.[19] Gwin and his crew aboard the *Tyler* received no pleas from the army for assistance and watched Federals retreat. Some Confederate artillery fire overshot their targets and splashed in the river around the gunboat, but the *Tyler* received no damage.

About 1:30 P.M., Gwin sent an officer ashore to ask for orders from Brigadier General Stephen A. Hurlbut. The general ordered Gwin to commence firing and, more important, told him where *not* to fire. After receiving this message, Gwin opened up with his 8-inch and 32-pounder guns at 2:50 P.M. and later reported that he silenced several Rebel batteries. Hurlbut confirmed Gwin's claim, stating that the naval fire was "most effectual."[20] It is evident that the Confederates feared the big guns on the gunboats and respected the damage they could cause. Throughout the two days of fighting at Shiloh, the *Tyler* and *Lexington* steamed up and down the river adjacent to the battleground providing fire support, most prominently countering the Rebel advances on April 6 and the following night.

Gwin moved the *Tyler* back to the landing about 4 P.M. and attempted to contact Grant for orders. Grant responded that Gwin should use his own judgment. The *Lexington* arrived almost immediately in order to help the *Tyler*. Shirk was to support Wallace, but the latter marched along inland roads to assist Grant, so the *Lexington* steamed from Crump's Landing against an increasing current and a rising river toward Pittsburg Landing.

What happened next was the most famous naval incident at the Battle of Shiloh and also the most misunderstood—not from controversy but how it was accomplished. Shortly after 4 P.M., the *Tyler* and *Lexington* steamed south about three-quarters of a mile from Pittsburg Landing and engaged Confederate batteries operating on the bank. The Rebels lobbed shells at the gunboats, but they did no damage. The return fire from the boats silenced the batteries.

The gunboat captains waited to see if other targets would present themselves. They provided fire support as the Union line wavered and retreated. One unintended consequence of the naval fire occurred in the vicious fighting at the Hornets' Nest. Shrapnel from the rounds tore through trees, ripping branches apart and cascading them down on the Union soldiers who were surrounded by several regiments of Confederates. This added to the rapidly deteriorating situation and may have helped persuade General Benjamin M. Prentiss to surrender.[21]

The boats steamed to a position opposite the steep ravine of Dill Branch, just south of Pittsburg Landing. Beginning about 5:30 P.M., the gunboats worked with field artillery batteries to stem a Confederate attack. The Rebels would have to cross the ravine to attack the landing. Gwin later reported, "Both vessels opened a heavy and well-directed fire on [the Confederates], [and] in a short time, in conjunction with our artillery on shore, succeeded in silencing their artillery, driving them back in confusion." Lieutenant Shirk reported the *Lexington* blasted the Rebels with a withering barrage, demoralizing their infantry, resulting in a "perfect rout" after about ten minutes of firing.[22] The Confederates were stymied and then repulsed.[23] The gunboats continued the fire until no targets presented themselves, and the supporting Confederate artillery was silenced.[24]

As twilight deepened on the battlefield, the gunboats patrolled the Tennessee River. The *Lexington* returned to Crump's Landing around 8:00 P.M. in the event Rebel forces attempted to flank Grant's army. But, as Lieutenant Shirk reported, "Finding that everything was quiet there, [I] returned to this place [Pittsburg Landing]."[25] The *Tyler* then initiated harassing fire as night descended. Brigadier General William "Bull" Nelson ordered Gwin to fire selectively on different areas of the battlefield to support the Union troops and keep the Confederates off balance. Gwin began the fire about 9 P.M. and continued until 1 A.M., when the *Lexington* took over. The *Tyler* fired one of its heavy guns every ten minutes, never consecutively at the same target. To confuse the Confederates, Gwin sometimes interspersed his heavy ordnance with "an occasional shrapnel from the howitzer." The *Lexington* continued the strategy from 1 A.M. until dawn at fifteen-minute intervals.[26] The Confederates, who had halted their attacks as twilight descended, were kept up all night, never knowing if the screaming, hissing rounds would be aimed at them or another group of men nearby. Much of the naval gunfire landed deep into the battlefield, far to the rear of the Confederate lines and near General P. G. T. Beauregard's camp. Beauregard assumed command in the afternoon following the death of General Johnston. The big naval shells landing close to his headquarters helped convince the Creole general to call off the advance of his forces as night fell.[27]

One of the great questions of the Battle of Shiloh remains: How did Gwin and Shirk provide the harassing fire? Gwin explained that he set his fuses at various lengths, providing for range differences of the shells.[28] But that does not answer the question. An understanding of the topography of Dill Branch yields other answers and adds to an appreciation of Gwin's genius. At first, it appears the *Tyler* and *Lexington* fired blindly into Dill Branch that night. Although the ravine was partially flooded, the gunners on the timberclads and their spotters in the wheelhouses or on the engine boxes could not see above the lip of the ravine. Fragments of naval rounds and fuses have been found in Fraley Field and the yard of the Shiloh Church, twelve thousand feet from the river at Dill Branch ravine and well beyond the effective range of the guns.[29] Several fragments have also been discovered in the ravine.[30] This is because the boats could not see their targets. If the gunfire was at too flat an angle, the rounds would lodge into the banks of the ravine. Gwin had been told to fire on Confederates who were in the vacated Union camps, but there was no line of sight. The gunners "walked" rounds by elevating their guns and then incrementally dropping them, perhaps one-half of a degree at a time, until the low point of aim was achieved. They then reversed the method, in effect, "hosing" a target. The northern side of the ravine deflects to the south near its western end, thus allowing Gwin and Shirk to aim at that point, changing their elevation and trajectory angle with each shot.[31] The effect was to spread their rounds over a great area, over the heads of the Union soldiers and, certainly, many Confederates as well. The former were comforted by the tremendous noise, the latter certainly were not. The fuses on the shells were set to explode the shells over and into the Confederate lines without harming the Federal troops.

The average height of the river in summer is about 342 feet above sea level (ASL). Flood stage is about 360 feet ASL. In April 1862, the river was running about 370 feet ASL.[32] The ravine is eighty feet deep, with a gradient slope of 40 percent to 70 percent.[33] This means that during the battle, the ravine was partially filled with river water, and the water was at least ten feet above flood stage. If the water level had been lower, the boats' chances of achieving great range with their rounds would have been vastly diminished. The gradient of the ravine made "skipping," or deflecting, the shells more effective. If the powder was heavily packed into the smoothbores, the maximum ranges achieved were well within reason.

Both sides agreed that the naval gunfire was annoying but relatively harmless, other than counter battery fire against Confederate artillery near the shore or those rounds aimed at infantry units within line of sight. The bulk of the rounds fired was not intended against specific targets but rather for harassment of enemy troops, particularly after night fell.

The periodic firing by the timberclads had psychological effects on both armies during that night, and this may be the most important contribution of the gunboats at Shiloh. The vessels provided a morale boost to the dispirited Union soldiers all through that night. The sound of the mighty guns comforted both Union soldiers and commanders after a long day of terrible fighting. After-action reports from Grant and his subordinate commanders prominently mentioned the gunboats, most offering high praise. An infantryman from the Seventieth Ohio spoke for perhaps most of the Union soldiers on the night of the sixth as he described the gunboats throwing "a hissing shell over to the enemy every quarter of an hour until daylight. The terrible shrieking of the large navy shells had a demoralizing effect upon the enemy, causing him to change his position several times during the night, besides robbing him of much needed sleep and rest; while it was soul-stirring music to our ears."[34]

The Confederates were very aware of the power of the gunboats, making them cautious of getting within range of the timberclads' big guns. Confederate commanders mentioned the gunboats fifty-one times in their after-action reports. One Confederate soldier agreed with his commanders, writing in his diary a description of the chaos wrought: "the gunboats' horror had seized on both men and officers."[35] Another Rebel soldier bemoaned the time spent under the naval guns: "It rained and rained almost the entire night, and the Yankee's Gunboats were shelling the woods all around with their big guns, and we were there in the mud and rain waiting for another day that the machines of death might begin their work."[36]

Eight high-level Confederate commanders mentioned retiring out of range of the enemy gunboats.[37] Major General Braxton Bragg, then a Confederate corps commander, issued orders that his men "fall back out of the range of the gunboats and encamp for the night." Leonidas Polk, another corps commander, also ordered his troops to fall back out of the gunboats' range. General P. G. T. Beauregard issued orders for the troops to pull back and referred to the timberclads numerous times, most in context with the Union forces being under the protection of the gunboats' guns. He described a plan to attack the enemy if they came out from under that shield and also significantly mentioned the Confederate troops' rest being "broken . . . by a discharge at measured intervals of heavy shells thrown from the gunboats." Writing to his men after the battle, Beauregard told his army, "You drove him [the enemy] from his camps to the shelter of his iron-clad gunboats, which alone saved him from complete disaster."[38]

The next day, April 7, the gunboats ceased fire at daylight to prevent friendly fire incidents, but the *Tyler* and *Lexington*, as they patrolled back and forth south of the landing, menaced the Confederates. As Lieutenant Shirk reported, the boats performed "acts of mercy, picking up the wounded who had found their way to the river and conveying them to the hospital boats."[39] Lieutenant Gwin reported to Flag Officer Foote, "Your old wooden boats rendered invaluable service."[40] Secretary of the Navy Gideon Wells concurred in a response to the gunboats' role at Shiloh, "This is another evidence of the gallant and invaluable service rendered by the Navy on the Western waters." Grant could only agree: he wrote in his after-action report, "In this repulse [on the evening of April 6], much is due to the presence of the gunboats *Tyler* and *Lexington* and their able commanders, Captains Gwin and Shirk."[41]

The Confederates' success on the first day of fighting was for the other days of battle stymied by a series of factors, including the death of General Johnston, the relative timidity of Beauregard, the arrival of Union reinforcements from the Army of the Ohio, and, certainly, the effects of the timberclad gunboats. Beauregard was not up to the task of completing the destruction of the Union army and withdrew his battered army to Corinth, where the final outcome would be decided in a few weeks with a Rebel loss. Several Confederate commanders credited the gunboats with covering fire that protected the Union transport vessels and added greatly to the Union defenses.[42]

Grant and Sherman had nothing but praise for the navy in this campaign. The mutual trust between the Western generals and Flag Officer Foote and his naval commanders cemented their relationship, setting the stage for upcoming successes in the Mississippi Valley. Both Grant and Sherman recognized that naval fire support provided not only a much-needed protective umbrella for troops in amphibious landings but the gunboats also struck fear in enemy commanders. The big naval guns and the terror they wrought immeasurably multiplied Union operational effectiveness on inland waters. From Shiloh to the end of the war almost exactly three years later, the Union army and navy worked together in the Western waters as a very effective joint operations team.

Notes

1. U.S. War Department, *Official Records of the Union and Confederate Navies in the War of the Rebellion*, 31 vols. (Washington, DC: GPO, 1922), 22:643 (this source is subsequently denoted by *ORN*); F. Y. Hedley, *Marching through Georgia: Pen-Pictures of Every-Day Life in General Sherman's Army, from the Beginning of the Atlanta Campaign until the Closing of the War* (Chicago, 1890), 37; Timothy B. Smith, *The Untold Story of Shiloh: The Battle and the Battlefield* (Knoxville: University of Tennessee Press, 2006), 56.

2. *ORN*, 22:643–45, 783.

3. *ORN*, 22:644.

4. Christian Zook to Father, March 24, 1862, 46th Ohio Infantry File, Shiloh National Military Park.

5. The name A. O. Tyler is misleading, and the confusion it created rippled through official reports and later through some historians' analyses. Rodgers thought that the name *Tyler* carried a negative connotation for the U.S. Navy. Former president John Tyler was a secessionist, and the commander wanted to change the vessel's name to "*Taylor*," apparently after former president Zachary Taylor. Rodgers began using "*Taylor*" on his reports. The name was never officially changed, but it was simply referred to by the single word *Tyler*. To confuse matters, beginning later in 1862 and lasting throughout the war, David Dixon Porter, perhaps in a show of support for his friend John Rodgers, consistently referred to the vessel as the *Taylor*. He continued this in his postwar publications: *Incidents and Anecdotes* (New York, 1885) and *The Naval History of the Civil War* (New York, 1886). Portions of this chapter that cover the outfitting and deployment of the timberclads are found in Gary D. Joiner, *Mr. Lincoln's Brown Water Navy: The Mississippi Squadron* (New York: Rowman and Littlefield, 2007), 23–24, 36–39, 49–51.

6. *ORN*, 22:283.

7. Jay Slagle, *Ironclad Captain: Seth Ledyard Phelps and the U.S. Navy, 1841–1864* (Annapolis, MD: Naval Institute Press, 1996), 116–17.

8. Paul H. Silverstone, *Warships of the Civil War Navies* (Annapolis, MD: Naval Institute Press, 1989), 158–60.

9. *ORN*, 22:356–57.

10. *ORN*, 22:427–28.

11. T. B. Smith, *Untold Story of Shiloh*, 56.

12. *ORN*, 22:643.

13. *ORN*, 22:644–47, 784; Edwin C. Bearss, *Hardluck Ironclad: The Sinking and Salvage of the Cairo* (Baton Rouge: Louisiana State University Press, 1966), 46.

14. U.S. War Department, *The War of the Rebellion: A Compilation of the Official Records of the Union and Confederate Armies*, ed. Robert N. Scott, 128 vols. (Washington, DC: GPO, 1884), 10.1:9–10, 22–23; 10.2:34. (This source is hereafter referred to as "*OR*." All references are to series 1 unless otherwise noted.)

15. Charles Dana Gibson and E. Kay Gibson, *Assault and Logistics: Union Army Coastal and River Operations, 1861–1866* (Camden, ME: Ensign, 1995), 78–79; T. B. Smith, *Untold Story of Shiloh*, 58.

16. *OR*, 10.1:27; Christian Zook to Father, March 24, 1862, Forty-sixth Ohio Infantry File, Shiloh National Military Park.

17. *OR*, 10.1:22; Unsigned, undated memoir, USS *Tyler* file, Shiloh National Military Park.

18. Some portions of this chapter concerning the actions of the *Tyler* and *Lexington* at Shiloh are found in Joiner, *Mr. Lincoln's Brown Water Navy*, 52–54.

19. *ORN*, 22:762, 764; *OR*, 10.1:259, 261.

20. *ORN*, 22:762–63; *OR*, 10.1:205.

21. *OR*, 10.1:166, 279; James Lee McDonough, *Shiloh: In Hell before Night* (Knoxville: University of Tennessee Press, 1977), 164.

22. *ORN*, 22:763–64.

23. Shelby Foote, *The Civil War, A Narrative: Fort Sumter to Perryville* (New York: Random, 2005), 343.

24. *ORN*, 22:763–64; Mildred Throne, ed., *The Civil War Diary of Cyrus F. Boyd: Fifteenth Iowa Infantry, 1861–1863* (Baton Rouge: Louisiana State University Press, 1953) 34; Spencer Tucker, *Andrew Foote: Civil War Admiral on Western Waters* (Annapolis, MD: Naval Institute Press, 2000), 188–89.

25. *ORN*, 22:763–64.

26. *ORN*, 22:763–64.

27. Tucker, *Andrew Foote*, 189.

28. *ORN*, 22:763–64.

29. Stacy Allen, historian, Shiloh National Military Park, conversation with author, July 22, 2005.

30. Various archaeological reports in the archives of Shiloh National Military Park.

31. "Pittsburg Landing, Tennessee," USGS 7.5-minute topographic quadrangle map of Pittsburg Landing, Tennessee; National Geographic TOPO! Tennessee 3-Dimensional seamless digital topographic data.

32. Stacy Allen, historian, Shiloh National Military Park, conversation with author, July 22, 2005.

33. "Pittsburg Landing," 7.5 minute topographic quadrangle map, National Geographic TOPO! Tennessee data.

34. T. W. Connelly, *History of the Seventieth Ohio Regiment: From Its Organization to Its Mustering Out* (Cincinnati, OH: Peak, n.d.), 24; *OR*, 10.1: 109, 166.

35. *OR*, 10.1:397, 442; William A. Brown Diary, April 6, 1862, archives, Shiloh National Military Park.

36. W. J. McMurray, *History of the Twentieth Tennessee Regiment Volunteer Infantry, C.S.A.* (Nashville, TN: Publication Committee, 1904), 210.

37. *OR*, 10.1:418, 423, 425, 432, 480, 499, 534, 601.

38. *OR*, 10.1:385–87, 397.

39. *ORN*, 22:763.

40. *ORN*, 22:763–64.

41. *ORN*, 22:765–66.

42. *OR*, 10.1:385–87, 397, 418, 423, 425, 432, 455,480, 499, 534, 582, 601, 622, 616.

6

GENERAL BEAUREGARD'S
"COMPLETE VICTORY" AT SHILOH
AN INTERPRETATION

Grady McWhiney

Atelegram, sent from the Shiloh battlefield on the evening of April 6, 1862, to Confederate officials in Richmond, told what had happened, or at least what General Pierre Gustave Toutant Beauregard thought and hoped had happened: "We this morning attacked the enemy in strong position . . . , and after a severe battle of ten hours, . . . gained a complete victory, driving the enemy from every position."[1]

President Jefferson Davis still had no reason to doubt the accuracy of this report when he informed the Confederate Congress two days later that "the enemy was driven in disorder from his position and pursued to the Tennessee River, where, under cover of his gun-boats, he was at the last accounts endeavoring to effect his retreat by aid of his transports." Davis admitted that "details of this great battle are as yet too few and incomplete to enable me to distinguish with merited praise all of those who may have conspicuously earned the right to such distinction . . . ," yet he announced, "with entire confidence, that it has pleased Almighty God to crown the Confederate arms with a glorious and decisive victory over our invaders."[2]

The Confederate Senate, in response to the president's announcement, quickly passed a resolution thanking General Beauregard and his troops for the "exhibition of skill and gallantry displayed" in gaining this "signal triumph."

During the next few days, it became distressingly apparent to everyone in Richmond and elsewhere in the South that the Confederates had not achieved a "signal triumph" at Shiloh. Beauregard had neither destroyed General Ulysses Simpson Grant's army nor forced it to retreat across the river; indeed, the very day that Beauregard's telegram arrived in Richmond, the combined Union armies of Grant and General Don Carlos Buell had driven the Confederates back to Corinth. "The news today from Ten[nessee] is not so favorable," a former member of the president's cabinet wrote on April 9. "Gen'l Beauregard telegraphs that he had fallen back from the river to his original position at Corinth."[3]

There is no doubt what happened at Shiloh; the dispute that began almost immediately after the battle and continues today is over whether Beauregard should have called off the first day's action when he did. Jefferson Davis, who mistrusted Beauregard, became convinced "that, when General [Albert Sidney] Johnston fell, the Confederate army was so fully victorious that, had the attack been vigorously pressed, General Grant and his army would before the setting of the sun have been fugitives or prisoners."[4]

Other writers agreed. Just after the war Edward Alfred Pollard, editor of the *Richmond Examiner* and certainly no friend of Jefferson Davis, described Beauregard's decision as the "extraordinary abandonment of a great victory." Confederate units were ready to "sweep the enemy from the field," claimed Pollard. "The sun was about disappearing, so that little time was left to finish the glorious work of the day. The movement commenced with every prospect of success. But just at this time the astounding order was received from Gen. Beauregard to withdraw the forces beyond the enemy's fire!"[5]

Similar complaints against Beauregard appeared periodically in the pages of such journals as the *Southern Historical Society Papers*. "A great victory was just within the grasp of the Confederates" at Shiloh, insisted Colonel William Allan in 1884, but Beauregard "allowed [it] to slip away from them." James Ryder Randall, Confederate journalist and author of *Maryland, My Maryland*, announced in 1896 that "Beauregard's unfortunate order of retreat [on the first day at Shiloh] saved the Federals from capture or destruction." John Witherspoon Du Bose stated in 1899 that "Beauregard, going on the field on a bed, wasted by protracted illness, . . . recalled the troops from the very arms of victory." Major Robert W. Hunter proclaimed in 1907 that if Beauregard had allowed the attack to continue, "Grant would have been crushed before Buell's reinforcements could have saved him." In 1914, Confederate veteran Philip D. Stevenson summarized the views of Beauregard's critics. "Why," he asked rhetorically, when the Yankees were "disorganized and whipped, huddled together like sheep," did the Confederates fail to "go forward and complete their work? Alas!" he concluded, "they had changed commanders! And their new commander ordered them to halt and retire! And lo! The victory was lost!"[6]

Beauregard, some of his friends and supporters, and a number of historians have insisted that his decision to stop the Confederate attack when he did "was the right one." They have accused General Braxton Bragg, who commanded on the Confederate right at Shiloh, and Colonel William Preston Johnston, son of Albert Sidney Johnston, of misstatements designed to diminish Beauregard's military reputation and to magnify Albert Sidney Johnston's.[7]

The pro-Beauregard accounts argue that their hero stopped the action because, first, the Confederates were "tired, hungry, and spiritless" after fighting all day; second, there was no real possibility that they might "break the Union line late in the evening" because the Federal enjoyed advantages of firepower and terrain that "a series of disjointed attacks [directed by Bragg] at that late hour upon a battery of over fifty pierces" could never overcome; and third, Beauregard "wanted to get his army in hand before darkness" so that he would be prepared for whatever might happen the next day.[8]

Let us try to look at the military situation as Beauregard and others who were there saw it on that Sunday afternoon in April. The best of these eyewitness sources, of course, are the letters, diaries, and official reports that were written during or shortly after the battle. The memoirs and recollections, written later, generally are less reliable; after a time, people tend to forget or to distort the way things happened. But selective recollections and incorrect statements are not invariably or exclusively confined to memoirs; documents written at the time the events happened may also be full of misrepresentations and lies. For writers of official military reports, whose reputations and careers can depend on what they say, the temptation to distort the truth is sometimes overpowering. That is why working with battle reports is so dangerous; commanders rarely admit to failures or mistakes. Therefore, statements made in official reports that are not substantiated by one or more relatively independent eyewitnesses should be viewed with some skepticism.

In his official report, dated April 11, 1862, Beauregard not only failed to state that he had ordered the Confederate attack to cease on April 6; he even suggested that the capturing of enemy "stores and munitions" was as important to him as the defeat of Grant. "By a rapid and vigorous attack on General Grant," explained Beauregard, "it was expected he would be beaten back into . . . the river, or captured, in time to enable us to . . . remove to the rear all the stores and munitions that would fall into our hands . . . before the arrival of General Buell's army on the scene. It was never contemplated, however, to retain the position thus gained." In his summary of the first day of battle, which he says ended "after 6 P.M., . . . when the enemy's last position was carried, and his forces finally broke and sought refuge behind a commanding eminence covering the Pittsburg Landing," Beauregard again placed great emphasis upon retrieving what he called the "spoils of war." Darkness was close at hand," he insisted. "Officers and men were exhausted. . . . It was, therefore impossible to collect the rich and opportune spoils of war scattered broadcast on the field left in our possession, and impracticable to make any effective dispositions for their removal to the rear. I accordingly . . . directed our troops to sleep on their arms, . . . hoping, from news received by a special dispatch, that delays had been encountered by General Buell, . . . and that his main force, therefore, could not reach the field of battle in time to save General Grant's shattered fugitive forces from capture or destruction on the following day."[9]

Much later, after he had been accused of stopping the attack too soon on that critical April evening, Beauregard gave quite a different account of his actions. In an article published in *Battles and Leaders*, he claimed that he called off the Confederate attack because (1) units of Buell's army had already crossed the river and joined Grant; (2) the Federals were protected by both gunboats and "some sixty guns that . . . commanded all the approaches" to the landing; and (3) the Confederates were exhausted and out of ammunition and "no serious effort was [being] made to press the victory by the [Confederate] corps commanders."[10]

This summary of what Beauregard said caused him to end the assault, which might best be described as a postwar fantasy, is a mixture of hindsight, exaggeration, and misrepresentation designed to make Beauregard appear sagacious. He was two miles or more behind the front lines, at Shiloh Church, when he ordered the action halted on the evening of April 6, 1862.[11] From time to time during the afternoon, staff officers may have brought Beauregard information on various activities, but without visiting the front himself, which he failed to do, his knowledge of what was happening there was always fragmentary, dated, and imprecise; nor did he have any understanding of arrangements behind the Union lines. Yet, he stated grandly, "Comprehending the situation as it was, at six P.M. I dispatched staff officers with orders to cease hostilities."[12]

Let us examine each of Beauregard's claims. If, as Beauregard asserted in his article, he had known that units of Buell's army had already joined Grant's forces, it is most unlikely that he would have sent a telegram to the Confederate government on the evening of April 6, 1862, announcing a "complete victory."

Nor was there any way for Beauregard to have known at that time how many guns protected the Federals near Pittsburg Landing. He says sixty guns threatened the Confederates, but this appears to be far in excess of the actual number. Grant, in his official report, mentioned only "four 20-pounder Parrott guns and a battery of rifled guns" and later said that about "twenty or more pieces of artillery" protected the Federals at nightfall. Historian Kenneth P. Williams, citing two unofficial accounts, stated that the total number of guns assembled was fifty, including some "moderately heavy siege weapons."[13]

Actually, whether they numbered twenty or fifty, these guns may have been less formidable than their numbers suggest. Grant and other observers stated that most of the weapons on the Federal line were rifled guns and siege pieces, where were not as effective against infantry assaults as smoothbores firing canister; the Army of the Potomac's chief of artillery considered rifled guns generally less useful than smoothbores, and he regarded the rifled twenty-pound Parrots as "unsafe," more dangerous to the users than to the enemy because they often burst during firing. Regular-army artillerymen consistently favored smoothbore Napoleons over rifled guns.[14]

Reports also indicate that elements of two units that formed part of the Union defense line near Pittsburg Landing were battered and short of ammunition. The commander of Battery D, First Missouri Light Artillery, reported that during the day, he had lost fourteen horses and expended over two hundred rounds of ammunition; the commander of Battery H, First Missouri Light Artillery, reported losing twenty horses and being out of canister after having fired 275 rounds.[15]

The Union gunboats, which Beauregard said "opened on our eager columns a fierce and annoying fire . . . of the heaviest description," did far less damage than he supposed. Few shells from the gunboats were hitting the Confederates at the front because the guns, elevated to fire over the high river bank, could hit only points some distance from the river's edge. "They were comparatively harmless to our troops nearest the bank," reported Confederate General Leonidas Polk, "and became increasingly so as we drew near the enemy." A brigade commander called the shelling "more noisy than destructive," and General Braxton Bragg, who was at the front, stated that the fire from the gunboats, "though terrific in sound and producing some consternation at first, did us no damage, as the shells all passed over and exploded far beyond our positions."[16]

Extant records also fail to support the other claims of Beauregard. His charge that his corps commanders at the front made "no serious effort . . . to press the victory" seems to be nothing more than a malicious attempt to discredit the official testimony of Generals Leonidas Polk, William Joseph Hardee, and Bragg about what happened in the late afternoon of April 6, 1862, after the fall of the Hornets' Nest and the capture of union General Benjamin Mayberry Prentiss and his men about 5:30 P.M.[17]

One can understand why the reports of his corps commanders galled Beauregard. "The field was clear [followed the surrender of Prentiss]," stated Polk. "The first of the forces of the enemy were driven to the river and under its bank. We had one hour or more of daylight still left; were within from 150 to 400 yards of the enemy's position, and nothing seemed wanting to complete the most brilliant victory of the war but to press forward and make a vigorous assault on the demoralized remnant of his force." At this point, Polk insisted, the Union gunboats opened their noisy but relatively harmless fire, and Beauregard, unaware of the true situation at the front, made the mistake of stopping the action. Polk's exact words are: "Here the impression arose that our forces were waging an unequal contest; that they were exhausted and suffering from a murderous fire, and by an order from the commanding general they were withdrawn from the field." Beauregard certainly was not pleased with Polk's report.[18]

Nor was he any happier with Hardee's report, which declared that the Confederates "were within a few hundred yards of Pittsburg [Landing], where the enemy were huddled in confusion, when the order to withdraw was received." Even more upsetting to Beauregard was Hardee's statement that after the death of General Albert Sidney Johnston, there was "a lull in the attack on the right and precious hours were wasted. It is, in my opinion," announced Hardee, "the candid belief of intelligent men that, but for this calamity, we would have achieved before sunset a triumph signal not only in the annals of this war, but memorable in future history."[19]

Beauregard was equally displeased with the report of Bragg, whom Beauregard had recommended for promotion to the rank of full general on the night of April 6. Bragg's final report, which was not sent to the War Department until three months after the battle, also charged that Beauregard had stopped the action too soon. "The enemy had fallen back in much confusion [after the surrender of Prentiss]," noted Bragg, "and was crowded in unorganized masses on the river bank, vainly striving to cross." At this point, Bragg said, he had ordered the Confederates nearest the river "to move forward at all points and sweep the enemy from the field." General Patton Anderson remembered that one of Bragg's staff officers told him "to go wherever the fight is thickest." This forward "movement commenced with every prospect of success," claimed Bragg, but "just at this time an order was received from the commanding general to withdraw the forces beyond the enemy's fire."[20]

Eyewitness accounts, written both at the time and later, indicate that the Confederates were still pressing the Federals when Beauregard stopped the action. Bragg's chief engineer, Colonel Samuel H. Lockett, recalled, "I was with General Bragg, and rode with him along the front of his corps. I heard him say over and over again, 'One more charge, my men, and we shall capture them all.'" In a letter to his wife written a day after the battle ended, Bragg announced, "We literally swept . . . [the enemy] before us capturing his camps, artillery, men, horses, arms &c. &c. One whole battery was brought to me with the officers, men & horses all complete, and very impressive. It was now nearly sun set. We were close on the bank of the river just above Pittsburg, the landing place, driving . . . [the enemy] back, full well." Colonel Lockett remembered only a single enemy position still resisting at this point, and the Confederates could see confused Union masses huddled near the riverbank.[21]

Men from Generals John K. Jackson's and James Ronald Chalmers's brigades actually had crossed Dill's Branch and charged up its banks in the face of heavy Union fire, but there were too few of them to break the Federal line without help. Jackson reported that his "men advanced under a heavy fire from light batteries, siege pieces, and gunboats. Passing through the ravine, they arrived near the crest of the opposite hill upon which the enemy's batteries were, but could not be urged farther without support. Sheltering themselves against the precipitous sides of the ravine, they remained under this fire for some time." Jackson, "believing any further forward movement should be made simultaneously along our whole line," sought support from his division commander, General Jones Mitchell Withers, but before reinforcements arrived, Jackson "was ordered by a staff officer to retire. This order was announced to me as coming from General Beauregard," stated Jackson, "and was promptly communicated to my command."[22]

Support for Jackson and Chalmers was on the way, according to several sources, when Beauregard's order to withdraw arrived. General Patrick Ronayne Cleburne and Colonel R. G. Shaver claimed when they were "halted by . . . General Beauregard." Several regiments were assembled just behind the front ready to move forward when Beauregard's messengers arrived. General Daniel Ruggles, commander of a Confederate division, reported that he was "advancing toward the river" with "a considerable force" when he received Beauregard's order to retreat. Another division commander, General Withers, reported that he was sending forward reinforcements "when, to my astonishment, a large portion of the command was observed to move rapidly by the left flank from under the fire of the enemy. Orders were immediately sent to arrest the commander officers and for the troops to be promptly placed in position for charging the batteries. Information was soon brought, however, that it was by General Beauregard's orders, delivered thus directly to brigade commanders, that the troops were being rapidly [withdrawn]."[23]

We can never be certain why Beauregard stopped the battle when he did on that April evening. Years after the event, one of his staff officers claimed that Bragg rode to Beauregard's headquarters shortly after the Hornets' Nest fell and said "in an excited manner: 'General, we have carried everything before us to the Tennessee River. I have ridden from Owl to Lick Creek, and there is none of the enemy to be seen.' Beauregard," according to this story, "quietly replied: 'Then, General, do not unnecessarily expose your command to the fire of the gun-boats.'"[24] Other than this unsubstantiated recollection, there is absolutely no evidence that Bragg met Beauregard during the battle.

Colonel Lockett of Bragg's staff recalled that Beauregard's order, brought to Bragg at the front by a messenger, was "the victory is sufficiently complete; it is needless to expose our men to the fire of the gun-boats.'" Lockett said that upon hearing the order, Bragg exclaimed: "'My God, was a victory ever sufficiently complete? . . . Have you given the order to any one else?'" Told that the order had been delivered to other commanders as well, Bragg looked to his left, saw General Polk's forces withdrawing, and sobbed, "'My God, my God, it is too late!'"[25]

There seems to be little doubt that Bragg objected to the withdrawal order, though his words may not have been exactly those Lockett remembered. "We drove the enemy from every position, captured nearly all his artillery, and were hotly pursuing him under my command when we were recalled," Bragg informed his wife soon after the battle. He admitted in his official report that his troops were "greatly exhausted by twelve hours' incessant fighting" when the withdrawal order arrived, yet he insisted that a final assault had "every prospect of success." Years later, Sidney Johnston's son wrote that Bragg believed Beauregard's order cost the South the battle.[26]

It is unclear just how strong the Union position was when Beauregard called off the attack. Union reports can be cited to indicate either its strength or its weakness. Historians—many of them pro-Grant—have generally insisted that the Federal line would have held.[27] But one can never be sure about what will happen in a battle.

The terrain over which the Confederates were advancing, though rough, was by no means as difficult to cross as some writers have suggested. "Anyone who thinks the Rebel attack in this area could have succeeded should spend some time tramping around in this ravine," asserted one historian.[28] I took his suggestion, spent much of a day in the summer of 1982 "tramping around in this ravine," and can report that even a fifty-four-year-old man accompanied by a much-younger person had no problem crossing Dill's Branch or getting up and down its banks. Of course, we were not under enemy fire at the time. Test the terrain yourself; you will find nothing in the area, for example, comparable to what the Federals faced at Missionary Ridge. Chalmers's and Jackson's men already had demonstrated that they could charge across Dill's Branch and up its northern bank despite Federal resistance; it does not appear impossible that Confederate reinforcements, which were advancing when Beauregard's order stopped them, could have done the same.[29]

Of course, the claim by Beauregard that many Confederate units were disorganized and exhausted is true, but so were most Union units. General Buell reported that the river's edge "swarmed with a confused mass of men" and that "all efforts" to get this "throng of disorganized and demoralized troops" back into "the fight utterly failed." The commander of a Union regiment, who acknowledged that his retreat to the river without orders might subject him "to the criticism of military men," found it "difficult to rally and form the regiment" even behind the Federal guns. Another Federal officer complained that his regiment was retreating "in good order until we were run into by the retreating artillery, cavalry, and rabble, which very much scattered my command." General Buell stated that by nightfall on April 6, "7,000 [of Grant's men] were killed or wounded, 3,000 were prisoners, [and] at least 15,000 were absent from the ranks and hopelessly disorganized."[30]

When General William Nelson, who crossed the river at Pittsburg Landing about 5:00 P.M. with reinforcements from Buell's army, arrived, he "found a semicircle of artillery, totally unsupported by infantry, whose fire was the only check to the audacious approach of the enemy," and soon "the left of the artillery was completely turned by the enemy and the gunners fled from their pieces." Nelson's men "drove back the enemy and restored the line of battle. "This was at 6:30 P.M.," noted Nelson, "and soon after the enemy withdrew, owing, I suppose, to the darkness. I found cowering under the river bank when I crossed from 7,000 to 10,000 men, frantic with fright and utterly demoralized, who received my gallant division with cries, 'We are whipped; cut to pieces.' They were insensible to shame or sarcasm—for I tried both on them—and, indignant at such poltroonery, I asked permission to open fire upon the knaves."[31]

"Darkness was close at hand" was another excuse that Beauregard and his defenders used to justify his stopping the battle when he did. But this argument, which seems plausible enough, is seriously flawed. Beauregard, by his own admission, issued the withdrawal order at 6:00 P.M., at least thirty minutes before sundown, and considerably longer before real darkness. Beauregard's headquarters were approximately two miles from the front. Captain Clifton H. Smith, who delivered the withdrawal order to Bragg and returned with him to Beauregard's headquarters, testified that when they arrived back at Shiloh Church, it was just dark enough to prevent easy recognition. In other words, at least an hour, and probably longer, passed between the time Beauregard issued his order to end the attack and the onset of darkness.[32]

Whether or not the Confederates could have broken the last Union defense line during that time or later can never be determined and is, therefore, a nonhistorical question. More likely questions are why did Beauregard stop the battle when he did, and was his decision to do so the right one considering the existing military circumstances and the information that either he had at his disposal or he might readily have obtained?

As we have seen, the reasons given by Beauregard and his friends for stopping the attack—Union reinforcements, devastating artillery and gunboat fire, the poor effort by his own corps commanders to complete the victory, exhausted soldiers, and darkness—seem to be based on hindsight designed more to protect Beauregard's military reputation than to clarify his motives. Perhaps Colonel William Preston Johnston, one of Beauregard's postwar enemies, was closer to the mark. "General Beauregard at Shiloh [Church], two miles in the rear with the debris of the army surging back upon him, the shells bursting around him, sick with his two months' previous malady, pictured in his imagination a wreck at the front," wrote Johnston. "Had his officer been with Bragg, and not greatly prostrated and suffering from severe sickness, I firmly believe his order would have been to advance, not to retire."[33]

The illness of Beauregard may account not only for his failure to visit the front before halting the attack but also for his apparent willingness to accept the advance of captured Union General Prentiss. In explaining to his wife two days later why the attack on April 6 ended when it did, General Bragg wrote, "Gen'l Prentiss—a prisoner—had just told Gen'l Beauregard that they were defeated and in route across the river. The General tho[ough]t it best no doubt to spare our men, and allow them to go. But unfortunately Buell came."[34] If Bragg's account is correct, Prentiss may have saved Grant's army from destruction twice on April 6—once when he bought precious time for the Federals by his stubborn defense at the Hornets' Nest and again when he influenced Beauregard to end the attack by telling him that Grant was whipped and retreating across the river.

Regardless of what or who influenced Beauregard to stop the attack, his decision to do so indicates unsound military judgment. Before ending the action, he at least should have consulted the commanders at the front. Had his health been good, he might have done so. Stopping the attack without either consulting the generals directing the advance or going to the front himself to see the situation was a serious mistake.

Both the friends of Beauregard and the historians who attempt to justify his decision to halt the fighting when he did seem to overlook the basic reason why the Confederates were at Shiloh on April 6, 1862. They were there to capture or to destroy Grant's army before it could be reinforced by Buell's. To accomplish anything less would be a failure.

If Beauregard believed that Grant was whipped and retreating, that should have been all the more reason to press on and destroy him rather than to stop and rest for the night. An aggressive commander would have refused to use the lateness of the hour or the tiredness of his troops as excuses to end a battle, especially one in which the enemy was in retreat and backed up against a deep and wide river. By continuing to attack the Federals, even in darkness, the Confederates had everything to gain and little more to lose than they lost the next day. After all, their best hope of victory was to do as much damage to Grant as they possibly could before Buell's fresh forces arrived.

The "complete victory" that Beauregard failed to gain but so rashly claimed in his telegram to Richmond on the night of April 6 turned out to be a disaster for the Confederacy. And that disaster may well have been caused by the failure of Beauregard to follow the advice offered in the delayed official report of one of his corps commanders, Braxton Bragg. This report, written after Bragg had replaced Beauregard as army commander, was self-serving and full of hindsight. Curiously, in it, Bragg advocated tactics that he would never employ himself, yet his advice was sound. In part, it read, "[Shiloh offers us] a valuable lesson, by which we should profit—never on a battlefield . . . lose a moment's time, but leaving the killed, wounded, and spoils [of war] . . . , press on with every available man, giving a panic-stricken and retreating foe no time to rally, and reaping all the benefits of a success never complete until the enemy is killed, wounded, or captured."[35]

Notes

This article first appeared in the *Journal of Southern History* 44, no. 3 (August 1983): 421–34. Used by permission.

1. U.S. War Department, *The War of the Rebellion: A Compilation of the Official Records of the Union and Confederate Armies*, ed. Robert N. Scott, 128 vols. (Washington, DC: GPO, 1884), 10.1:384. (This source is hereafter referred to as "*OR*." All references are to series 1 unless otherwise noted.)

2. *OR*, (1884), 52.2:298.

3. Thomas Bragg Diary, April 9, 1862, Southern Historical Collection, University of North Carolina, Chapel Hill.

4. Jefferson Davis, *The Rise and Fall of the Confederate Government*, 2 vols. (New York: Appleton, 1881), 2:68. Davis's mistrust of Beauregard is well documented. As early as January 1862, it was clear to observers in Richmond that the president disliked Beauregard. "In speaking of the . . . Generals, their qualities & c., the. . . . never names Beauregard," noted a cabinet member; " . . . he does not like him or think much of him." Bragg Diary, January 8, 1862. See also Bragg's diary, April 7, 1862. After Johnston's death, a War Department clerk, who knew how Davis felt about Beauregard, predicted that the general was "a doomed man." John B. Jones, *A Rebel War Clerk's Dairy at the Confederate States Capital*, 2 vols. (Philadelphia, 1866), 1:118. See also Jefferson Davis to James Lyon, August 13, 1876, Jefferson Davis Papers, Manuscript Division, Library of Congress, Washington, DC; Jefferson Davis to Lucius B. Northrop, April 9, 1879, Jefferson Davis Papers, Duke Univer-

sity, Durham, NC; Jefferson Davis to E. Kirby Smith, October 29, 1862, Edmund Kirby-Smith Papers, Southern Historical Collection, University of North Carolina, Chapel Hill.

5. Edward Alfred Pollard, *The Lost Cause: A New Southern History of the War of the Confederates* (New York, 1866), 240–41.

6. Colonel William Allan, "A Review of Alfred Roman's Military Operations of General Beauregard," *Southern Historical Society Papers* 12 (June 1884): 264; James R. Randall, "General W. H. C. Whiting: A Chevalier of the Lost Cause," *Southern Historical Society Papers* 24 (1896), 276; John Witherspoon Du Bose, "Confederate Generals—Their Ability," *Southern Historical Society Papers* 35 (1907): 132; P. D. Stevenson, "Missionary Ridge," *Southern Historical Society Papers* 42 (April 1914): 17.

7. See, for example, P. G. T. Beauregard, "The Campaign of Shiloh," in *Battles and Leaders of the Civil War*, ed. Robert U. Johnson and Clarence C. Buel, 4 vols. (New York: Century, 1887–88), 1:590–91; Alexander Robert Chisolm, "The Shiloh Battle-Order and the Withdrawal Sunday Evening," in Johnson and Buell, *Battles and Leaders*, 1:606; Thomas Jordan, "Battle of Shiloh: Refutation of the So-called 'Lost Opportunity, on the Evening of April 6th,' 1862," *Southern Historical Society Papers* 16 (1888): 297–318; Thomas Jordan, "The Battle of Shiloh," *Southern Historical Society Papers* 35 (1907): 217; Thomas Jordan, "Notes of a Confederate Staff-Officer at Shiloh," in Johnson and Buell, *Battles and Leaders*, 1:601–3; James L. McDonough, *Shiloh—In Hell before Night* (Knoxville: University of Tennessee Press, 1977), 168–83 (quotation on 177); T. Harry Williams, *P. G. T. Beauregard: Napoleon in Gray* (Baton Rouge: Louisiana State University Press, 1954), 141–42.

8. T. H. Williams, *P. G. T. Beauregard*, 142 (first and fourth quotations); Mc-Donough, *Shiloh*, 175–78 (second quotation on 175); Jordan, "The Battle of Shiloh," 217 (third quotation).

9. *OR*, 10.1:385 (first three quotations), 387 (last three quotations).

10. Beauregard, "Campaign of Shiloh," 590–91.

11. *OR*, 10.1:402; William Preston Johnston, "Albert Sidney Johnston at Shiloh," in Johnson and Buell, *Battles and Leaders*, 1:565.

12. Beauregard, "Campaign of Shiloh," 591. James McDonough thinks Beauregard's "decision was the right one and was probably based, at least in part, on intelligence . . . supplied by his staff officers," but no sources are cited to support this statement. *Shiloh*, 177–78.

13. *OR*, 10.1:109 (first quotation); Ulysses S. Grant, "The Battle of Shiloh," in Johnson and Buell, *Battles and Leaders*, 1:474 (second quotation); Kenneth P. Williams, *Lincoln Finds a General: A Military Study of the Civil War*, 5 vols. (New York: Macmillan, 1949–59), 3:374 (quotation), 526.

14. Grady McWhiney and Perry D. Jamieson, *Attack and Die: Civil War Military Tactics and the Southern Heritage* (Tuscaloosa: University of Alabama Press, 1982), 59, 122–23.

15. *OR*, 10.1:167–68.

16. *OR*, 10.1:387, 410, 455, 466.

17. Prentiss placed the time of his surrender at 5:30 P.M.; Beauregard, however, implied that it took place "after 6 P.M." *OR*, 10.1:279, 387; quotation in Beauregard, "The Battle of Shiloh," 590–91.

18. *OR*, 10.1:410. The reaction of Beauregard to the reports of his corps commanders is evident in various articles written in his defense. See for example Jordan, "Battle of Shiloh," 309–12.

19. *OR*, 10.1:569.

20. P. G. T. Beauregard to Jefferson Davis, April 6, 1862, Braxton Bragg Papers, William P. Palmer Collection, Western Reserve Historical Society, Cleveland, Ohio; *OR*, 10.1:463, 466–67, 497, 467.

21. *OR*, 10.1:472, 533–34, 550–51, 555, 582; S. H. Lockett, "Surprise and Withdrawal at Shiloh," in Johnson and Buell, *Battles and Leaders*, 1:605 (quotation); Braxton Bragg to Elise Bragg, April 8, 1862, Braxton Bragg Papers, William K. Bixby Collection, Missouri Historical Society, St. Louis.

22. *OR*, 10.1:550–51, 555.

23. *OR*, 10.1:582 (first quotation), 542, 538, 559, 472–73 (second quotation on 472), 533–34 (third quotation on 534).

24. Chisolm, "Shiloh Battle-Order," 606.

25. Lockett, "Surprise and Withdrawal at Shiloh," 605.

26. Bragg to Elise Bragg, April 8, 1862, Braxton Bragg Papers, William K. Bixby Collection, Missouri Historical Society, St. Louis; Johnston, "Albert Sidney Johnston at Shiloh," 568; *OR*, 10.1:467; *OR*, 10.1:467.

27. *OR*, 10.1:204–5; John Euclid Magee Diary, April 6, 1862, , Duke University Library, Duke University; K. P. Williams, *Lincoln Finds a General*, 3:378–81; T. H. Williams, *Beauregard*, 142; Bruce Catton, *Grant Moves South* (Boston: , 1960), 237–42.

28. McDonough, *Shiloh*, 175n.

29. *OR*, 10.1:472, 533–34, 550–51, 555, 582.

30. *OR*, 10.1:292 (first four quotations), 216, 215 (fifth and sixth quotations), 224 (seventh quotation); Don Carlos Buell, "Shiloh Reviewed," in Johnson and Buell, *Battles and Leaders*, 1:522 (final quotation).

31. *OR*, 10.1:323–24. See also 328.

32. *OR*, 10.1:387; Beauregard, "Campaign of Shiloh," 591; Jordan, "Battle of Shiloh," 311, 308. Jordan reports that Smith claimed that it took him only about twenty minutes to ride from Beauregard's headquarters to Bragg's position at the front. That would have meant that Smith reached the front just before sundown. How long Smith remained at the front before starting back with Bragg to Beauregard's headquarters or how long that ride took them, Smith does not state.

33. Johnston, "Albert Sidney Johnston at Shiloh," 568.

34. Bragg to Elise Bragg, April 8, 1862, Braxton Bragg Papers, William K. Bixby Collection, Missouri Historical Society, St. Louis.

35. *OR*, 10.1:470.

7

VICTORY FOR NEITHER SIDE
CONFEDERATE SOLDIERS' REACTIONS
TO THE BATTLE OF SHILOH

Charles D. Grear

Late on April 6, 1862, from the Shiloh battlefield, commanding general Pierre Gustave Toutant Beauregard wrote to the Confederate government in Richmond, "We this morning attacked the enemy [at Shiloh], and after a severe battle of ten hours, . . . gained a complete victory."[1] Confederates fought hard that day and pushed the Union army to the banks of the Tennessee River. With ideas of certain victory, Confederate soldiers encamped for the night in the captured Union camps waiting for the sun to rise and allow the completion of their triumph. When the sun crested the horizon the following day, Beauregard and his soldiers found the Union army reinforced. The revitalized Northerners pushed the Southerners off the battlefield, forcing them to retreat back to Corinth, Mississippi. The Confederates no doubt won the first day of the fighting, but did they win the battle? Beauregard contended that "a rapid and vigorous attack on General Grant . . . enable[d] us to profit by the victory."[2]

Controversy shrouds many battles in the Civil War, but probably none is debated more than the fighting around Shiloh Church. An aspect of the battle that receives little attention is the question of the reactions of the common Confederate soldier. What influenced him? Did Rebel soldiers think they were the victors or the vanquished in the battle? Did the order to halt on April 6, sleeping among the dead and dying that night, the constant shelling by the gunboats, or the death of General Albert Sydney Johnston contribute to the men's reactions? What standards did the men use to draw their conclusions? Confederate soldiers recorded their reactions in their letters, diaries, and, much later, in reminiscences. A thorough examination of these documents reveals that although reactions concerning specific aspects of the battle differ among the men who fought it, many of the Confederate soldiers came to believe, when thinking about the battle as a whole, that neither side could call Shiloh a victory.

Before the battle, Confederate soldiers experienced a wide array of emotions. Because many looked to the impending fight for their first experience of warfare, a majority of the men were in high spirits. Frank M. Gailer, a Confederate quartermaster, wrote before the engagement, "I have a great anxiety to see and be in a great battle."[3] Silas T. Grisamore of the Eighteenth Louisiana Infantry wrote of the morning of April 5, a day before the battle began, "The appearance of daylight was awaited with anxiety and suspense for the bloody work to begin."[4] Of course, not all comments were upbeat; others like George W. Jones of Stanford's Mississippi Battery had "the shakes badly."[5] Overall, the men looked forward to the battle with anticipation of a victory that would reverse the tide of the war in the West.[6]

Confederate enthusiasm continued in the ranks throughout the early hours of the battle. As they pushed Union soldiers out of their camps, their anxiety about combat diminished. Sam R. Watkins of the First Tennessee Infantry recalled, "I had been feeling mean all the morning as if I had stolen a sheep, but when the order to charge was given, I got happy. I felt happier than a fellow does when he professes religion at a big Methodist camp-meeting. I shouted. It was fun then. Everybody looked happy. We were crowding them."[7] Basil W. Duke, a lieutenant of John Hunt Morgan, described the feelings of his men as "glowing enthusiasm. . . . and spirited impatience to close with the enemy."[8] Events early in the first day kept the men's spirits high. According to Major Grisamore, "There was every appearance of the most complete surprise of the enemy, as we found the pots on the fire with breakfast cooking in them, the washtubs with clothes in them, and everything topsy turvy throughout his [Sherman's] camp."[9] The morale of Confederate soldiers increased greatly at the outset of the fighting, but developments later in the day would dampen the soldiers' feelings of the ecstasy.

Toward the end of the day, men ran out of ammunition and began, like one of the regiments under John K. Jackson's command, to stream to the rear to replenish their cartridge boxes. Because of the lack of ammunition, his command "could not be urged farther without support."[10] The only response the men received while looking for ammunition was the exhortation to return to the front and use their bayonets. Some units had other problems with ammunition. After fighting for hours, the guns of the men of the Fourth Tennessee Infantry became so fouled that the men could not reload them. Lack of ammunition or the inability to reload a weapon made the Confederates feel vulnerable and ineffective. These feelings would directly contribute to a change in attitude toward the end of the day.[11]

Mounting Confederate casualties took their toll on the reactions of the Confederate soldiers. Major Grisamore recorded that "the result of the charge made upon the enemy by the 18th [Louisiana Infantry] Regiment was disastrous, especially to our company. The loss of officers and men killed, wounded, and captured was about 200."[12] Grisamore's unit was not alone in its experience. Lieutenant Colonel Ferguson also of the Eighteenth Louisiana battalion described his feelings when the fighting ended: "Those that were unhurt had to tell all about how near they came to being killed. . . . I quit them in despair."[13] Having close friends killed or wounded in combat and sights of bloody and maimed soldiers also had a negative effect. "It was truly horrendous," Louisiana soldier Edmond Enoul Livaudais wrote as he described how his regiment "ascended the hill [ravine] to see all sides those unfortunate men of the Eighteenth coming down bathed in their blood; some had been wounded in their face, others, in the body, arm, etc. They fled into our ranks, asking us for water and help."[14] The loss of close friends, the scenes of death, the smell of blood and burning gunpowder, and feelings of despair—all these greatly affected the Confederates but the order to halt was not expected.

Before daylight closed on the evening of April 6, an order from General Beauregard to halt the advance on the enemy passed through the ranks. This order damped the Southern soldiers' morale. The disgust among the ranks in response to the order is predictable. John Smith Kendall of the Fourth Louisiana Infantry expressed his frustration: "Our advance was suddenly checked by the order to retire. 'What the hell does that mean?' one man cried, expressing the views of the whole brigade, 'what do we want to retire for?' But we did, and in no very good humor."[15] J. K. P. Blackburn of the Eighth Texas Cavalry, better known as Terry's Texas Rangers, said: "When the order was read, instead of creating enthusiasm amongst the men it created indignation and disgust because it was apparent to all in the firing line that the hard earned victory that had cost so much blood and so many lives was to be thrown away for the want of one more charge."[16] Though upset about the order, Kendall still "felt very proud of our success."[17] Beauregard's order, the lack of ammunition, and the scenes of battle produced profound reactions among the men, but their achievements of the day—surprising the enemy, taking his camps, confiscating his supplies, and pinning him against the bank of the Tennessee River—convinced the Confederates that "our victory had been won," and "we whipped the Yankees."[18] In their minds at the close of the first day, they felt they were victors in the largest battle in the Civil War to date.

Many contemporaries and historians have examined the death of Albert Sydney Johnston during the first day of the battle—how he died, where he died, and the implications of his death on the tactics of the remainder of the battle. One aspect of his death that is overlooked is the impact it produced among the rank and file. During the fighting of the first day, the common soldier did not know about the death of the general, but some did have a sense that something serious had happened. Sam R. Watkins in his popular history of *"Co. Aytch"* of the First Tennessee stated, "We saw General Albert Sidney Johnson surrounded by his staff and Governor Harris, of Tennessee. We saw some little commotion among those who surrounded him, but we did not know at the time that he was dead. The fact was kept from the troops."[19] Slowly, word of the general's death spread throughout the ranks. Frank L. Richardson of the Thirteenth Louisiana Infantry noted, "It was whispered that Sydney Johnston had fallen, but we didn't know how true it was."[20] Howell Carter of the First Louisiana Cavalry recorded that when confirmation of the general's death reached him and his fellow soldiers, "The chilliness of gloom crept over our entire command."[21] Overall, the common Confederate soldier did not know of the death of Johnston until the guns had fallen silent, and, thus, it had no impact on their thoughts and actions during the first day's battle.

After sunset on April 6, new events unfolded around the men. All that night, Southern soldiers had to endure the firing of artillery shells from Union gunboats and the groans of wounded and dying soldiers. re on the Confederate soldiers has received very little attention from historians.

Though it receives relatively little attention, the navy played a crucial role in the battle of Shiloh. The gunboats, wooden vessels with eight-inch smoothbores and thirty-two-pound howitzers, entered the fighting at 2:50 P.M., when the USS *Tyler* opened fire on the Confederate advance. The shelling instantly created confusion among the Confederate ranks and contributed to Beauregard's decision to halt his men several hours later. According to one of his staff officers, "It is needless to expose our men to the fire of the gunboats."[22] The soldiers realized the situation when the gunboats fired upon them. According to William A. Brown, the Federal soldiers "were reforming under cover of their gunboats," and "horror had seized on both [Confederate] man and officers."[23] The gunboats produced a fear of pursuing the Union Army because their presence and firepower invoked dread among the troops. The men wanted, according to a report of the battle by Brigadier General A. P. Stewart, "to aid in the pursuit of the enemy, which was checked by the fire from the gunboat."[24]

The shelling not only halted the Confederate advance but also forced them to return to the Union camps they overran earlier in the day. According to a private in Stanford's battery, "Their gunboats shelled us so heavily that we had to retreat back to their encampment."[25] Other soldiers noted that the Federals supplemented the firing of the gunboats with field artillery. Sam Houston Jr., son of the famous Texas general, president, and governor, recorded that

> those few shots fired by the gun-boats seemed the signal for a cannonading, which, considering its brief duration, was the most terrific I ever witnessed. The enemy had massed their entire force of field artillery along the riverbank, where was also planted a heavy land battery. So incessant was the firing, that it could only be likened to exaggerated musketry; one could find certain cadences in the din and almost torture it into a tune; while the deep bass of the Gunboats' one hundred and twenty four pounders, heightened the vagary.[26]

The deafening noise and the dread of the big guns made some of the men thankful that this was the last charge on April 6.

As time passed for those men leading the push against the Union army at the river, they began to realize that the shells "passing far over our heads must have rendered it rather warm for those in our rear."[27] Leonidas Polk explained in his battle report why it was safe for the men nearest the riverbank. "The height of the plain on which we were, above the level of the water, was about 100 feet, so that it was necessary to give great elevation to his guns to enable him to fire over the bank. The consequence was that shot could take effect only at points remote from the river's edge. They were comparatively harmless to our troops nearest the bank, and became increasingly so as we drew near the enemy and placed him between us and his boats."[28] The sounds and anxiety of a strong defensive position protected by artillery and gunboats temporarily stalled the Confederate advance until they realized that the threat was elsewhere. Frank L. Richardson, of the Thirteenth Louisiana Infantry, described the barrage: "The roar of these cannon was grand and terrific. As it was the first time we had ever been under the line of mortars, it was startling. They were, however, elevated too high and could not have done much damage."[29] By time they realized the guns could not harm them, they had received Beauregard's orders to halt.

Though the gunboats halted the forward advance only temporarily and produced few casualties near the river, the cannons had a greater consequence on the men farther from the front—where the shells were landing. Richardson, who witnessed the ineffective impact the shells had on the men in the front, directly felt the impact of the shells "just before sunset. We faced about and moved towards the enemy's abandoned camps in the rear."[30] Confederate units on the front after receiving Beauregard's order to halt, in relative safety from the gunboats, received orders from "General [Braxton] Bragg to fall back out of the range of the gunboats and encamp for the night" in the captured Union camps.[31] Unfortunately for the Confederates, by 5:35 P.M. the *Lexington* joined *Tyler* in shelling them. To reach the abandoned Union camps, the Thirteenth Louisiana Infantry had to leave the plains near the river and pass through woods. "The gunboats were shelling these woods. Trees were split open and great branches cut down," wrote one of the soldiers. "The shot and shell that passed over our heads in the plain fell here, and crashed through the woods." Once they realized their situation, Richardson and the men in his regiment "dodged from tree to tree. . . . It was about dusk. The shell and shot looked like shafts of lightning, cutting through the forest. The roar was like that of many thunder claps breaking over the head at once. We got beyond the range of their guns, into the Federal camps on the other side. The stars began to shine out; the shells continued to burst over the woods behind us long after we had laid down to rest."[32] The shelling continued throughout the night, but similar to the men along the front lines, Richardson and his comrades found that the terror was only temporarily. Though the shells landed among the men, they quickly realized that even the heavy naval ordinance had a limited destructiveness, and the damage was confined to the woods between the river and the last Union camps the Confederates had overrun.

During the night of April 6, Federal ships worked relentlessly all night transporting men and supplies, and the Union gunboats USS *Tyler* and *Lexington* kept up a steady bombardment. Most Confederates were camped too far from the river to hear the transportation of the Union soldiers, but they definitely heard the firing of the naval guns and the explosion of the shells. Though, initially, the firing of naval ordnance created a panic among the men, this fear quickly diminished once they realized that the cannons had a limited range and only affected a small area because of the topography.[33]

The shelling halted the Confederate advance. As darkness crept over the men and the muskets and rifles fell silent, Lieutenant William Gwin of the *Tyler* decided to change his tactics. He devised an idea and received permission to "throw an 8-inch shell into the camp of the enemy every ten minutes during the night and thus prevent their sleeping."[34] The Union gunboats fired their guns at fifteen-minute intervals starting at 9:00 P.M. and continuing until daylight.[35] Initially, this provided a relief for the men still in the woods, which James M. Williams of the Twenty-first Alabama Infantry Volunteers described in a letter to his wife, Lizzie: "Night found us in the last camp of the enemy under a galling fire of shells from the gun-boats; at dark this ceased and our regiment moved back to the first camp we captured where we lay all night in their tents."[36] The men recognized the range of the guns and camped in relative safety. Though out of danger from the shells themselves, however, they still had to endure the sounds of the firing of cannons and the explosion of the ordnance all night. Duke of Morgan's cavalry regiment remembered, "All night long, the huge pieces upon the gunboats thundered at intervals, with a roar which seemed like that of a bursting firmament. . . . These huge missiles came screaming louder than a steam whistle, striking off the tops of trees, and filling the air with dense clouds of smoke when they burst, but doing no damage."[37] Men positioned close to the river for the night suffered more from the sounds of the gunboats. Blackburn of the Terry's Texas Rangers said they "slept on the battleground that night as best we could. . . . with the gunboats on the river firing over us all night to disturb our slumber."[38]

Throughout the day, Confederates had pillaged the Yankee camps. Joseph Dimmit Thompson of the Thirty-eighth Tennessee Infantry said they "all helped ourselves to whatever we could find. I took a fine carpet sack and filled it with useful trinkets; took pants, cap, drawers, books, blankets, knives, forks, India rubber, knapsacks, haversacks, etc . . . We found apples, cheese, ham and good things, and ate all we could."[39] Though, in the words of J. B. Ulmer of Wirt Adams's Texas Cavalry, "the fiery missiles of the gunboats cleft the air above us with their awful shrieks, we reveled in the fatness of the enemy's camp."[40] The excitement of pillaging the Union camps along with the relative safety from the gunboat shells temporarily buoyed the morale of the exhausted Confederates but other influences lurked in the shadows and impacted the men's reactions to the battle.

That night, most Southern soldiers had to sleep in the camps that their Union foes had occupied the night before. These sites had also been the scenes of fighting during the day that had just ended. After the excitement of pillaging evaporated, those Confederates who could do so bedded in the Yankee tents for the night. Throughout the night, most Confederates slept in a torrential downpour of rain and among large numbers of dead and wounded men from both sides. "Tired and sad," Major Grisamore and his men "lay down and endeavored to obtain a little rest, but before midnight the rain began to fall, and the agonizing voices of the wounded were heard in distressing cries all night long."[41]

Other men suffered from the trauma of the fighting they had just gone through. August Hervey Mecklin recorded in his diary that he "attempted it [sleep] but the balls would whistle and the musketry would roar [in] my ears."[42] The horrors of combat took their psychological toll on the men, and the combination of rain, the presence of the dead and wounded, and the constant noise of the gunboats' cannons kept some of the exhausted men awake for the entire night. Joseph Thompson, whose unit camped that night in the last Union camps to be overrun, a position where fighting had occurred late in the day and that was well in range of the gunboats, said, "As early as 9 o'clock, they [the Yankees] commenced throwing shell at us from their boats and continued all night. We were forced to stand behind trees for shelter; and there we stood all night long!! At midnight, a heavy rain set in accompanied by peal after peal of thunder, together with the roaring of cannon and the bursting of shell. The flashes of lightning revealed the gastly features of the dead. The groans and piteous shrieks of the wounded was heart-rendering in the extreme. There we stood, all wet to the skin!! Oh, what a night of horrors that was!! It will haunt me to the grave."[43] The experiences of the first day and night plagued many of the men and made them begin to reconsider if they had been the true victors.

The Confederates had undeniably been the victors on April 6, but events that transpired next brought confusion about who, if anyone, had won the battle as a whole. Did the Confederates feel they had won, and by what criteria? Their feelings of victory changed to defeat as the sun rose the morning of April 7. Thomas Chinn Robertson wrote in a letter home, "We were all hoping it [the order] was to march back to our camp at Monterey, but the booming of cannon and whistle of shells told us that we had bloody work to perform."[44]

In his diary, William Micajah Barrow of the Fourth Louisiana Infantry recorded the changes in the men's outlooks; his April 6 entry is: "hard fighting all day. we whipped the Yankees." By the end of the second day of fighting, he recorded, "This morning I awoke early. . . . The regiment was drawn up in line (what was left of it) we marched to battle and I was taken prisoner about one o'clock."[45] Sam R. Watkins stated, "On Monday the tide was reversed. . . . Now those Yankees were whipped, fairly whipped, and according to all the rules of war they ought to have retreated. But they didn't. . . . Victory was again to perch upon their banners."[46] April 7, brought no gains for the Confederates but a day of hard fighting and retreating.[47] Though it is clear that the Confederates lost the second day of the battle, this is the point where many Confederates begin to disagree as to whether the enemy had defeated them or they were victorious because they had achieved their goals. Though the men had a stake in the outcome of the battle, they did not have to declare Shiloh a victory, unlike Beauregard, in order to keep their jobs. They knew that even if they claimed defeat in the battle, the Confederacy would employ them as soldiers for the duration of the war. In other words, they had job security, except if killed or wounded. Consequently, they were honest because they did not worry if their letters with their opinions fell into the possession of the Confederate government or military.

Confederate soldiers used many different aspects of the battle to argue their point of view. Some topics that Confederate soldiers disputed included whether the retreat was forced or planned by Beauregard, whether they brought back with them all the pillage they found, and whether they achieved the objectives of the battle. Confederate soldiers held on dearly to their points of view to deflect blame or to prove their virtues as good soldiers.

After sending the telegram on April 6, Beauregard needed to justify his statement of complete victory as his army retreated the next day. The commanding general reported, "It was never contemplated, however, to retain the position thus gained and abandon Corinth, the strategic point of the campaign."[48] Some of the men in the ranks agreed with Beauregard. Thomas D. Duncan, a Mississippian cavalryman, wrote sixty years later, well after the belief in the Lost Cause had gripped the South, "With no Confederate reenforcements in prospect, General Beauregard began, early in the afternoon, to withdraw the gray army from the unequal conflict. We retired in good order, and were deeply surprised that the Union forces made no attempt to pursue us beyond their encampment."[49] According to Beauregard and an aged Confederate soldier sixty years after the battle, the Southern retreat was planned in advance and was not marred by pressure from the Union army.

Other soldiers presented different views of the retreat. William E. Bevens of the First Arkansas Infantry provided a sterile view of the events of the second day: "Our men, fighting stubbornly all the while, were pushed back by superior force through and beyond the Yankee camps we had captured so easily the day before, and at last retreated to Corinth."[50] Bevens essentially stated that the Union army forced the Confederates to retreat, but nothing else of significance occurred, nor implied that it was disorderly. This view along with the former is rare. The dominant view of the common soldier is more critical.

The Confederate soldier viewed the retreat of the second day as a complete debacle. They felt defeated and ashamed while marching back to Corinth. Robert Patrick of the Fourth Louisiana Infantry recorded in his diary on April 7, "Our army fell back towards Corinth the most completely disorganised and demoralized army imaginable. If the Yankee army had been in a condition to have followed us they could have captured the whole concern."[51] Even some of Beauregard's officers agreed with the men; General Braxton Bragg wrote to his commanding general, "Our condition is horrible. . . . Troops utterly disorganized. Road almost impassable. . . . I find but few officers with their men." By 2 P.M., Bragg noted, "The whole road presents a scene of rout."[52]

John W. Taylor of the Fifteenth Mississippi Infantry corroborated Bragg's report in a letter to his parents: "We was badly scattered, I never seen any of my regiment until night. I fell in with the 22 Louisiana regiment and we ran until I give out. I escaped the balls but I do not know how it was for the men fell all around me."[53] Another member of the Fifteenth Mississippi, Mecklin, recorded, "I saw our men falling back one by one. Then I saw whole squads retreating. Soon the whole regiment was in full retreat. The retreat was a perfect rout. The men scattered in every direction. Our regiment never again formed itself."[54]

The accuracy of the Confederate soldiers' view of the retreat was confirmed by their foes. Alexander Oliphant, a Union soldier in the Twenty-fourth Indiana Infantry, said that the Confederates "ran—not retiring in good order, but they ran for their lives."[55] The men in the ranks disprove Beauregard's account of an orderly retreat. Beauregard's idea of victory through an orderly retreat is not plausible because, according to the men, an orderly retreat was nonexistent.

Another reason that Beauregard gave in defense of his claim of victory was that the men and the army left the field with wagonloads of spoils. This was part of his larger argument that the Confederate army did not engage the Union army at Shiloh to crush it but simply to weaken it as it prepared to invade the South from Pittsburg Landing. Beauregard explained his logic in his report after the battle: "By a rapid and vigorous attack on General Grant it was expected he would be beaten back into his transports and the river, or captured, in time to enable us to profit by the victory, and remove to the rear all the stores and munitions that would fall into our hands in such an event before the arrival of General Buell's army on the scene." By knocking the Union army back on its heels and taking their supplies, the commanding general planned "to leave it unable to take the field for the campaign for which it was collected and equipped at such enormous expense and with such profusion of all the appliances of war."[56] Thomas D. Duncan, the Mississippi cavalryman who wrote in the early twentieth century, demonstrated that at least some Confederate rank and file agreed—or came to agree—with Beauregard's justification for victory. "We marched back to Corinth," Duncan wrote, "taking with us all captured cannon and other arms, without a rear-guard fight."[57]

For a garnering of spoils that could be described as successful, as Beauregard did of this one, an army must bring back or destroy large stores of enemy supplies and equipment and then get back to its base with at least most of its own equipment intact. The Confederate army did destroy some Union supplies, but Beauregard reported a more complete outcome, which, according to many of the soldiers, was not reality. Other officers and especially the enlisted men disagreed with their commanding general. Bragg reported, "Our artillery is being left all along the road by its officers."[58] The previous day, the Confederate army had captured thirty-three Union cannons, but while the Confederates retreated to Corinth, the Union army recaptured many of those pieces, plus some Rebel guns. Even supplies and mementos that the Confederate soldiers took while pillaging the Union camps were discarded during the march to Corinth. Joseph Thompson in a letter written almost two weeks after the battle described the fighting on April 7: Union soldiers surrounded the camp, forcing the Rebel soldiers to leave quickly and "to throw away their haversacks, blankets, and everything that would retard their flight for it was death to him who lagged behind. I had my Yankee knapsack buckled so tightly that I could not get rid of it. . . . In trying to get it off I fell into a creek, and my trinkets . . . went a flying. I thank God that I got off with my life."[59] What Richardson of the Thirteenth Louisiana Infantry described of the retreat supports Thompson's view: the retreat as so unplanned and disorganized that it "had prevented most of them from carrying away the valuables they had collected. The only property which I appropriated was an India rubber cloth, to protect me from the rain. Life was so uncertain during the battle that it didn't seem worth while to increase my store of worldly goods."[60] The men had left with such great alacrity that it would be difficult to think that they felt they won the battle, but the argument amongst the men over fulfilling the objectives of the battle only intensified.

Beauregard's claim is only partially correct that he fulfilled his objective of taking all of the supplies of the Union army and thus staggering their ability to advance deeper into the Confederacy. Though they carried away little ordnance from the Union camps, some men, such as the appeasing Colonel Duke, agreed with the general: "The battle of Shiloh was, after all, a Confederate success. The army of invasion was crippled and reduced to a cautious offensive, little better than inactivity. The Federal arms were stayed and blunted, and the Southern people, reanimated, prepared for fresh and vigorous resistance."[61] Other soldiers reasoned that the Confederate army demoralized its opponent through the number of Union casualties in the battle. With inflated numbers, Robert T. Moore of Alabama wrote home two weeks after the battle, "I don't think that the Yankees will ever fight us anymore, I think they are tiard of it. It is said that we lost twenty five hundred men, and the yankees lost twenty thousand."[62] Mecklin summed these points up, "Our loss was great, though not as great as the enemy. We left the enemy in possession of the field. Our men destroyed several of their campgrounds. All things compared we have gained a dearly fought victory."[63]

The idea that the battle of Shiloh weakened the Union army through making it cautious to move deeper into the South allowed some men to reason that the Confederates were the victors.

The realities of the overall war situation in the spring of 1862 came to influence many soldiers' point of view. Unknown to the soldiers in the days following the battle was that on April 8, while they were still trudging back toward Corinth, the key Confederate outpost at Island No. 10 on the Mississippi River fell to Union forces, and its forty-two hundred Confederate defenders went into captivity. By the end of April, Admiral David Farragut had captured New Orleans, giving the Union navy control of most of the Mississippi River. By June, Memphis fell to the Union army.[64] Though initially, it appeared to some soldiers that Beauregard had fulfilled his objective of a major raid with a Confederate victory at Shiloh, they soon realized their mistake and used retrospect to try to find victory and assign blame.

One thing that many soldiers argued was that the initial objective of the battle was not a major raid but the annihilation of the Army of the Tennessee. Many looked at Johnston for the answers. George W. Jones of Stanford's Mississippi battery wrote in his diary after the battle, "What a pity that General A. S. Johnston was killed. If he had not received that fatal wound, Grant and his army would have been either killed, drowned in the Tennessee River, or taken prisoners."[65] Duke, though he approved of Beauregard's reasoning, also commented about Johnston's objective to take down Grant's men: "It is a point conceded, now, on all sides, that had the Confederate army pursued its success on the evening of the first day, the army under General Grant would have been annihilated, and Buell never could have crossed the river. Had General Johns[t]on survived, the battle would have been pressed vigorously to that consummation."[66] The idea that the objective of the battle at Shiloh was to annihilate the Army of the Tennessee was the interpretation held by most Confederate soldiers.

Most soldiers who thought the objective was to eliminate the Union army made their opinion known through criticizing Beauregard, specifically his order to halt on April 6. The opinions of the Confederate soldiers range from disappointment to disgust. A disappointed Duncan recollected that the Confederate army ended the first day of fighting "with a seeming victory in our grasp, with the brave, though depleted and disorganized army of blue at bay at the river's brink."[67] Watkins expressed his disgust with the commanding general when he wrote, "Those four letters, h-a-l-t, O, how harsh they did break upon our ears. The victory was complete, but the word 'halt' turned victory into defeat."[68] After the war, Confederates, such as Duke and Richardson, even stated that this was the moment that the war changed for the Confederacy. Duke wrote, "On that afternoon, (after Beauregard issued the order) the second chance which the Confederacy had, to win the war, was thrown away."[69] Richardson of the Thirteenth Louisiana in retrospect disagreed with the order to halt because "[l]ittle did we know that this short truce would turn the fortunes of war against the whole Confederacy. Our cause was lost from that hour."[70] Disagreements over the objective of the battle of Shiloh created many reactions, indeed, from the men.

The experiences of the men with the battle of Shiloh did not end when the guns fell silent and the enemy disappeared from view. "The Railroad platform is almost covered with coffins and wounded soldiers—every train brings some anxious parent looking after their sons," one soldier commented about the scene in Corinth, the city to which the soldiers had retreated. A Louisianan passed by a church full of wounded soldiers and saw a large box "filled with feet and arms & hands. It was so full that 2 horrible & bloody feet protruded out of the top."[71] Disease also ran rampant through the camps of the Confederates. Captain James I. Hall of Company C of the Ninth Tennessee Infantry wrote home in late April about his company: "The health of the company is not good almost all the boys are complaining the sickness is caused by exposure during and after the battle. We are in [a] bad fix."[72] Other men noted a feeling of helplessness toward their wounded friends. "Our wounded were suffering, and we could obtain but a few articles of diet suitable for them."[73]

Witnessing these bloody scenes of the mutilated, sick, dying, and dead had a profound effect on Confederate morale and the soldiers' view of the battle. In many cases it changed the men forever. After the retreat to Corinth, scenes of carnage plagued the city and the camps. Compounding the horrific scenes of the battlefield was the opportunity to think about the events of April 6 and 7 and to recognize the changes the battle had produced in themselves and their comrades. Many recorded the changes in their own behavior and that of their friends. Before the battle, "the camp, once so gay, so joyous," according to Livaudais, "now lay under the pall of death. Everywhere prevailed a mournful silence."[74] Other soldiers noted these changes. On April 8, Major Silas T. Grisamore noted, "At this time everything was gloom and sadness about camp."[75] As the men recovered, John Pugh of the Washington Artillery described the scene in Corinth in detail: "[E]veryone was hushed in sadness. . . . For a week or more after our return [to Corinth], everything was as quiet as if the whole country around was one church. The loss of friends, and the horrible scenes which they had just witnessed, together with their almost miraculous escape, seemed to quiet everyone."[76] Though the silence of the camp ended after a few weeks, the battle had a more profound effect on the men and how they lived their lives. Captain Hall attributed some of the permanent changes in the men of his company to the battle of Shiloh.

> While in camp at Columbus, for want of other employment, the men and officers, many of them had both acquired a fondness for gambling, . . . [especially] cock fighting. As we marched down toward Corinth, the whole country was scoured in the search for fighting birds and whenever the army would halt in their march a crowd of soldiers would collect to witness a cock fight. The throng was so thick sometimes that men on the outskirts of the crowd would climb up into trees to get a better view. . . . [A]lthough I remained in the army three years after this [the battle of Shiloh], I do not remember ever seeing or hearing of another cockfight in our Regiment or in fact, in any part of the army with which I was there in.[77]

The battle of Shiloh took its toll on the men and the people of the Confederacy.

Not only did the battle have an immediate effect on the emotions of the men but it also made them question the future of the war. A Texan revealed these attitudes and feelings a month after the conclusion of the battle. William P. Rogers wrote home to his wife on May 1 concerned about the future of the war and Confederacy: "God only knows my dear Wife what is ahead of us. For the future of our country I greatly fear—All is gloomy now all is despondency here among the people—You meet with [no] smiling face nor joyous brow."[78] L. Yandell, a medical officer in the Fourth Tennessee Infantry, described the reality of the war that filled his mind in a letter to his father two weeks after the battle. "God grant that it may end soon, and yet I do not see any ray of hope for its early termination. The future grows darker. Those persons who reason themselves into the belief that peace will soon come or at least that the war will soon cease, are blinded and mislead by their wishes."[79] Most reactions of the men were negative and confused over the future of the war and the Confederacy.[80]

Confederate soldiers had a variety of reactions to the battle based on many different aspects of their experience during the days of April 6 and 7 and the months that followed.

No consensus developed as to whether the battle of Shiloh had been a victory or a defeat. Considerable opinion existed in favor of both views. When men looked at the battle in its totality, they determined, with reason, that it was a draw. Kendall of the Fourth Louisiana Infantry concluded in his memoirs that the battle "was a victory for neither side. The enemy did not follow us, and we abandoned the field."[81] Other men recorded their opinions in letters to loved ones in the immediate days after the battle. The day after the battle ended, J. M. Stevens wrote to his wife, "I can't say whether we are whip[p]ed or not though I don't think we are or will be."[82] When he wrote to his wife, James W. Williams of the Twenty-first Alabama gave other reasons for his confusion: "How the battle of Shiloh is looked upon by the country I do not know, but I believe it to have been one of the fiercest and most desperately fought conflicts of the whole war—The Yankees fought bravely and only gave way inch by inch, before our advancing lines strewing the ground with their dead & wounded and our own."[83] Yandell, thinking like a medical officer, claimed, "Our army and the Federal army both suffered severly. I dont think either can claim a victory."[84]

Confederates disputed whether they were victorious or defeated when they examined specific aspects of the battle such as Beauregard's order to halt, the death of General Johnston, the shelling of the gunboats, sleeping with the dead and wounded, the retreat to Corinth, and disputes over the objective of the campaign. When viewed in its totality, most Southern soldiers concluded that because they won the first day of fighting by forcing the Union army to retreat, and the Union did the same the following day, at great cost in men and supplies for both sides, the battle resulted in a draw. Overall, the battle left Confederate soldiers confused and uncertain about their future and that of their country. One thing that many men did not debate is that "the terrible scenes of the two days April 6 & 7—The Battle of Shiloh—are indelibly fixed in my memory."[85]

Notes

1. U.S. War Department, *The War of the Rebellion: A Compilation of the Official Records of the Union and Confederate Armies*, ed. Robert N. Scott, 128 vols. (Washington, DC: GPO, 1884), 10.2:91 (this source is hereafter referred to as "*OR*." All references are to series 1 unless otherwise noted); Grady McWhiney, "General Beauregard's 'Complete Victory' at Shiloh: An Interpretation," *Journal of Southern History* 49 (August 1983): 421.

2. *OR*, 10.1:385.

3. Wiley Sword, *Shiloh: Bloody April* (New York: Morrow, 1974), 109.

4. Arthur W. Bergeron, ed., *The Civil War Reminiscences of Major Silas T. Grisamore, C.S.A.* (Baton Rouge: Louisiana State University Press, 1993), 33.

5. George W. Jones Diary, April 5, 1862, Greenville Public Library, Greenville, Mississippi, as quoted in Larry J. Daniel, *Shiloh: The Battle That Changed the Civil War* (NEW York: Simon and Schuster, 1997), 130.

6. Sword, *Shiloh*, 109.

7. Sam R. Watkins, *"Co. Aytch": First Tennessee Regiment* (Dayton, OH: Morningside Bookshop, 1992), 34.

8. Basil W. Duke, *A History of Morgan's Cavalry* (Bloomington: Indiana University Press, 1960), 142.

9. Bergeron, *Civil War Reminiscences*, 34.

10. *OR*, 10.1:402; Sword, *Shiloh*, 286, 318, 322, 363; Daniel, *Shiloh*, 256.

11. Sword, *Shiloh*, 319.

12. Bergeron, *Civil War Reminiscences*, 36.

13. Ferguson Memoir, Army of the Mississippi File, Shiloh National Military Park, as quoted in Daniel, *Shiloh*, 241.

14. Earl C. Woods, ed., *The Shiloh Diary of Edmond Enoul Livaudais* (New Orleans, LA: Archdiocese of New Orleans, 1992), 30.

15. John Smith Kendall, "Recollections of a Confederate Officer," *Louisiana Historical Quarterly* 29 (October 1946): 1067.

16. J. K. P. Blackburn, L. B. Giles, and E. S. Dodd, *Terry Texas Ranger Trilogy* (Austin, TX: State House Press, 1996), 114. The entire regiment of Texas cavalrymen was not present for the battle, only a small detachment under the command of General Nathan Bedford Forrest.

17. Ibid.

18. Donald E. Sutherland, ed., *Reminiscences of a Private: William E. Bevens of the First Arkansas Infantry* (Fayetteville: University of Arkansas Press, 1992), 73; Wendell Holmes Stephenson and Edwin Adams Davis, eds., "The Civil War Diary of William Micajah Barrow, September 23, 1861–July 13, 1862," *Louisiana Historical Quarterly* 17 (October 1934): 722.

19. Watkins, *"Co. Aytch,"* 33; Sword, *Shiloh*, 272–73.

20. Frank L. Richardson, "War as I Saw It," *Louisiana Historical Quarterly* 6 (January 1923): 102.

21. Howell Carter, *A Cavalryman's Reminiscences of the Civil War* (New Orleans: American, 1979), 25.

22. T. B. Smith, *Untold Story of Shiloh*, 55; Sword, *Shiloh*, 283–84; Samuel H. Lockett, "Surprise and Withdrawal at Shiloh," in *Battles and Leaders of the Civil War*, ed. Robert Underwood Johnson and Clarence C. Buel (New York: Yoseloff, 1884), 1.605.

23. William A Brown Diary, April 6, 1862, Shiloh National Military Park, as quoted in T. B. Smith, *Untold Story of Shiloh*, 63.

24. *OR*, 10.1:428. Further descriptions of this halt created by the gunboats, see Colonel A. J. Vaughan's report, *OR*, 10.1:425.

25. Buck to sister, April 12, 1862. Stanford's Battery Files, Shiloh National Military Park, as quoted in T. B. Smith, *Untold Story of Shiloh*, 44.

26. Sam Houston Jr., "Shiloh Shadows," *Southwestern Historical Quarterly* 34 (April 1931): 331.

27. Ibid.

28. *OR*, 10.1:410. This quotation can also be found in Sword, *Shiloh*, 344.

29. Richardson, "War as I Saw It," 102.

30. Ibid., 103.

31. *OR*, 10.1:418.

32. Sword, *Shiloh*, 344; Richardson, "War as I Saw It," 103.

33. Timothy B. Smith, *The Untold Story of Shiloh: The Battle and the Battlefield* (Knoxville: University of Tennessee Press, 2006), 28, 54; Daniel, *Shiloh*, 265.

34. Sword, *Shiloh*, 344, 374; *OR*, 10.1:324.

35. Sword, *Shiloh*, 374; *OR*, 10.1:324.

36. John Kent Folmar, ed., *From That Terrible Field: Civil War Letters of James M. Williams, Twenty-first Alabama Infantry Volunteers* (Tuscaloosa: University of Alabama Press, 1981), 55.

37. Duke, *History of Morgan's Cavalry*, 152–53.

38. Blackburn, Giles, and Dodd, *Terry Texas Ranger Trilogy*, 121.

39. John G. Biel, ed., "The Battle of Shiloh: From the Letters and Diary of Joseph Dimmit Thompson," *Tennessee Historical Quarterly* 1, no. 17 (Fall 1958): 265; also quoted in Sword, *Shiloh*, 343–44, 372.

40. J. B. Ulmer, "A Glimpse of Albert Sidney Johnston through the Smoke of Shiloh," *Southwestern Historical Quarterly* 10 (April 1907): 296; Watkins, *"Co. Aytch"*, 34–35.

41. Bergeron, *Civil War Reminiscences*, 35–36; Daniel, *Shiloh*, 263.

42. Augustus Hervey Mecklin, Diary 1862, Mississippi Department of Archives and History, Jackson, Mississippi, 54; as quoted in Sword, *Shiloh*, 376.

43. Biel, "Battle of Shiloh," 265–66.

44. Thomas Chinn Robertson to unknown person, April 9, 1862, Department of Archives and Manuscripts, Louisiana State University, Baton Rouge, Louisiana, as quoted in Sword, *Shiloh*, 385–86.

45. Stephenson and Davis, "Civil War Diary of William Micajah Barrow," 722.

46. Watkins, *"Co. Aytch"*, 35.

47. Sword, *Shiloh*, 401.

48. *OR*, 10.1:385.

49. Thomas D. Duncan, *Recollections of Thomas D. Duncan: A Confederate Soldier* (Nashville, TN: McQuiddy, 1922), 45, 62.

50. Sutherland, *Reminiscences of a Private*, 73.

51. I. Jay Taylor, ed., *The Secret Diary of Robert Patrick, 1861–1865* (Baton Rouge: Louisiana State University Press, 1959), 36.

52. *OR*, 10.1:294.

53. John W. Taylor to Father and Mother, 11 April 1862, Southern Historical Collection, University of North Carolina Library, Chapel Hill, North Carolina, as quoted in Ben Wayne, *A Hard Trip: A History of the 15th Mississippi Infantry, C.S.A.* (Macon, GA: Mercer University Press, 2003), 77.

54. Augustus Hervey Mecklin Papers, Mississippi Department of Archives and History Library, Jackson, Mississippi, as quoted in Wayne, *Hard Trip*, 77.

55. Oliphant to mother, April 8, 1862, Alexander Oliphant Letters, Twenty-fourth Indiana File, Shiloh National Military Park as quoted in Daniel, *Shiloh*, 281.

56. *OR*, 10.1:385, 389.

57. Duncan, *Recollections* 62.

58. *OR*, 10.1:294.

59. Larry J. Daniel, *Cannoneers in Gray: The Field Artillery of the Army of Tennessee, 1861–1865* (Tuscaloosa: University of Alabama, 1984), 44; Biel, "Battle of Shiloh," 266.

60. Richardson, "War as I Saw It," 223.

61. Joseph Allan Frank and George A. Reaves, *"Seeing the Elephant": Raw Recruits at the Battle of Shiloh* (New York: Greenwood, 1989), 168; Duke, *History of Morgan's Cavalry*, 155.

62. Robert T. Moore, "A Letter of R. T. Moore, August 22, 1861; and a letter of William T. Moore, April 21, 1862," *Alabama Historical Quarterly* 23 (1961): 300–301.

63. Augustus Hervey Mecklin Papers, Mississippi Department of Archives and History Library, Jackson, Mississippi; as quoted in Wayne, *Hard Trip*, 78.

64. Daniel, *Shiloh*, 314.

65. Mike Spradlin, ed., "The Diary of George W. Jones: An Impartial History of Stanford's Mississippi Battery," *Camp Chase Gazette*, April 1981, 145.

66. Duke, *History of Morgan's Cavalry*, 154.

67. Duncan, *Recollections*, 60–61.

68. Watkins, *"Co. Aytchy,"* 34.

69. Duke, *History of Morgan's Cavalry*, 152.

70. Richardson, "War as I Saw It," 103.

71. Larry J. Daniel, *Soldiering in the Army of Tennessee* (Chapel Hill: University of North Carolina, 1992), 66, 69; Daniel, *Shiloh*, 302.

72. James R. Fleming, *Band of Brothers: Company C, 9th Tennessee Infantry* (Shippensburg, PA: White Mane, 1966), 96.

73. Bergeron, *Civil War Reminiscences*, 41.

74. Woods, *Shiloh Diary*, 20.

75. Bergeron, *Civil War Reminiscences*, 41.

76. Barnes F. Lathrop, "A Confederate Artilleryman at Shiloh," *Civil War History* 1, no. 8 (1962): 382, 385; also quoted in Daniel, *Shiloh*, 302; Frank and Reaves, *"Seeing the Elephant,"* 127.

77. Fleming, *Band of Brothers*, 26.

78. Eleanor Damon Pace, ed., "The Diary and Letters of William P. Rogers, 1846–1862," *Southwestern Historical Quarterly* 32 (April 1929): 288.

79. L. Yandell to father, April 21, 1862, Baird Collection, Western Kentucky University Library, Bowling Green, Kentucky, as quoted in Frank and Reaves, *"Seeing the Elephant,"* 173.

80. Some men did react optimistically to the battle, such as Philip Daingerfield Stephenson. Stephenson recorded a buoyant view of battle in his memoirs.

> I was in camp when our men came back from Shiloh, and they came back, heads up, like heroes, still *full of fight!* It was no retreat, much less a rout. It was simply a withdrawal in the most orderly and leisurely manner, losing and leaving little, but bringing off several thousand prisoners, many pieces of artillery, several thousand small arms and a large quantity of plunder. There never was an army that showed more of a spirit of victory after a battle, than did our army after Shiloh. Their stories of the battle bore all the marks of triumph. For instance, they told me how completely they *surprised* the enemy the first day, finding some asleep in their tents, others cooking, and all totally unprepared. They described the *richness* of the camp and how they slept the night of the first day in the enemy's tents and helped themselves.

His opinion differed from majority of the men because of his ignorance. He did not participate in the battle but instead spent the duration of the battle behind lines suffering from dysentery. Nathaniel C. Hughes Jr., ed., *The Civil War Memoir of Philip Daingerfield Stephenson, D.D.: Private, Company K, 13th Arkansas Volunteer Infantry, Loader, Piece No. 4, 5th Company, Washington Artillery, Army of Tennessee, CSA* (Baton Rouge: Louisiana State University Press, 1995), 59.

81. Kendall, "Recollections of a Confederate Officer," 1069.

82. J. M. Stevens to wife [Mary], April 8, 1862, Shiloh National Military Park as quoted in Frank and Reaves, *"Seeing the Elephant,"* 169.

83. Folmar, *From That Terrible Field*, 56.

84. L. Yandell to father, April 10, 1862, Baird Collection, Western Kentucky University Library, Bowling Green, Kentucky; quoted in Frank and Reaves, *"Seeing the Elephant,* 169.

85. Folmar, *From That Terrible Field*, 55.

8

AFTER SHILOH

GRANT, SHERMAN, AND SURVIVAL

Brooks D. Simpson

The story is so oft-told that it seems all too familiar, a staple of the traditional Civil War narrative. Immediately after Shiloh, Ulysses S. Grant
dropped his previous notion that the war might be a short contest decided in
a handful of battles: the Confederate resistance suggested to him that this war
might go on for some time. Whether it would go on with him was another
matter altogether. He came under criticism so intense that for a while it looked
as if he might be removed from command. Only the wisdom of the all-know-
ing Abraham Lincoln shielded him from his critics: "I can't spare this man; he
fights." At the same time, Grant bonded with one of the few people willing to
be his friend under fire, William Tecumseh Sherman. That friendship proved
critical to Union fortunes when Grant, humiliated by the sanctimonious Henry
W. Halleck, contemplated going on leave, only to be saved by Sherman. Grant
decided to stick around, Halleck left for Washington, and the Union survived
what may have been its biggest detour on the road to Appomattox.

To be sure, Grant himself was responsible for a good deal of this narrative.
"Up to the battle of Shiloh I, as well as thousands of other citizens, believed
that the rebellion against the government would collapse suddenly and soon,
if a decisive victory could be gained over any of its armies," he recalled in
his *Memoirs*. But when the Confederates mounted their attack at Shiloh, "I
gave up all idea of saving the Union except by complete conquest." After an
extensive review of what he believed to be misapprehensions and misunder-
standings of the battle, he concluded that Shiloh "has been less understood,
or, to state the case more accurately, more persistently misunderstood, than
any other engagement between National and Confederate forces during the
entire rebellion."[1]

The impact of Shiloh and its aftermath upon Grant, long a staple of any
biographical narrative of his life, deserves closer scrutiny. Some parts of

the oft-told tale have been challenged by scholars who have perused the evidence with care, but one characteristic of Civil War scholarship seems to be that revised understandings do not always succeed in supplanting the traditional tale. Grant certainly came under criticism after Shiloh and under different circumstances might have lost his command. But did he owe his retention to the intervention of the president? In retrospect, Grant may well have come to see Shiloh as decisive in transforming his understanding of the conflict and in convincing him to wage harsher war against the Confederates. Was that indeed the case at the time? Much would be made of how Shiloh forged a friendship between Grant and Sherman that proved essential to eventual Union victory. How does one explain how that relationship came about? How did Grant come to explain the battle, especially in the light of newspaper criticism?

On the evening of April 7, 1862, Ulysses S. Grant was exhausted, as was his command. For two days they had engaged in relentless combat, having been pushed back to the vicinity of Pittsburg Landing on April 6 before receiving reinforcements and counterattacking the following day. At times, it had seemed a close-run thing, for the initial Confederate attack came as a surprise, and it drove several Union divisions back in some disorder before the bluecoats rallied. Even then, several thousand soldiers fled panic-stricken to the landing itself: it took most of the day and into the evening before long-expected reinforcements finally arrived. Moreover, Grant did not enjoy a warm relationship with Don Carlos Buell, whose forces crossed the Tennessee River late on the afternoon of Sunday, April 6, and continued to take up positions during the rainy night, and Grant could not understand why one of his own division commanders, Lew Wallace, had taken so long to arrive. Grant was down one division commander mortally wounded (William H. L. Wallace) and another captured (Benjamin Prentiss), and the Confederates had dealt his command a rather savage blow. Although the Monday counterattack recaptured the ground that had been lost on Sunday, by battle's end Grant did not mount much of a pursuit, in part because it seemed he was less than sure whether Buell and his commanders would comply with his orders. As it was, these two bloody days, with their astonishing list of losses, had also taken their toll on Grant physically and psychologically. He could not stand the cries of the wounded at a field hospital the night of April 6, choosing instead to spend the night standing under a tree in the drenching rain, despite suffering from a painful ankle injury; the following day, as he crossed one field, he observed that one could transverse it without ever actually touching the ground because it was covered by dead soldiers.[2]

Grant did what he could to anticipate mounting a pursuit on April 8, although he was under orders from Halleck not to go too far forward. Meanwhile, he reported the results of the day to Halleck—"the complete repulse of the enemy"—and shared his thinking with Buell.[3] The following morning, as he launched what turned out to be a half-hearted and easily stalled pursuit, he took the time to congratulate his men for defeating "a numerically superior force of the enemy composed of the flower of the southern army commanded by their ablest Generals. . . . In numbers engaged no such contest ever took place on this continent. In importance of result, but few such have taken place in the history of the world." He shared the same sense of exultation with his wife, Julia, adding that the losses for both sides would exceed twenty thousand men, as it did.[4]

Such carnage required a quick response to police the battlefield. Burial parties set to burying the dead of both sides, and by April 9, that job was largely accomplished, although it meant that the Confederate dead were buried in several mass trenches. That same day, Grant filed his first extended report of the battle. On April 6, he asserted, the Confederates drove in his pickets, but by the time the Confederates reached the main army, all five divisions "were drawn up in line of battle ready to meet them." If there was a question of surprise or preparedness, Grant did not mention it. After a day-long struggle during which Grant's men grudgingly gave ground, the lead elements of Buell's army arrived just as the Confederates made a "desperate effort" but were driven back. Reinforcements arrived during the night, and Grant, "feeling that a great moral advantage would be gained by becoming the attacking party," ordered a counterattack at dawn. After another day of heavy combat, the Confederates retreated: exhaustion and the weather precluded an immediate pursuit.[5]

At a time when he admitted he had yet to see the reports of his subordinates, Grant singled out Sherman as "a gallant and able officer" who, despite having been "severely wounded in the hand" and "again wounded and had three horses killed under him," "displayed great judgment and skill in the management of his men."[6] The words were important. Grant said nothing about Sherman's role in the period leading up to the battle, especially his reassurances that there was no sign of an imminent attack, or about the deployment of Sherman's men in camp, which was not optimal for purposes of resisting an assault. At the same time, Grant refrained from making any adverse assessment of his other division commanders, refusing to discuss the nature of his orders to Lew Wallace and Prentiss on April 6.

Within two weeks, Grant had reason to assess Sherman's loyalty in comparison to that of another one of his division commanders, John A. McClernand. McClernand had tarried in filing a report on his command at Fort Donelson. When it finally arrived, over two months after the fact, Grant was dismayed by what he read, and he could not refrain from sharing his own observations as he forwarded the document to Halleck. The report, he remarked, was "a little highly colored as to the conduct of the First Division"; Grant did not recall McClernand having made a suggestion about mounting what turned out to be the decisive counterattack on February 15.[7] Nor did Grant find reassuring Lew Wallace's report about Shiloh, which arrived at headquarters several days later. Wallace did what he could to explain and excuse his arrival at Pittsburg Landing after the close of combat on April 6, asserting that he complied with the orders he received. Grant did not agree, although, for the moment, he restricted his dissent to a flat endorsement that highlighted his disagreement with Wallace's account.[8]

Even more depressing was the criticism Grant received in the newspapers. Initial reports had proclaimed a great victory and celebrated Grant's generalship, but within a week, he came under fire in article after article that harshly condemned his performance. The New York *Tribune* asserted that "there was no more preparation by Gen. Grant for an attack than if he had been on a Fourth of July Frolic"; in the Cincinnati *Gazette*, Whitelaw Reid went so far as to declare that some of Grant's men had been bayoneted in their tents. The themes were always the same: Grant was incompetent, he had failed to prepare his men to withstand an assault, and he had been caught by surprise. Added to the second-guessing that abounded around Pittsburg Landing, especially among those officers and men seeking to advance their reputation at Grant's expense or to excuse their own performance, these reports wounded him. Perhaps, he hoped, the war would soon be over. "I am looking for a speedy move, one more fight and then easy sailing to the close of the war," he wrote Julia on April 15. He certainly hoped as much, because the criticism of his performance stung. Had Julia read the papers? "I will come in again for heaps of abuse from persons who were not here."[9]

Grant was about to come in for even more abuse from his commanding officer. Halleck arrived at Pittsburg Landing on the evening of April 11. He confided to his wife that the officers "seemed very glad to see me," for "this army is undisciplined and very much disorganized"—just what Halleck was prepared to discover, given his previous criticisms of Grant's administrative abilities. "Immediate and active measures must be taken to put your command in condition to resist another attack by the enemy," he admonished Grant three days later, adding, "Your army is not now in condition to resist an attack."[10] Halleck followed this up by issuing more instructions to bring Grant's and Buell's commands into disciplined order, complete with drill and reminders about proper procedures in following the chain of command. An observer watched as Halleck paced back and forth in front of Grant, "scolding in a loud and haughty manner" while Grant "sat there, demure, with red face, hat in lap, covered with the mud of the field, and undistinguished from an orderly."[11]

It did not take long for Halleck to realize that although Grant may not have managed a tidy army, the problems in command went far beyond him, especially in those units that had seen their baptism of fire at Shiloh. In compliance with Halleck's orders, Grant had provided for a board of officers to examine the competency and behavior of officers suspected of failing to meet expectations. Sherman took advantage of this opportunity to rip through several subordinates, demonstrating just how widespread the problem was. It may have been as important a service as Sherman performed for Grant, for two days after Sherman had forwarded to Grant charges against several of his officers, Halleck received a telegram from Secretary of War Edwin M. Stanton: "The President desires to know why you have made no official report to this department respecting the late battles at Pittsburg Landing. And whether any neglect or misconduct of General Grant or any other officer contributed to the sad casualties that befell our forces on Sunday."[12]

If Halleck had wanted to rid himself of Grant, he now had the perfect opportunity to do so. He believed that Grant had not been prepared for what befell him on April 6: his criticisms of Grant's administrative skills and of his ability to maintain good order and discipline appeared to be confirmed by what he had encountered over the preceding dozen days. But Halleck stayed his hand. "The said casualties of Sunday the sixth were due in part to the bad conduct of officers who were utterly unfit for their places & in part to the numbers & bravery of the enemy," he wired Washington. "I prefer to express no opinion in regard to the misconduct of individuals till I receive the reports of commanders of Division. A Great Battle cannot be fought or a victory gained without many casualties."[13]

Why did Halleck say this? Why did a general who had busied himself less than two months before this message with discrediting Grant neglect this opportunity to take him out, once and for all? Just days before issuing this reply, Halleck had declared, "I never saw a man more deficient in the business of organization. Brave and able in the field, he has no idea of how to regulate & organize his forces before a battle."[14] Such an indictment would seem to justify Lincoln's inquiry. Yet, Halleck destroyed the very basis for a case against Grant when he wired Washington: "The newspaper accounts that our divisions were surprised are utterly false. Every division had notice of the enemy's approach hours before the battle commenced."[15]

Such a claim would not seem to be supported by the record, leaving one to wonder why Halleck offered it. Perhaps it helped that he had thought highly of Sherman's performance during the battle. Within two days of his arrival at Pittsburg Landing, Halleck concluded that Sherman had "saved the fortune of the day" on April 6 and then had "contributed largely to the glorious victory of the 7th."[16] The truth, of course, was somewhat more complex. After all, it had been Sherman who had downplayed reports of enemy activity just beyond his lines, and it had been Sherman who had been less than efficient in discerning the enemy's presence and intent. Had he been so disposed, Grant might well have fingered Sherman for the collapse of intelligence and security that had contributed to the success of the Confederate attack on April 6. That he chose instead to celebrate Sherman's generalship once the battle had commenced suggested that he had chosen not to sacrifice Sherman's reputation to protect his own. That choice had fortunate consequences, even as it illustrated Grant's understandable preference for officers who were loyal to him over those who offered criticism. At the same time, both Grant and Sherman, eager to discredit critical newspaper reports detailing a Union army overrun in a moment of absolute surprise, went too far when it came to defending themselves from charges that they had not anticipated the Confederate attack.[17]

Sherman was blunt: there was no surprise at Shiloh. He read the newspapers. "I see we were surprised, that our men were bayoneted in their tents, that officer had not had breakfast &c.—This is all simply false," he told his brother John, who just happened to be a United States Senator from Ohio.[18] Such stories were what passed for news when cowards talked to correspondents. Two days later, he assured his wife, Ellen, that "the hue & cry against Grant about surprise is wrong. I was not surprised and I was in advance." The next day, he repeated the same argument to his brother-in-law, Charles Ewing: "As to the Cock & bull story of surprise it is absurd—we had been skirmishing for two days, and on the morning of the Battle, Every regiment was armed & equipped & in Line of battle—Every Battery harnessed in position, and cavalry saddled up." Referring to Stanton's telegram relaying Lincoln's inquiry about what had happened, he remarked, "Halleck answered he thought the Confederate officers and soldiers were to blame, and were the cause of the dreadful slaughter." To his father-in-law, Sherman sounded the same themes, adding that "the attempt to throw blame on Grant is villainous."[19]

In retrospect, Sherman was rather defensive about his own behavior, in part because he knew that if fingers were to be pointed at anyone about surprise, some would have to be pointed at him. It was good to know that Halleck and Grant both praised him. At the same time, he sympathized with Grant, in large part because Sherman had undergone the same sort of bombardment by newsprint in 1861 in Kentucky, an episode that had left him to wrestle with accusations that he was insane and unfit to command. If he believed that he had regained his reputation and perhaps more at Shiloh, he knew that it would not have taken very much for the battle to represent the ultimate demise of his military career. Now, he worried that Grant would suffer as he once had. In defending Grant, he avenged himself by demonstrating that the press was always out to get someone. They both had been wronged by reporters.

One might well understand that officers and soldiers in Buell's command, in order to advance their claim that Buell had saved the day, would be critical of Grant's generalship. "Grant was whipped on Sunday & if it had not been for part of Buell's Army coming up Monday morning they would all have been taken prisoner," argued one Ohio soldier who served under Buell.[20] Nor were all of Grant's own men especially pleased by their general's performance. Many soldiers held him responsible for the army's unpreparedness to resist an attack they had no idea might come. One spoke of Grant's "imbecile character"; another thought that Buell's arrival "was all that saved Grant's Army." A visitor from Iowa came away from Pittsburg Landing appalled by Grant's leadership: "The criminal carelessness, or something worse, on the part of General Grant, whereby so many brave soldiers were slaughtered, admits of no . . . excuse."[21]

Still, for the next several days, Grant had to respond to reports about misbehavior by his men, highlighting the issue of lax discipline. At the same time, he was aware that McClernand and Lew Wallace were seeking to protect their reputations at his expense. By April 25, Grant had just about had enough. Although the army would move as soon as the roads dried, he told Julia that he was "no longer boss." It was now Halleck's command, "and I am truly glad of it. I hope the papers will let me alone in the future." He had been reduced to doing paperwork from breakfast through dinner: he claimed, rather unpersuasively, that he did not read the papers and as a result saved himself from "much uncomfortable feeling."[22] It was a weak cover. To an old army friend, he noted that even as his army was preparing to move to fight another battle, one that he hoped "will wind up the big battles," newspaper critics "are giving me fits" on Shiloh. Some day, he believed, people would understand that with thirty-five thousand men "we kept at bay" eighty thousand attacking Confederates on April 6 and that "we could not have been better prepared had the enemy sent word three days before when they would attack." Indeed, he himself would have attacked, he claimed, had he not chosen to await Buell's arrival.[23]

Grant relayed the same message to his father. Those officers and soldiers who had fought on April 6 retained their confidence in him: his critics in uniform "showed the white feather" and were now anxious to place the blame elsewhere. "As to the talk about a surprise here, nothing could be more false. If the enemy had sent us word when and where they would attack us, we could not have been better prepared."[24] Such claims were simply incredible ... especially when they appeared in the *Cincinnati Commercial* a week after Grant wrote them. In an astonishingly stupid act, Jesse Grant had forwarded his son's private comments to a newspaper. Four days later, another letter, this one from Grant staff officer William S. Hillyer, popped up in the same paper. "What prompts this systematic defamation," Hillyer asked. "In whose way is he? Whose sins has he to bear—whose shortcomings to cover?" The critics were obviously trying to conceal the "naked deformity of their own base cowardice, and screen themselves behind the pretence of bad generalship." Even Halleck "says the talk of surprise is sheer nonsense."[25]

It was a bad business to go to war with critical reporters. Even worse was the death of Charles F. Smith on April 25. Smith had never recovered from an infection that set in after he had suffered a deep cut in his leg in March. Grant missed him at Shiloh. Now, just at a time when he needed all the friends he could get, he was deprived of the wise counsel and support of someone whom he held in great esteem. That he was increasingly alone became evident when he finally received McClernand's report about Shiloh, in which the division commander had once more held forth in ignorance about what had been going on in other commands. A revised report from McClernand several days later retained the same flaw. Grant had only one ally: "In Gen. Sherman the country has an able and gallant defender and your husband a true friend," he wrote Julia.[26]

At month's end, the army began to move. Grant believed a battle was imminent. "Before this reaches you," he wrote Julia, "probably another battle, and I think the last big one, will have taken place or be near at hand." As to the newspaper reports he had not read, he told her to "give yourself no trouble": everyone else understood the situation, and the criticisms came from "persons who were not here" and from officers "who disgraced themselves and now want to draw off public attention." One issue troubled him enough for him to make especial mention of it: "We are all well and me as sober as a deacon no matter what is said to the contrary." As for Halleck, Grant judged him "one of the greatest men of the age."[27]

Undoubtedly, Grant appreciated Halleck's support, even if he found his superior's repeated admonishments irritating. That very day, however, Halleck decided to reorganize his command. Originally, Grant, Buell, and John

Pope were going to retain command of their forces, defined variously as corps and as wings, minus a reserve formed from elements from each command. Within days, however, Halleck changed his mind. He transferred George H. Thomas's division from Buell to what was Grant's corps/wing, now headed by Thomas; McClernand would head the reserve; Grant was elevated to second-in-command, although the confusing wording of the order stated that he also retained command of his old corps/wing (an organizational format that as set forth would have been impossible).[28]

Grant complained to Halleck that he believed that many people believed that "my position differs but little from that of one in arrest," especially as Halleck transmitted orders directly to McClernand and Thomas, "both nominally under my command." Grant asked that he be restored to command or relieved from duty. He believed that Halleck was not disposed "to do me any injustice, but suspicions have been aroused that you may be acting under instructions, from higher authority, that I know nothing of"; Grant reminded Halleck that "there has been a studied persistent resistance to me by persons outside the army, and it may be by some in it."[29]

In reply, Halleck revealed his impatience with Grant's self-pity. He explained that as second-in-command, Grant no longer was in charge of either Thomas's right wing or McClernand's reserve (thus offering a reasonable clarification of his muddled order): "You have precisely the position to which your rank entitles you" as the second senior officer in Halleck's command. Had Halleck stopped there, all would have been fine, but he offered an assertion that was at best questionable and could be treated as deceptive: "For the last three months I have done every thing in my power to ward off the attacks which were made upon you. If you believe me your friend, you will not require explanation; if not, explanation on my part would be of little avail."[30]

This last assertion, simply put, was not true. After Fort Donelson, it had been Halleck who got Grant into hot water with General-in-Chief George McClellan by criticizing Grant's inattentiveness to administrative detail, his inability to instill discipline in his command, and his failure to communicate regularly with Halleck to keep him informed of circumstances. Halleck had also passed along word that there were rumors that Grant had started drinking to excess again, reigniting old army rumors with someone who was all too willing to believe them. It had been Lincoln who had intervened to call Halleck to account; in turn, Halleck backed off once he received the position he had long sought, that of directing Buell as well as Grant. Halleck's complaints had set the context for second-guessing Grant after Shiloh: ironically, it had been Halleck who had forestalled Grant's possible removal at that time, when it looked as if Lincoln was quite willing to spare the former storekeeper from Galena.[31]

And, yet, this was not the only myth surrounding the story of the command structure set up by Halleck or of Grant's retention. Long after the war, in 1892, there appeared Alexander K. McClure's *Abraham Lincoln and Men of War-Times*. McClure, a Pennsylvania Republican, told how he had visited the White House late one night after Shiloh to plead the case for Grant's removal.

> I appealed to Lincoln for his own sake to remove Grant at once, and, in giving my reasons for it, I simply voiced the admittedly overwhelming protest from the loyal people of the land against Grant's continuance in command. I could form no judgment during the conversation as to what effect my arguments had upon him beyond the fact that he was greatly distressed at this new complication. When I had said everything that could be said from my standpoint, we lapsed into silence. Lincoln remained silent for what seemed a very long time. He then gathered himself up in his chair and said in a tone of earnestness that I shall never forget: "*I can't spare this man; he fights.*"[32]

Given Stanton's telegram inquiring of Halleck whether Grant was negligent at Shiloh, it is fair to infer that at least at one time Lincoln was quite prepared to spare Grant. The remainder of McClure's tale called its veracity into question, because he claimed that the person who had devised the very command relationship that Grant so despised was none other than the president himself. According to McClure, Lincoln explained to him that it was his idea to send Halleck to Pittsburg Landing after Shiloh; that would allow time to pass and tempers to cool. That done, the new command arrangement reassured people that Lincoln had faith in Grant: it sought to rehabilitate his reputation (and, McClure claimed, it worked). Eventually, of course, Halleck would become general-in-chief, and with his departure, Grant would regain his command: "It was Lincoln, and Lincoln alone, who saved him from disgrace and gave to the country the most lustrous record of all the heroes of the war," McClure concluded.[33]

It is one of the oddities of Civil War scholarship that while scores of historians have repeated without question McClure's quoting of Lincoln on Grant's indispensability, most have not shown a similar disposition to credit this tale about a masterful manipulation of command relationships—although the latter supports the former in McClure's telling. In truth, Halleck had planned before any battle took place to assume command of the joint forces of Grant and Buell once they united; there is no other documentary reference to the process outlined by McClure that would suggest that Lincoln's hidden hand was at work. Given that Lincoln would later ponder whether to remove Grant during the Vicksburg campaign and given Stanton's telegraphic inquiry, it seems safe to say that this tale of Lincoln's confidence in Grant ought to be retired, despite the fondness some historians have for it.[34]

For the criticism of Grant did not cease with his appointment as Halleck's second-in-command. Grant continued to nurse his wounded ego. For a man who claimed that he did not read the paper, he certainly seemed to have a fair idea of what they said. "I am thinking seriously of going home, and to Washington, as soon as the present impending fight or footrace is decided," he wrote Julia on the same day he protested his position to Halleck. "I have been so shockingly abused that I sometimes think it almost time to defend myself." That proved a passing fancy: he had heard of the appearance of both his own and Hillyer's letter in the papers. "This should never have occurred," he groused.[35]

Senators and congressmen also debated Grant's performance at Shiloh. The general had his defenders, including Galena's own congressman, Elihu B. Washburne, who held forth on his general's virtues on the House floor on May 2 and followed the party line when it came to explaining Grant's detractors. "The glorious victory you won at Pittsburg Landing has evok[ed] much criticism from the men who are never satisfied with anything, but who always keep out of harm's way, and from the cowardly scoundrels who fled from the field," he wrote Grant.[36] The general appreciated the help. "To say that I have not been distressed at these attacks upon me would be false," he replied, "as I have a father, mother, wife & children who read them and are distressed by them." Criticism also weakened his ability to command effectively. Once more, he defended his actions at Shiloh (although this time he did not mention the question of surprise), adding, "Looking back at the past I cannot see for the life of me any important point that could be corrected"—a rather astonishing assertion, given the situation.[37]

Washburne may have done his best, but not everyone was convinced by his case. Joseph Medill, editor of the pro-Republican *Chicago Tribune*, reminded the congressman of what had happened: "It was a most reprehensible surprise followed by an awful slaughter. Our cause was put in terrible peril. Want of foresight, circumspection, prudence and generalship are all charged upon this wretched man. But we need not dispute about it. I admire your pertinacity and steadfastness in behalf of your friend, but I fear he is played out. The soldiers are down on him."[38]

Grant may have complained about newspapermen, but he had no problem with having a few frequent the headquarters mess. Albert D. Richardson of the *New York Tribune* and Thomas W. Knox of the *New York Herald* stayed near Grant: Richardson recalled how in the evening Grant "reclined on the logs, or stood before the camp fire, smoking and talking of the Mexican war, or of Shiloh." Perhaps Richardson and Knox owed their proximity to the fact that they wrote for New York newspapers, for Grant was well aware of the criticism directed at him in Chicago and Cincinnati. "After we have done our best, to have such a torrent of obloquy and falsehood poured among my own troops is too much," he told one reporter. "I am not going to lay off my shoulder-straps until the close of the war, but I should like to go to New Mexico, or some other remote place, and have a small command out of the reach of the newspapers."[39]

Reporters were not the only ones to note Grant's depression. Pope later recalled how Grant would visit Pope's headquarters and spend the entire day in Pope's tent "sitting about and lying on a cot," talking about resigning. Nor was criticism of Grant limited to the papers. "Bitter and acrimonious controversies were raging in the camp about the management and the result of the late battle," Pope recalled, "in which he was largely the sufferer."[40] Grant's relationship with Halleck also continued to deteriorate. As the armies gathered north of Corinth, Grant discerned that an attack on the Confederate right promised results. But he returned from a visit to army headquarters crestfallen and reported that Halleck had contemptuously brushed it aside. "He pooh-poohed it," Grant told Rawlins, "and left me to understand that he wanted no suggestions from me."[41]

Grant was left to watch and wait. He believed that the coming clash at Corinth would be "the last great battle to be fought in the valley of the Mississippi"; Halleck's deliberateness was due to his determination "to make sure work" of the task.[42] Finally, on May 30, Union forces discovered that Pierre G. T. Beauregard had pulled out of the city. There would be no decisive battle, although Grant tried to speak well of the result. "There will be much unjust criticism of this affair," he told Washburne, "but future effects will prove it a great victory."[43] He would not always be as kind: later, he would characterize the campaign as a siege from beginning to end.[44]

Grant had been waiting for the conclusion of the campaign against Corinth to address his personal situation. Several of his subordinates had already commenced casting about for alternatives, notably David Hunter's command along the South Carolina coast.[45] Grant applied for a twenty-day leave for himself and several staff officers. While Halleck authorized the leave, he instructed Grant to remain a few days until the situation settled.[46] In later years, it would be told, primarily by Sherman, that Grant was on the point of leaving when Sherman visited his headquarters tent and intervened. In later years, Sherman made much of the ensuing conversation. Was it true that Grant was leaving? Yes. Why? "Sherman, you know. You know that I am in the way here. I have stood it as long as I can, and can endure it no longer." Sherman responded by reminding Grant that the newspapers had once labeled Sherman "crazy" but that Shiloh had given him "new life, and now I was in fine feather." If Grant left, he would drop out of the contest; if he stayed, "some happy accident might restore him to favor and his true place." Grant promised to wait and to contact Sherman once more should he prepare to leave; a few days later, he told Sherman that he had decided to stay.[47]

Cheered by the news that Grant had decided not to go on leave, Sherman wrote him an enthusiastically reassuring letter. "For yourself you could not be quiet at home for a week, when armies were moving," he remarked: it had been the press that had brought him into disrepute, and some day he and Grant would have their revenge.[48] He sounded a similar theme to his wife. Grant was "as brave as any man should be . . . but his rivals have almost succeeded through the instrumentality of the Press in pulling him down." Grant was "not a brilliant man" and had himself courted the press, "but he is a good & brave soldier tried for years, is sober, very industrious, and as kind as a child. Yet he has been held up as careless, criminal, a drunkard, tyrant and everything horrible." It was all the result of jealous rivals and cowards feeding lies to a press insatiable for the latest sensation, Sherman said.[49]

Just how true a friend Sherman was soon became evident. After the battle at Shiloh, Ohio's lieutenant general, Benjamin Stanton, visited Pittsburg Landing and listened as soldiers complained about Grant. Upon returning to Ohio, he published a blistering attack against Grant, highlighting his "blundering stupidity and negligence." Sherman decided to respond and accused Stanton of lying. What ensued was an exchange of fiery letters that drew in other members of the Sherman family. At a time when Grant found several of his own subordinates critical of his performance or seeking to evade responsibility for their own shortcomings and when he was seeking to evade Halleck's scowl, Sherman's blunt and energetic defense proved a welcome relief. Nor did it hurt that Sherman could mobilize a family of defenders who would carry forward the fight: it might have been different had Sherman followed the examples set by McClernand and Lew Wallace and pointed a finger at Grant.[50]

And, yet, one must not give Sherman too much credit for saving Grant for the Union. In truth, Halleck had requested him to remain for a few days; when Grant prepared to leave once more, Halleck "asked that I should remain a little longer if my business was not of pressing importance." Grant decided to stay, perhaps encouraged by Sherman's pep talk, but at least as much due to Halleck's queries: "and for the war, so long as my services are required I do not wish to leave." As he explained to Julia on June 3, "Necessity however changes my plans, or the public service does, and I must [yield]"; six days later, he added, "When I talked of going home and leaving my command here there was quite a feeling among the troops, at least expressed by Gen. officers below me, against my going." Grant appreciate the support and reminded Julia of how much he valued Sherman's service at Shiloh.[51]

Far more important to Grant's decision to remain was Halleck's decision on June 10 to disassemble his grand army, which restored Grant to the direct command of his own troops. Grant chose to establish his headquarters in Memphis, sixty miles west of Halleck at Corinth and for several weeks did what he could to bring order to an area filled with passionate secessionists. In this case, distance did not make Halleck's heart grow fonder, and before long, Grant was reading more hectoring telegrams. When he finally got orders to report to Halleck in early July, he might have feared the worst, only to learn that Halleck was going to Washington, D.C., to assume the post of general-in-chief.[52] Halleck's departure in itself did not assure Grant of a command. In 1866, Robert Allen, who at that time was a colonel in the quartermaster branch, reported that Halleck offered him command of the army.[53] Nothing came of this, and so Grant retained the field command he had secured after Corinth: it would not be until October that he gained a department-level command. But at least Halleck was gone.

Thus, it is time to reassess some of the traditional tales about the aftermath of Shiloh, especially as they regard Ulysses S. Grant. There is no evidence to suggest that at the time, Grant saw Shiloh as transforming his understanding of the nature of the effort needed to crush the Confederacy. It would not be until the summer of 1862 that Grant would reassess the determination of Confederates to secure their independence. That realization would come as a result of his experiences as the commander of an army of occupation, not as a result of Shiloh. It would also not be until then that he embraced escalating and broadening the scope of the conflict. Thus, Shiloh was not the turning point he and others made it out to be in this regard.[54] If anything, Shiloh came close to destroying Grant altogether. It would have been all too easy for his superiors to make him a scapegoat, and there are indications that Lincoln and Stanton were prepared to do just that . . . in part because of what Halleck had previously said about Grant. Ironically, it was Halleck who saved Grant from immediate dismissal, not Lincoln, although, in the end, Grant languished under Halleck's immediate oversight and nearly gave up. In turn, because Grant praised Sherman instead of singling him out for inadequate reconnaissance, intelligence-gathering, and preparation and because Sherman, unlike several of Grant's other division commanders, rushed to Grant's defense, the foundation of the Grant-Sherman alliance was set, facilitated in part by Grant's need to find someone to confide in after Smith, a man Grant idolized, died. One should not make too much of this, either: if Grant placed great trust in Sherman, Sherman still valued Halleck more as a general and if anything felt sorry for Grant, seeing in Grant's situation a moment akin to his earlier troubles in Kentucky. If, as Sherman later liked to claim, Shiloh made him, it almost unmade Grant, and that would have made it even more decisive than is usually assumed.

Notes

1. Ulysses S. Grant, *Personal Memoirs of U. S. Grant* (New York: 1885–86), 1:368–70. For a foreshadowing of this analysis, see Albert D. Richardson, *Personal History of Ulysses S. Grant* (Hartford, CT, 1868), 260; Adam Badeau, *Military History of Ulysses S. Grant* (New York, 1881), 1:94–96. Badeau's wording in particular is so close to that offered by Grant as to suggest ways in which Grant's memoirs were at times heavily dependent on the official military biography prepared by Badeau.

2. Grant, *Personal Memoirs*, 1:349–56.

3. Ulysses S. Grant to Henry W. Halleck, April 7, 1862, and Grant to Don Carlos Buell, April 7, 1862, John Y. Simon et al., eds., *The Papers of Ulysses S. Grant* (Carbondale: Southern Illinois University Press, 1967), 5:20–22 (hereafter indicated by *Papers*).

4. General Orders No. 34, District of West Tennessee, April 8, 1862, *Papers*, 5:21–22; Grant to Julia Grant, April 8, 1862, *Papers*, 5:27.

5. Grant to Pierre G. T. Beauregard, April 9, 1862, *Papers*, 5:30; Grant to Nathaniel H. McLean, April 9, 1862, *Papers*, 5:32–34.

6. *Papers*, 5:34.

7. Grant to McLean, April 21, 1862, *Papers*, 5:63.

8. Grant to Halleck, April 25, 1862, *Papers*, 5:68.

9. Grant to Julia Grant, April 15, 1862, *Papers*, 5:47. A rather full summary of press coverage can be found in Bruce Catton, *Grant Moves South* (Boston: Little, Brown, 1960), 251–55.

10. Halleck to Catherine Halleck, April 11, 1862, and Halleck to Grant, April 14, 1862, *Papers*, 5:48.

11. Brooks D. Simpson, *Ulysses S. Grant: Triumph over Adversity, 1822–1865* (Boston: Houghton Mifflin, 2000), 136.

12. See *Papers*, 5:49–51.

13. Halleck to Stanton, April 24, 1862, *Papers*, 5:51.

14. Halleck quoted in John F. Marzalek, *Commander of All of Lincoln's Armies: A Life of General Henry W. Halleck* (Cambridge, MA: Belknap, 2004), 122.

15. Kenneth P. Williams, *Lincoln Finds a General*, vol. 3 (New York: Macmillan, 1952), 405.

16. Ibid.; Wiley Sword, *Shiloh: Bloody April* (New York: Morrow, 1974), 433.

17. The best treatment of this issue is Catton, *Grant Moves South*, 255–59; see also Steven E. Woodworth, *Nothing but Victory: The Army of the Tennessee, 1861–1865* (New York: Knopf, 2005), 199, on the issue of tactical surprise.

18. Sherman to John Sherman, April 22, 1862, in Brooks D. Simpson and Jean V. Berlin, eds., *Sherman's Civil War: Selected Correspondence of William T. Sherman, 1860–65* (Chapel Hill: University of North Carolina Press, 1999), 206–8.

19. Sherman to Ellen Sherman, April 24, 1862, ibid., 208–9; Sherman to Charles Ewing, April 25, 1862, ibid., 210–11; Sherman to Thomas Ewing Sr., April 27, 1862, ibid., 211–13.

20. Joseph Allan Frank and George A. Reaves, *"Seeing the Elephant": Raw Recruits at the Battle of Shiloh* (Westport, CT: Greenwood, 1989), 141–43.

21. Ibid., 143; Sword, *Shiloh*, 434.

22. Grant to Julia Grant, April 25, 1862, *Papers of Ulysses S. Grant*, 5:72.

23. Grant to George P. Ihrie, April 25, 1862, *Papers*, 5:73–74.

24. Grant to Jesse R. Grant, April 26, 1862, reprinted in *Cincinnati Commercial*, May 2, 1862, *Papers*, 5:78–79.

25. William S. Hillyer, *Cincinnati Commercial*, May 6, 1862, *Papers*, 5:79–80.

26. Grant to Andrew C. Kemper, April 28, 1862, *Papers*, 5:89–90; Grant to John C. Kelton, May 1, 1862, *Papers*, 5:90; Grant to Julia Dent Grant, May 4, 1862, *Papers*, 5:110–11.

27. Grant to Julia Grant, April 30, 1862, *Papers*, 5:102–3.

28. *Papers*, 5:104–5.

29. Grant to Halleck, May 11, 1862, *Papers*, 5:114–15.

30. Halleck to Grant, May 12, 1862, *Papers*, 5:115.

31. See Simpson, *Grant*, 119–27.

32. Alexander K. McClure, *Abraham Lincoln and Men of War-Times* (Philadelphia: Times, 1892), 179–80.

33. Ibid., 180–82.

34. For example, Geoffrey Perret concedes that "other elements in McClure's account—particularly those relating to Halleck's role—are demonstrably untrue," yet he uses the quote (with this objection noted) in *Ulysses S. Grant: Soldier and President* (New York: Random House, 1997), 208 (see 500 for his reservation); by the time of *Lincoln's War* (New York: Random House, 2004), 142, he had abandoned this reservation, going so far as to render McClure's words as direct conversation in his effort to fashion a good story. Jean Edward Smith follows the more traditional approach of limiting his discussion to the famed quote itself in *Grant* (New York: Simon and Schuster, 2001), 205. In *Shiloh: The Battle That Changed the Civil War* (New York: Simon and Schuster, 1997), 308–9, Larry Daniel accepts McClure's entire tale.

35. Grant to Julia Grant, May 11, 1862, *Papers*, 5:115–16.

36. Washburne to Grant, May 6, 1862, *Papers*, 5:53.

37. Grant to Washburne, May 14, 1862, *Papers*, 5:119–20.

38. Catton, *Grant Moves South*, 261.

39. Richardson, *Personal History*, 257–58.

40. Peter Cozzens and Robert I. Girardi, eds., *The Military Memoirs of General John Pope* (Chapel Hill: University of North Carolina Press, 1998), 64–65, 91.

41. Richardson, *Personal History*, 260–61.

42. Grant to Julia Grant, May 13, 1862, *Papers*, 5:118; see also Grant to Julia Grant, *Papers*, 5:123–24.

43. Grant to Washburne, June 1, 1862, *Papers*, 5:136.

44. Grant, *Personal Memoirs*, 1:376.

45. Catton, *Grant Moves South*, 273; Simpson, *Grant*, 143.

46. Richardson, *Personal History*, 264.

47. William T. Sherman, *Memoirs of General William T. Sherman* (New York: Appleton, 1875), 1:255.

48. Sherman to Grant, June 6, 1862, in Simpson and Berlin, *Sherman's Civil War*, 232–33.

49. Sherman to Ellen Sherman, June 6, 1862, *Papers*, 234–37.

50. Sherman to Benjamin Stanton, June 10, 1862, *Papers*, 241–45; Charles B. Flood, *Grant and Sherman: The Friendship That Won the Civil War* (New York: Farrar Strauss Giroux, 2005), 121.

51. Grant to Julia Grant, June 9, 1862, *Papers*, 5:137–38, 140–41; Grant to Washburne, June 19, 1862, *Papers*, 5:145–46; Catton, *Grant Moves South*, 274–75.

52. Catton, *Grant Moves South*, 281, 287–88; Simpson, *Grant*, 143–46.

53. Badeau, *Military History*, 1:107–8.

54. See Brooks D. Simpson, "'The Doom of Slavery': Ulysses S. Grant, War Aims, and Emancipation, 1861–63," *Civil War History* 36 (March 1990): 36–56; Brooks D. Simpson, *Let Us Have Peace: Ulysses S. Grant and the Politics of War and Reconstruction, 1861–1868* (Chapel Hill: University of North Carolina Press, 1991), 23–29. Woodworth reflects this understanding (*Nothing but Victory*, 200).

CONTRIBUTORS
INDEX

CONTRIBUTORS

Charles D. Grear is an assistant professor of history at Prairie View A&M University. He received his PhD in history at Texas Christian University in 2005. Author of numerous articles, he is coauthor of the Texas history textbook *Beyond Myths and Legends: A Narrative History of Texas* (2008), author of several book chapters, and editor of an anthology *The Fate of Texas: The Civil War and the Lone Star State* (2008). Grear is book-review editor for H-CivWar and a recipient of the Lawrence T. Jones III Research Fellowship in Civil War Texas History from the Texas State Historical Association.

Gary D. Joiner received a PhD in history from Saint Martin's College, Lancaster University, United Kingdom. He is the Leonard and Mary Anne Selber Professor of History at Louisiana State University in Shreveport, where he is also director of the Red River Regional Studies Center. He is the author or editor of nine books including *Shiloh and the Western Campaign of 1862* (2007), *Mr. Lincoln's Brown Water Navy: Mississippi Squadron* (2007), and *One Damn Blunder from Beginning to End: The Red River Campaign of 1864* (2003), for which he won the Albert Castel Award in 2004 for best writing on the western theater of the Civil War and the A. M. Pate Jr. Award in 2005, given by the Fort Worth Civil War Roundtable for best research and writing on Trans-Mississippi Civil War history.

John R. Lundberg is an assistant professor of history at Houston Baptist University, Houston, Texas. He received his PhD from Texas Christian University in 2007. He is the author of *The Finishing Stroke: Texans in the 1864 Tennessee Campaign* (2002) and is currently working on a history of Granbury's Texas Brigade and a study of Unionism during the secession crisis in Texas.

Grady McWhiney (1928–2006) received his PhD from Columbia University in 1960. During his forty-four-year career, he taught at Troy State University, Millsaps College, University of California–Berkeley, Northwestern University, University of British Columbia, Wayne State University, University of Alabama, Texas Christian University, University of Southern Mississippi, and McMurry University. Among the many books he authored are *Braxton Bragg and Confederate Defeat* (1991), *Attack and Die* (1982), and *Cracker Culture* (2002).

Alexander Mendoza received his PhD from Texas Tech University in 2001 and is currently an assistant professor of history at the University of Texas at Tyler. He is the author of *Confederate Struggle for Command: General James Longstreet and the First Corps in the West* (2008).

Brooks D. Simpson is a professor of history at Arizona State University. He received his BA from the University of Virginia and his MA and PhD from the University of Wisconsin–Madison, the latter in 1989. Among his eleven books are *America's Civil War* (1996), *The Political Education of Henry Adams* (1996), *The Reconstruction Presidents* (1998), and *Ulysses S. Grant: Triumph over Adversity, 1822–1865* (2000), the latter of which was a *New York Times* Notable Book and a *Choice* Outstanding Academic Title for that year.

Timothy B. Smith received his PhD from Mississippi State University in 2001. A veteran of the National Park Service, working for seven years at the Shiloh National Military Park, he now teaches history at the University of Tennessee at Martin. Smith has authored several books, including *This Great Battlefield of Shiloh: History, Memory, and the Establishment of a Civil War National Military Park* (2004), *Champion Hill: Decisive Battle for Vicksburg* (2004), *The Untold Story of Shiloh: The Battle and the Battlefield* (2006), and *The Golden Age of Battlefield Preservation: The Establishment of America's First Five Civil War Military Parks* (2008). He is currently working on a history of Chickamauga and Chattanooga National Military Park and a study of the Civil War home front in Mississippi.

Steven E. Woodworth received his PhD from Rice University in 1987 and is a professor of history at Texas Christian University. He is the author, coauthor, or editor of twenty-six books. A two-time winner of the Fletcher Pratt Award of the New York Civil War Round Table (for *Jefferson Davis and His Generals* and *Davis and Lee at War* [1995]), Woodworth is also a two-time finalist for the Peter Seaborg Award of the George Tyler Moore Center for the Study of the Civil War (for *While God Is Marching On* and *Nothing but Victory* [2001]) and a winner of the Grady McWhiney Award of the Dallas Civil War Round Table for lifetime contribution to the study of Civil War history.

INDEX

CIVIL WAR CAMPAIGNS IN THE HEARTLAND

The area west of the Appalachian Mountains, known in Civil War parlance as "the West," has always stood in the shadow of the more famous events on the other side of the mountains, the eastern theater, where even today hundreds of thousands visit the storied Virginia battlefields. Nevertheless, a growing number of Civil War historians believe that the outcome of the war was actually decided in the region east of the Mississippi River and west of the watershed between the Atlantic and the Gulf of Mexico.

Modern historians began to rediscover the decisive western theater in the 1960s through the work of the late Thomas Lawrence Connelly, particularly his 1969 book *Army of the Heartland*, in which he analyzed the early years of the Confederacy's largest army in the West. Many able scholars have subsequently contributed to a growing historiography of the war in the West. Despite recent attention to the western theater, less is understood about the truly decisive campaigns of the war than is the case with the dramatic but ultimately indecisive clashes on the east coast.

Several years ago, three of my graduate students pointed out that the western theater possessed no series of detailed multiauthor campaign studies comparable to the excellent and highly acclaimed series Gary W. Gallagher has edited on the campaigns of the eastern theater. Charles D. Grear, Jason M. Frawley, and David Slay joined together in suggesting that I ought to take the lead in filling the gap. The result is this series, its title a nod of appreciation to Professor Connelly. The series' goals are to shed more light on the western campaigns and to spark new scholarship on the western theater.